wet moon

morning cold

7

ONI PRESS

AN ONI PRESS PUBLICATION

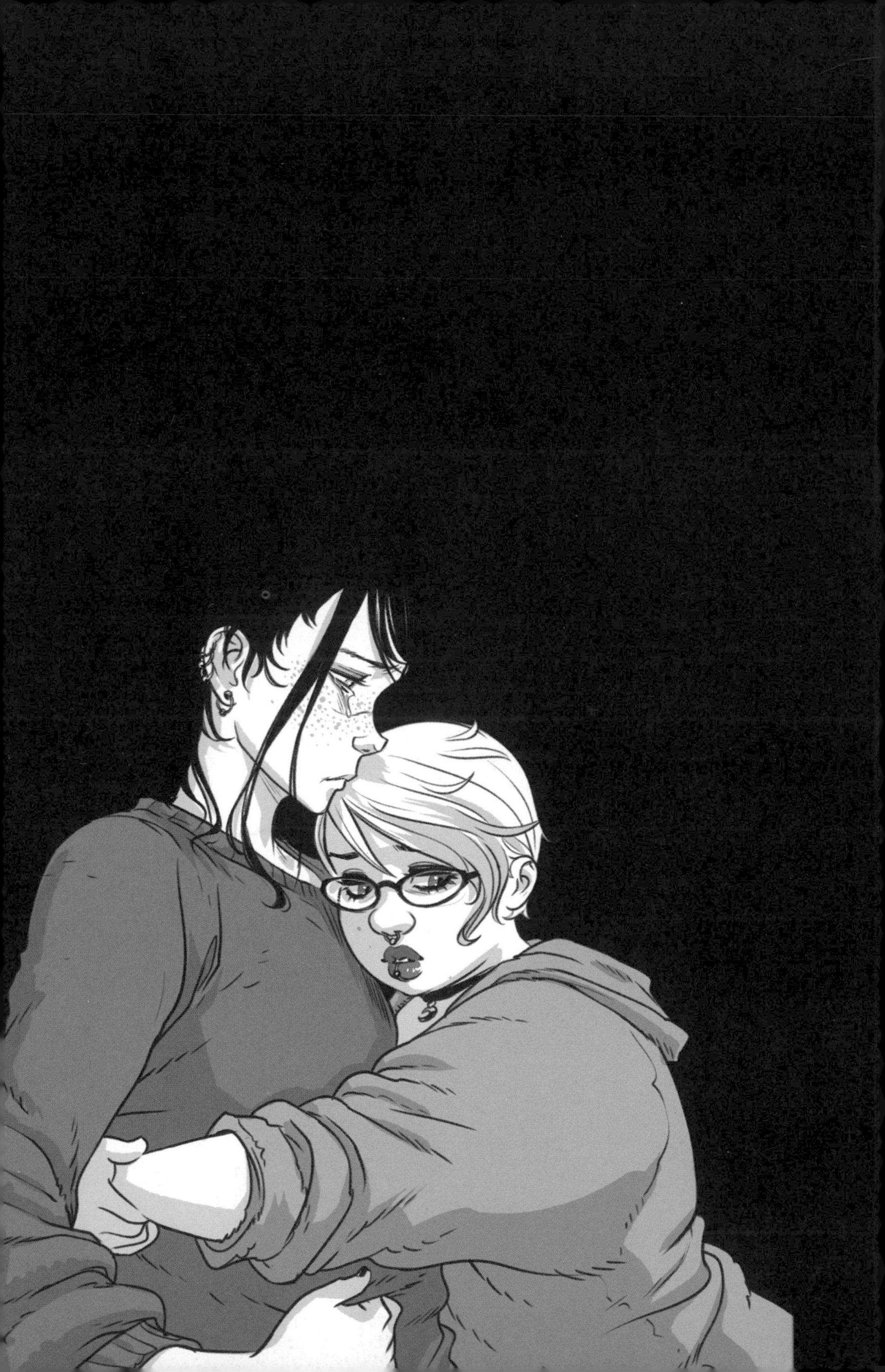

wet moon

morning cold

7

written and illustrated by **sophie campbell**

cover design by **sophie campbell**

book design by **hilary thompson & kate z. stone**

edited by **robin herrera**

PUBLISHED BY ONI PRESS, INC.

Joe Nozemack, *founder & chief financial officer*

James Lucas Jones, *publisher*

Charlie Chu, *v.p. of creative & business development*

Brad Rooks, *director of operations*

Melissa Meszaros, *director of publicity*

Margot Wood, *director of sales*

Sandy Tanaka, *marketing design manager*

Amber O'Neill, *special projects manager*

Troy Look, *director of design & production*

Hilary Thompson, *senior graphic designer*

Kate Z. Stone, *graphic designer*

Sonja Synak, *junior graphic designer*

Angie Knowles, *digital prepress lead*

Ari Yarwood, *executive editor*

Sarah Gaydos, *editorial director of licensed publishing*

Robin Herrera, *senior editor*

Desiree Wilson, *associate editor*

Alissa Sallah, *administrative assistant*

Jung Lee, *logistics associate*

Scott Sharkey, *warehouse assistant*

ONIPRESS.COM
FACEBOOK.COM/ONIPRESS
TWITTER.COM/ONIPRESS
ONIPRESS.TUMBLR.COM
INSTAGRAM.COM/ONIPRESS

First Edition: November 2018

ISBN 978-1-62010-545-0
eISBN 978-1-62010-546-7

Printed in China.
Library of Congress Control Number: 2018940555

1 2 3 4 5 6 7 8 9 10

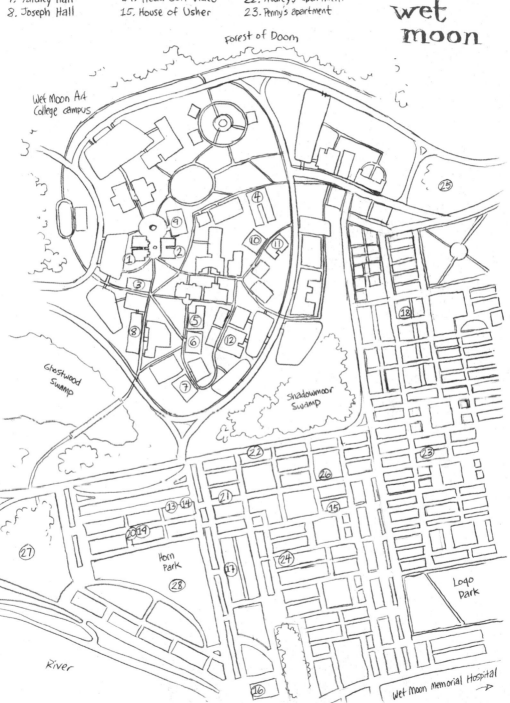

1. Bowden House
2. Vance House
3. Smith House
4. Westmiller House
5. Weitz Hall
6. Polsky Hall
7. Yardley Hall
8. Joseph Hall

9. Simmons Hall
10. Page Hall
11. Meyer Hall
12. Steve Hall
13. Burial Grounds
14. Head-Butt Video
15. House of Usher

16. Denny's
17. Marco's Diner
18. Trilby's Apartment
19. Swamp Things
20. Flower Power
21. Sundae Best
22. Audrey's apartment
23. Penny's apartment

24. Glen's apartment
25. Lorelei Cemetery
26. Polly Poster
27. Zurah Cemetery
28. softball field

wet moon

Forest of Doom

Wet Moon Art
College campus

Ghostwood
Swamp

Shadowmoor
Swamp

Horn
Park

Logo
Park

River

Wet Moon Memorial Hospital

29. The Lovedrop Residence
30. The Zuzanny Residence
31. The Bernarde Residence
32. The Swanhilde Residence
33. Wet Moon High School
34. The Druggie Bridge

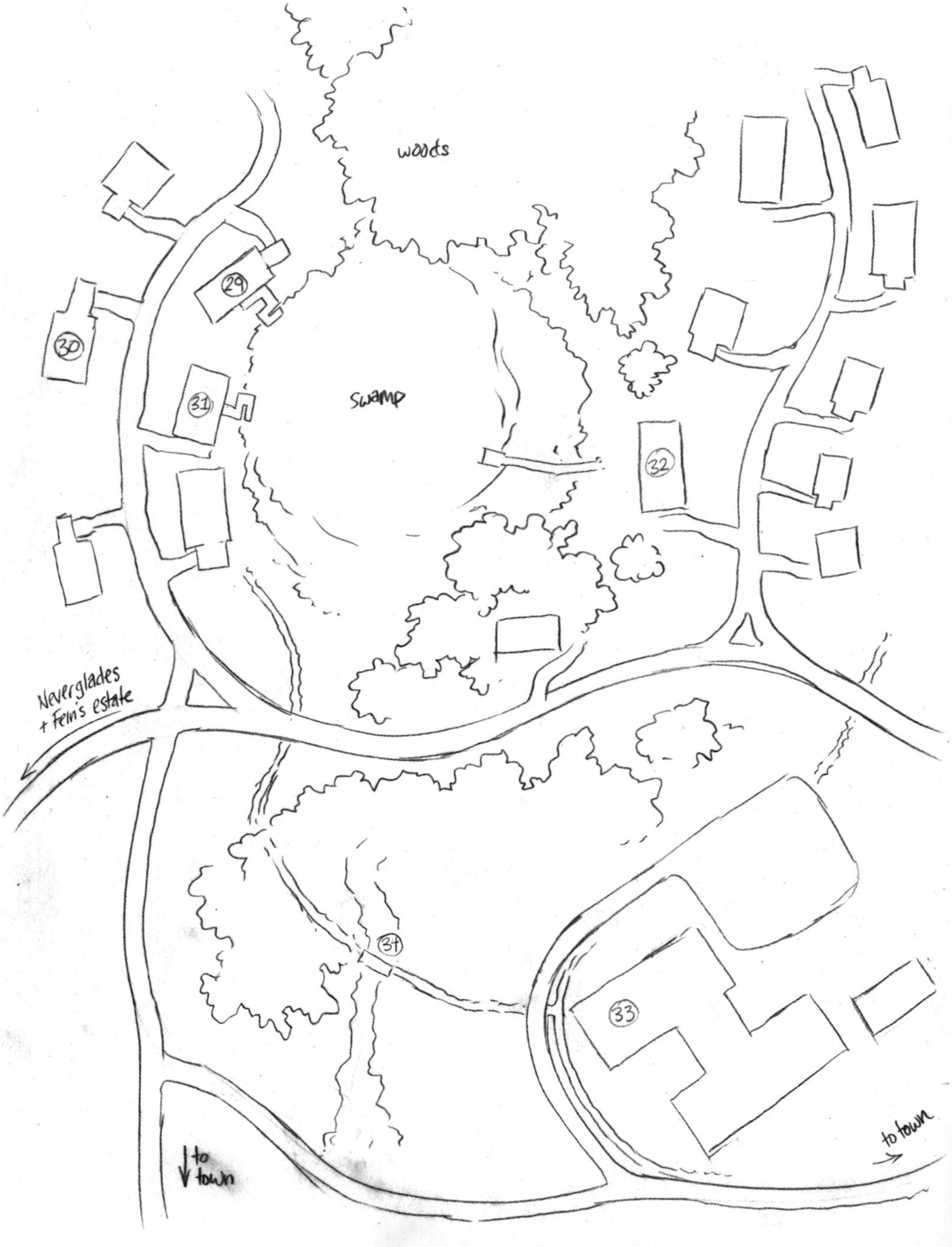

woods
swamp
29
30
31
32
33
34
Neverglades + Fern's estate
to town
to town

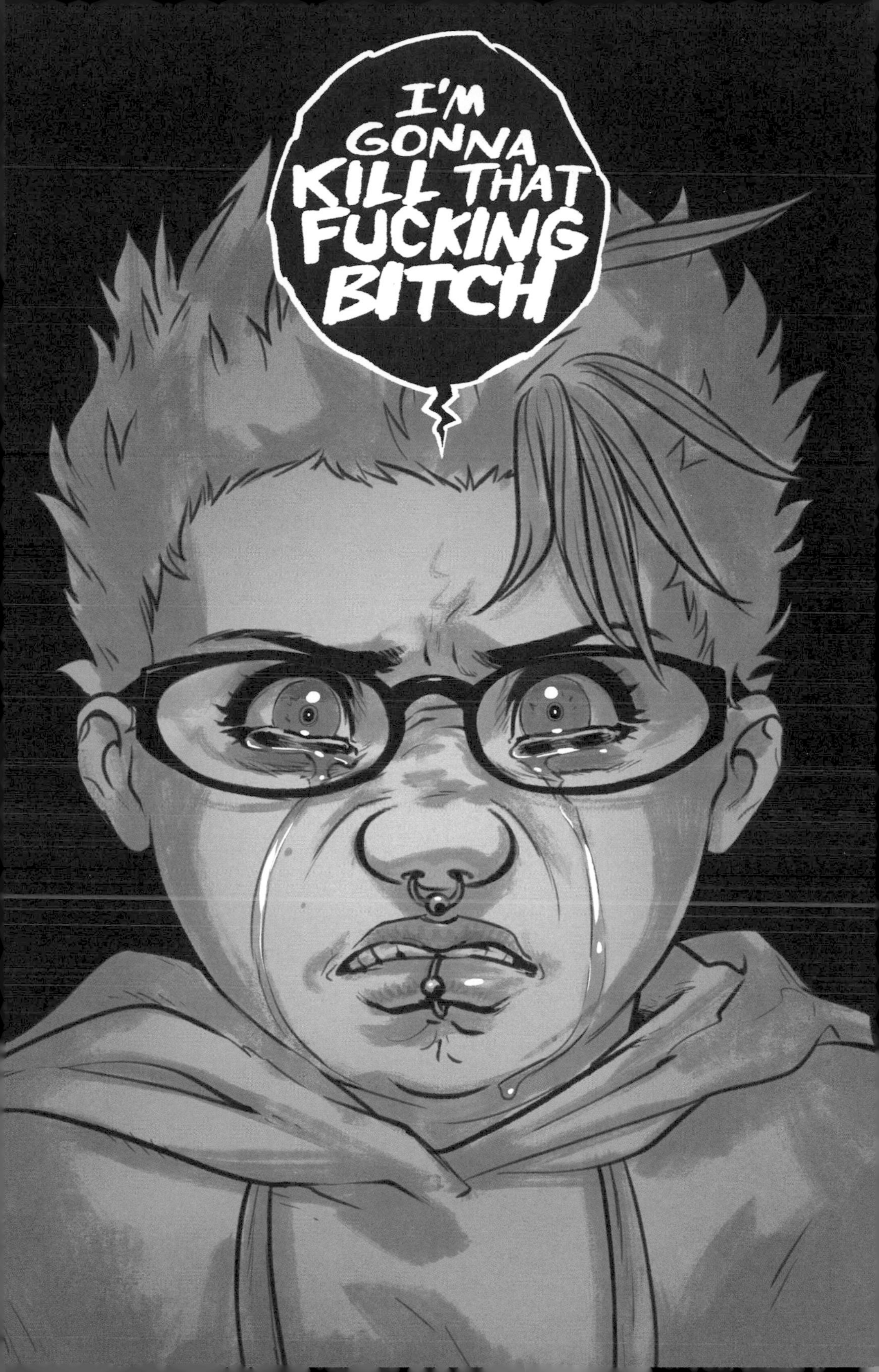
I'M GONNA KILL THAT FUCKING BITCH

31

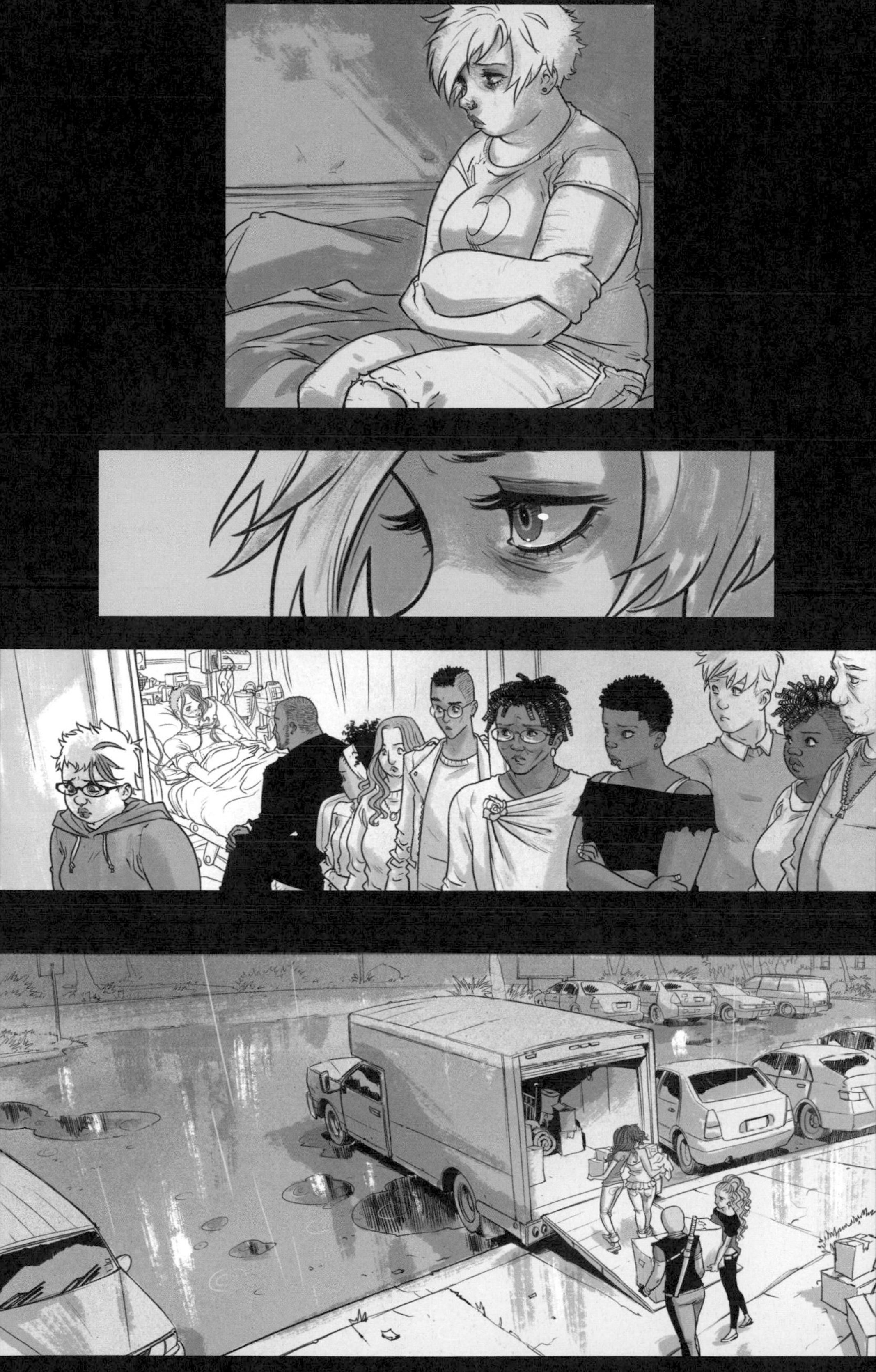

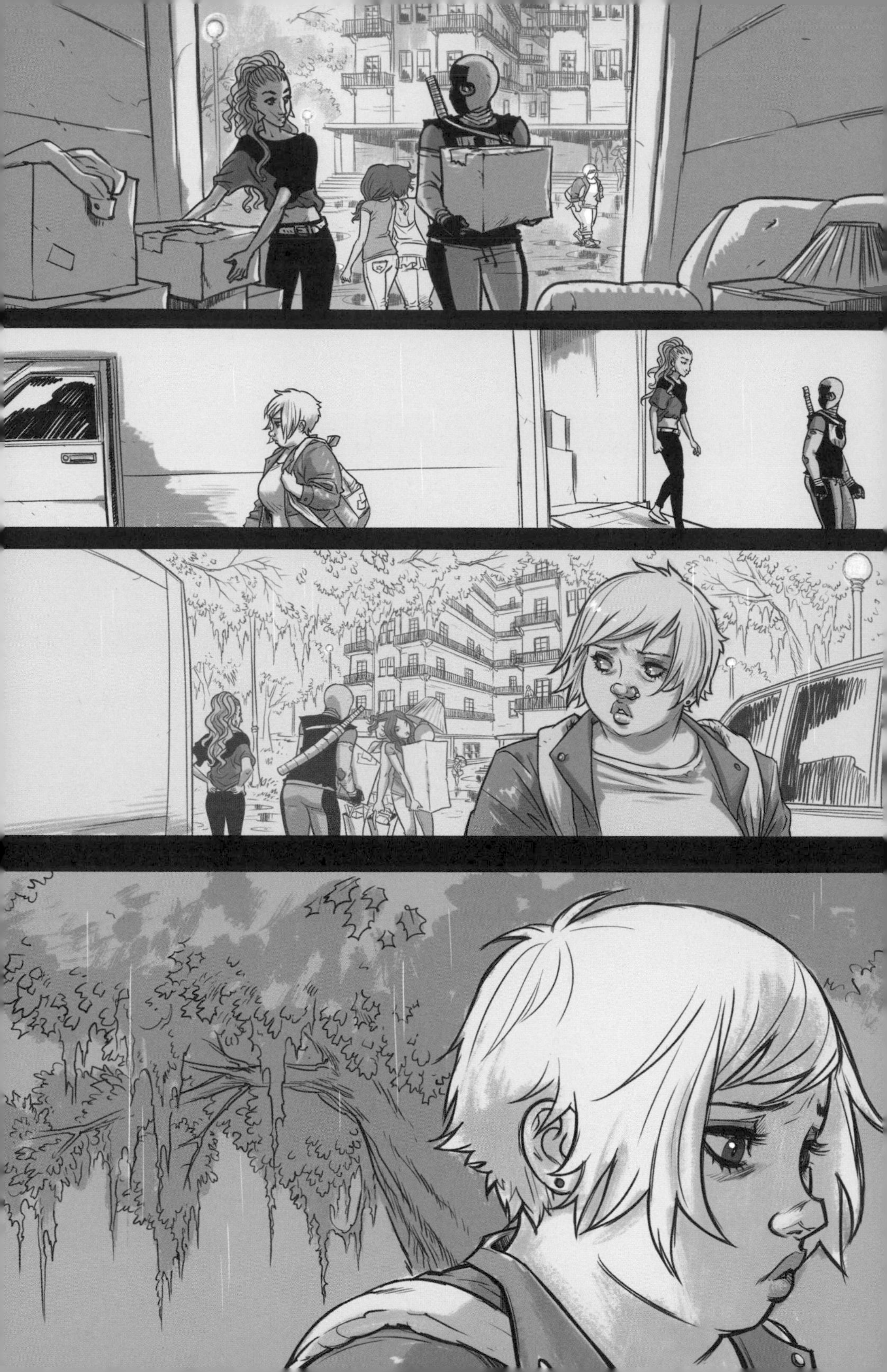

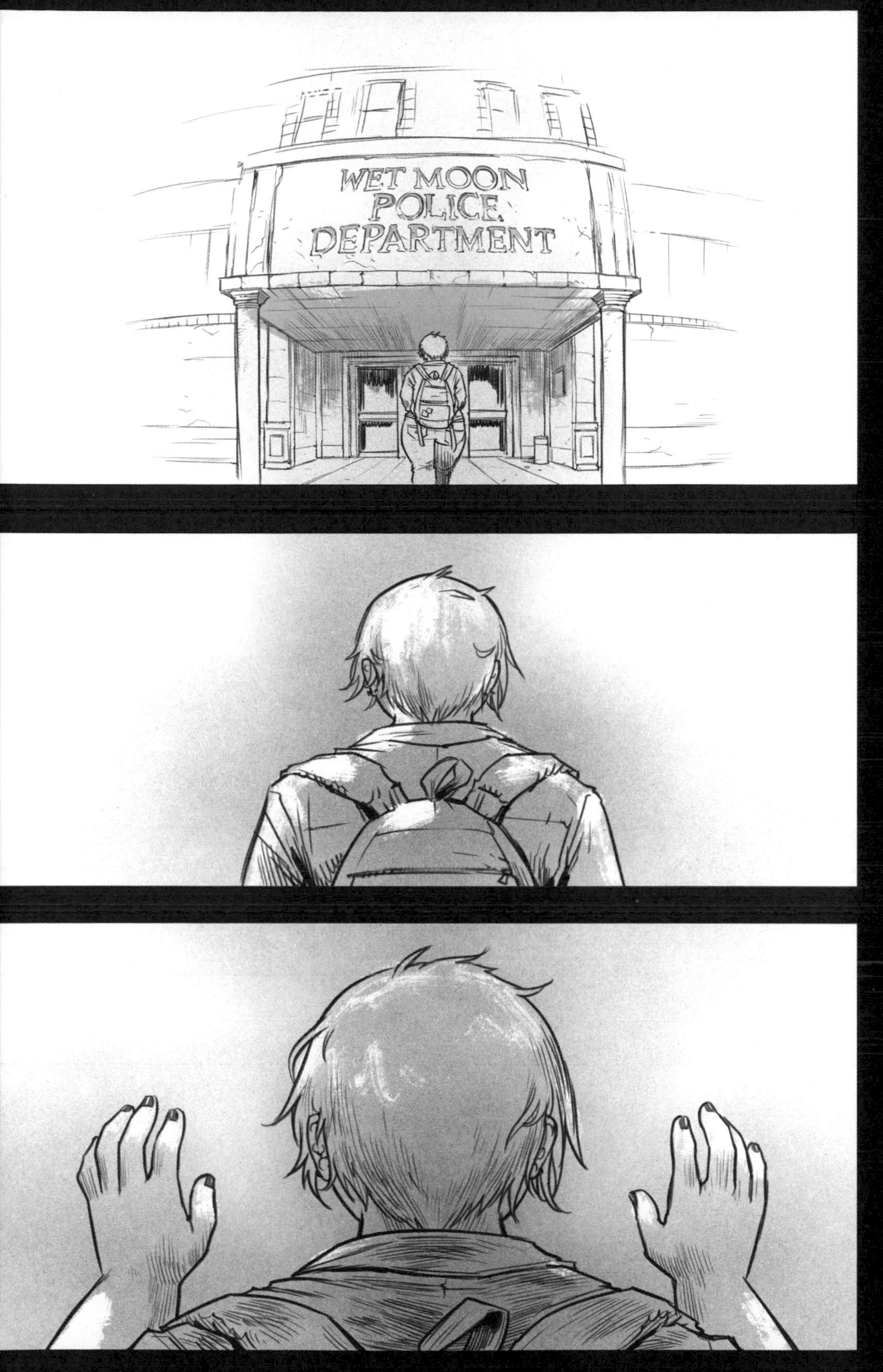
WET MOON
POLICE
DEPARTMENT

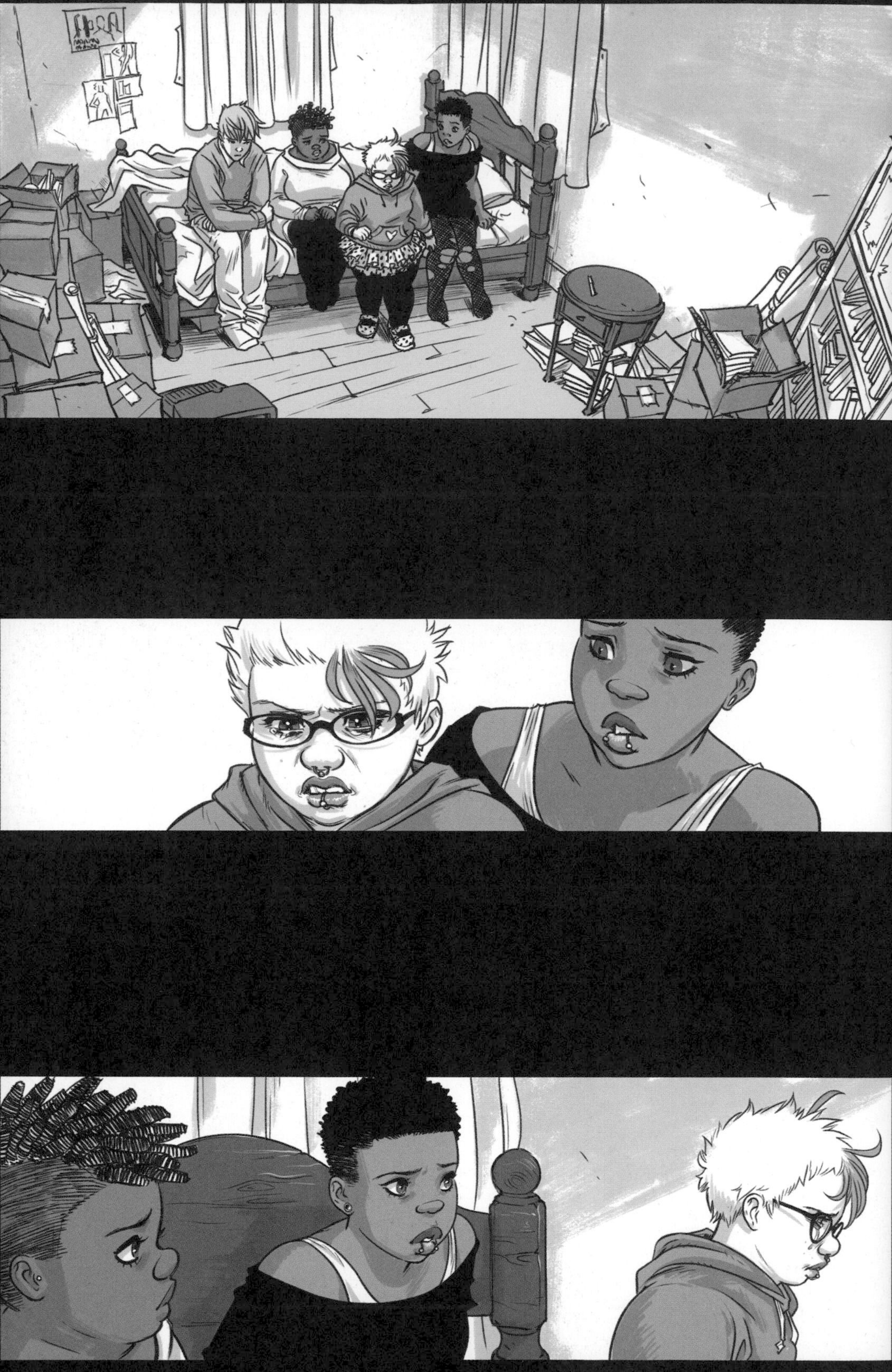

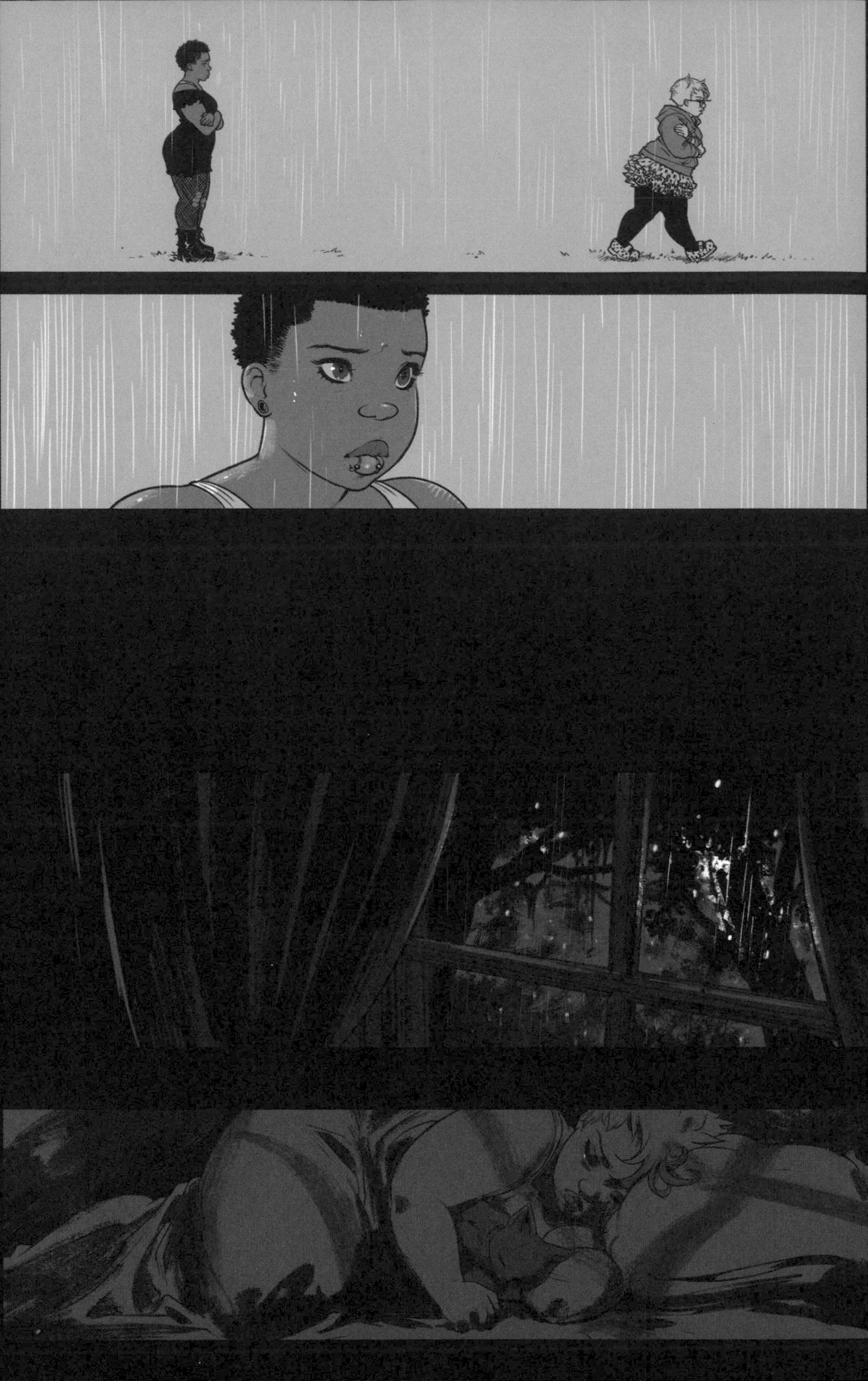

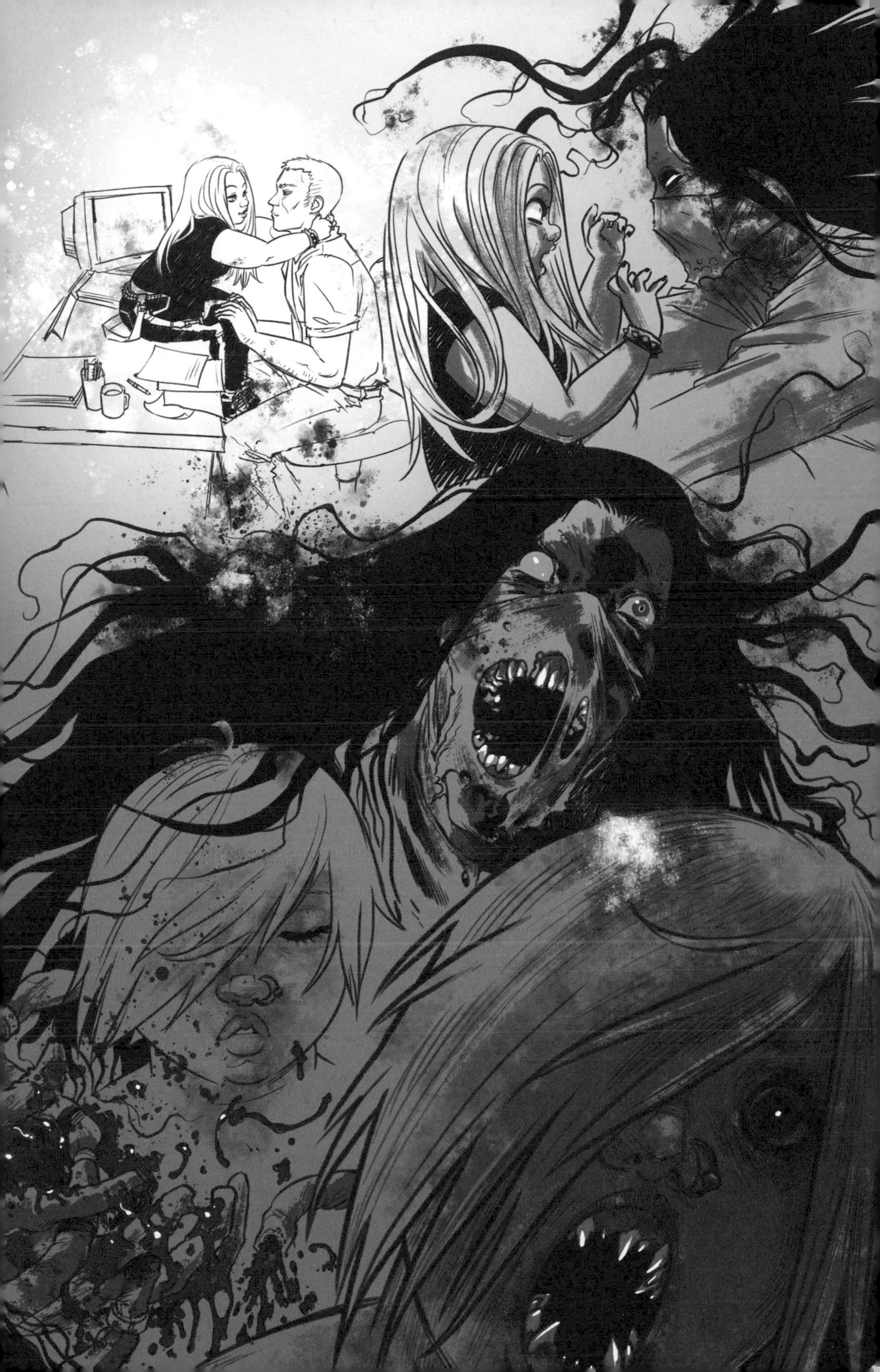

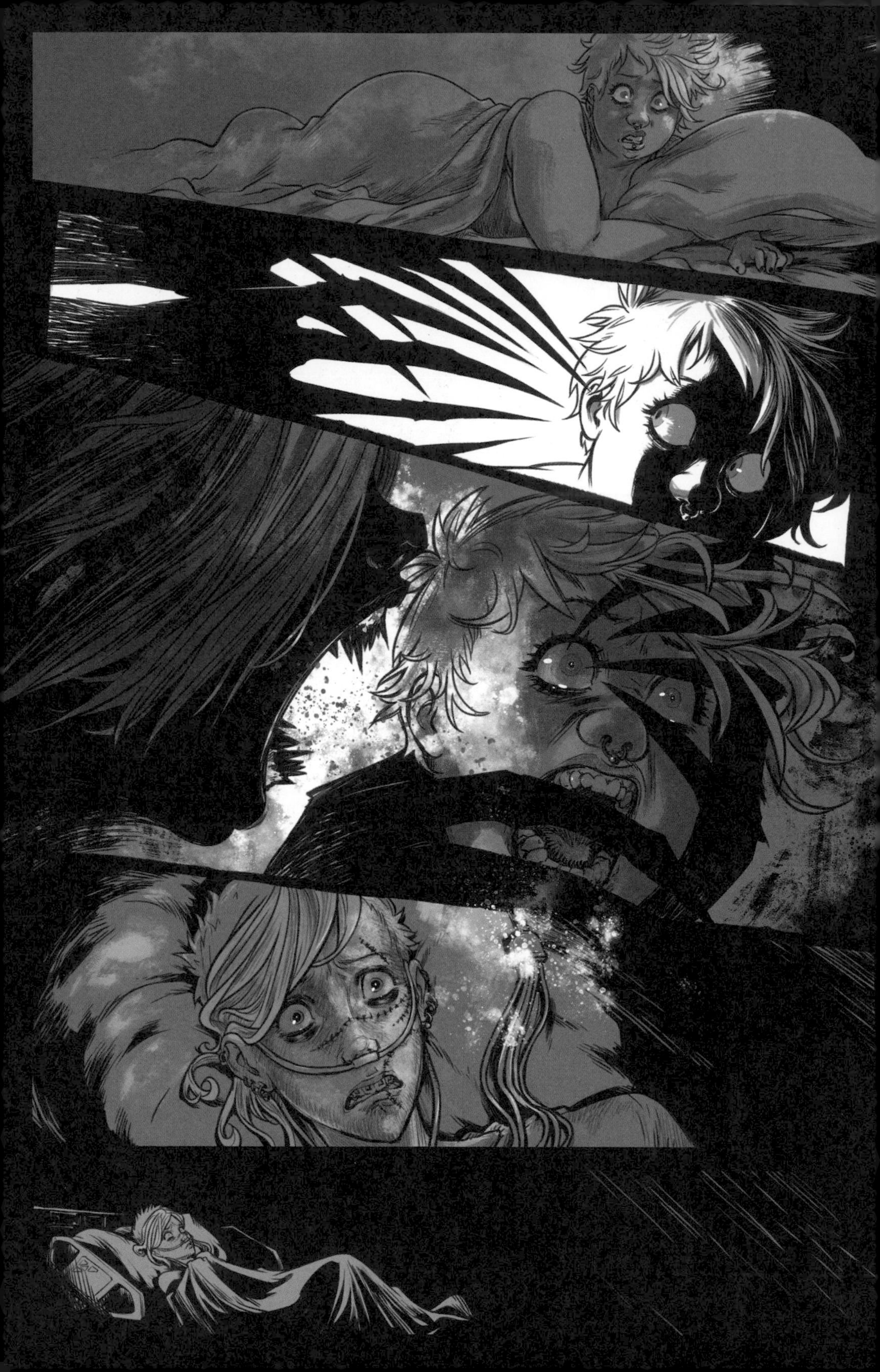

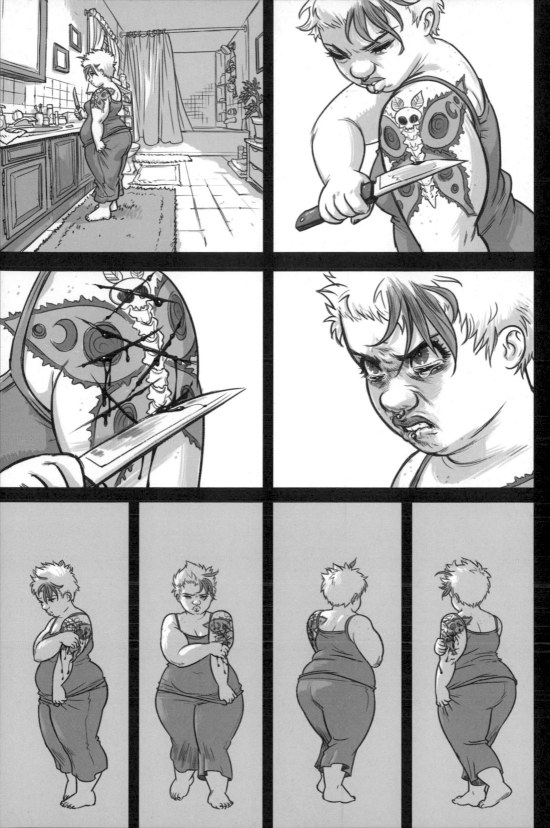

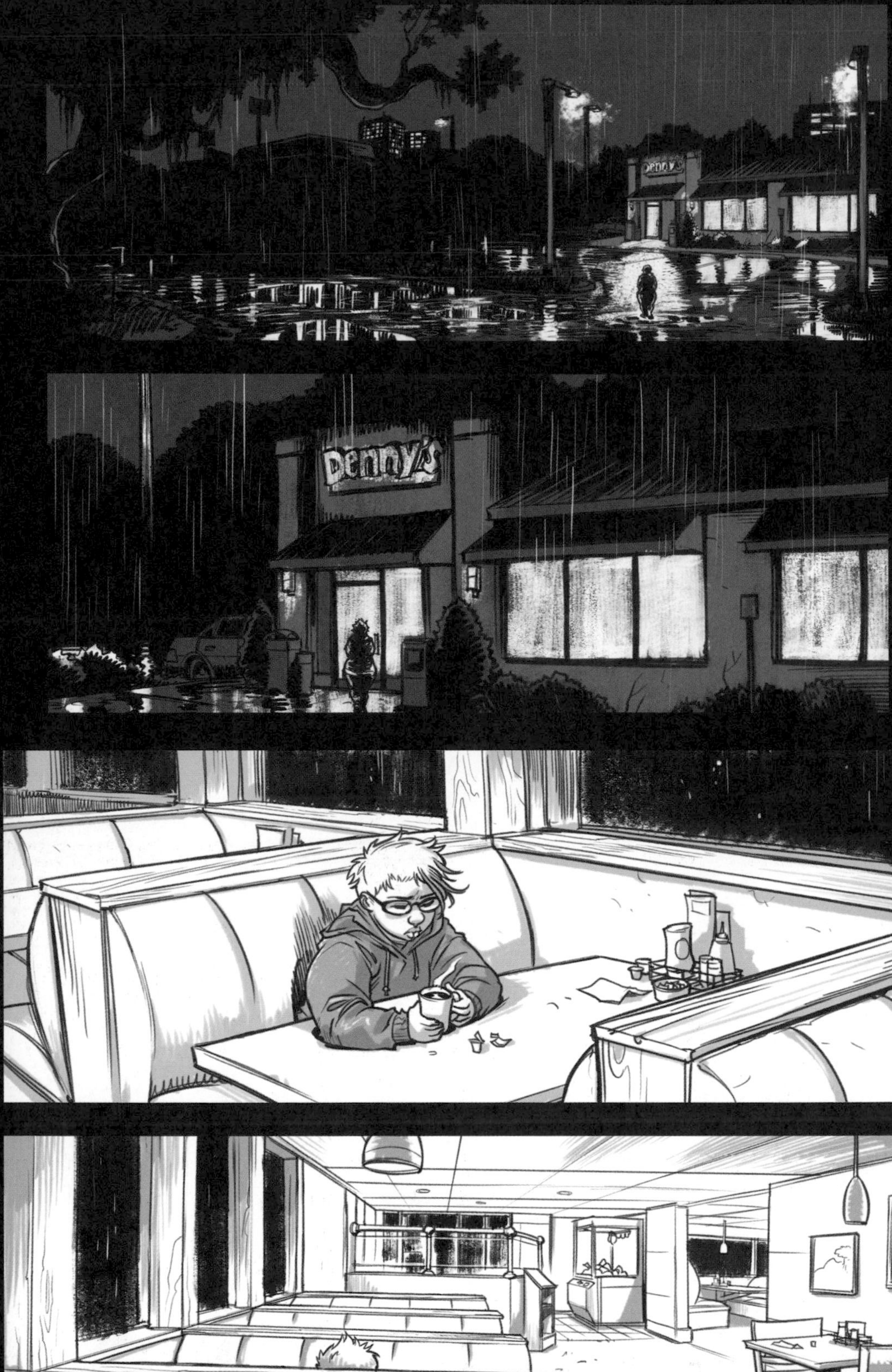
Denny's

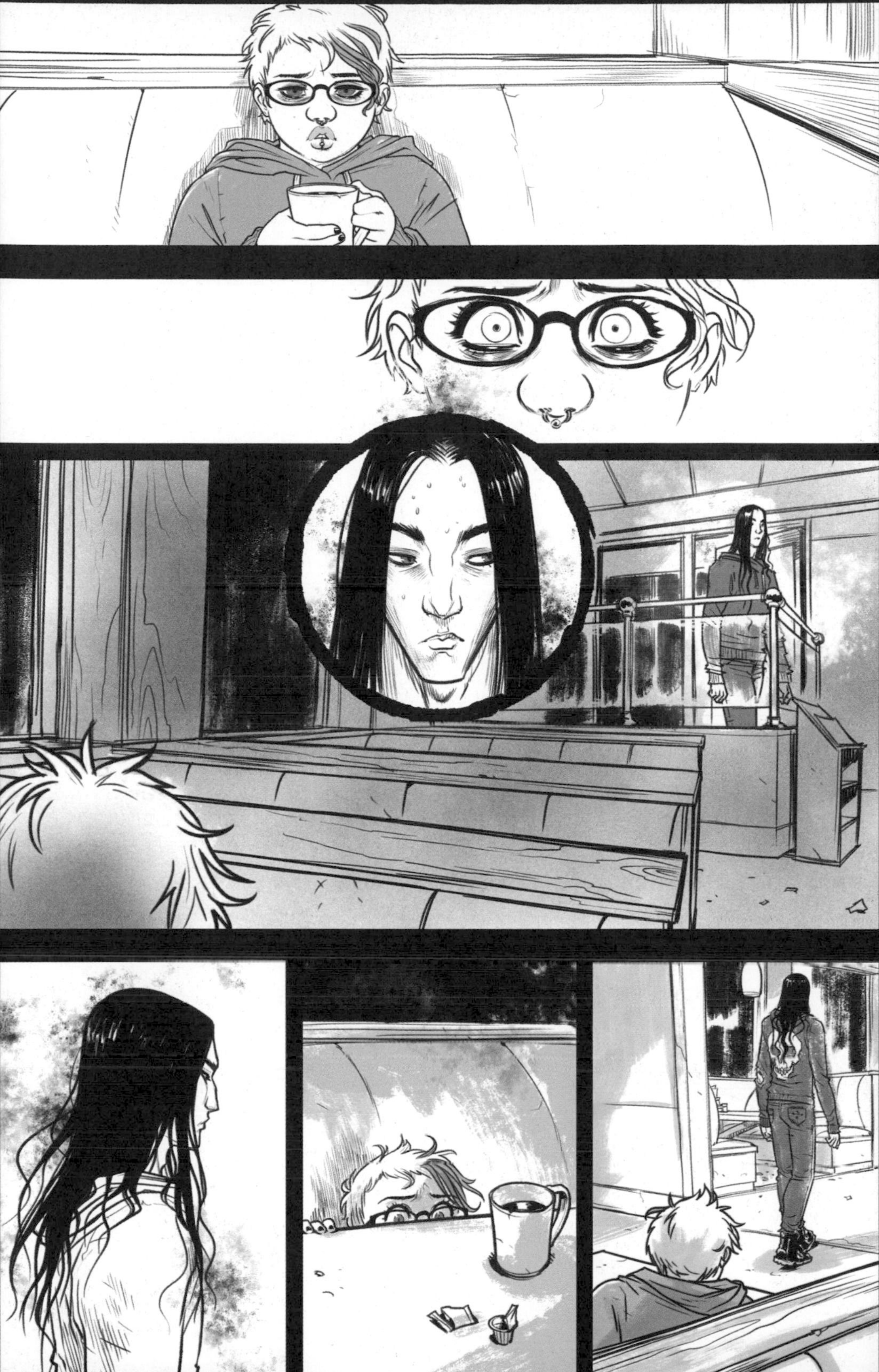

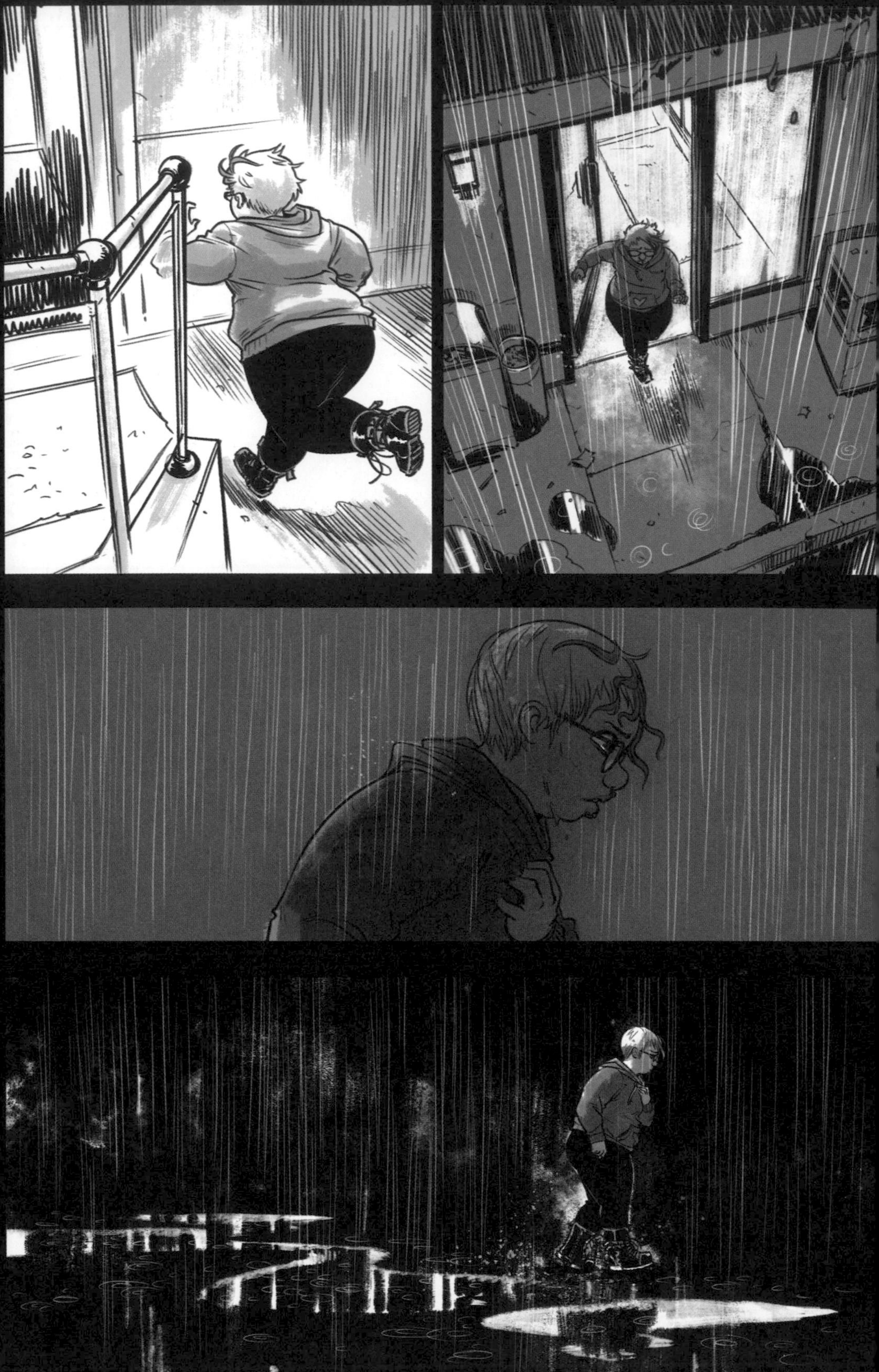

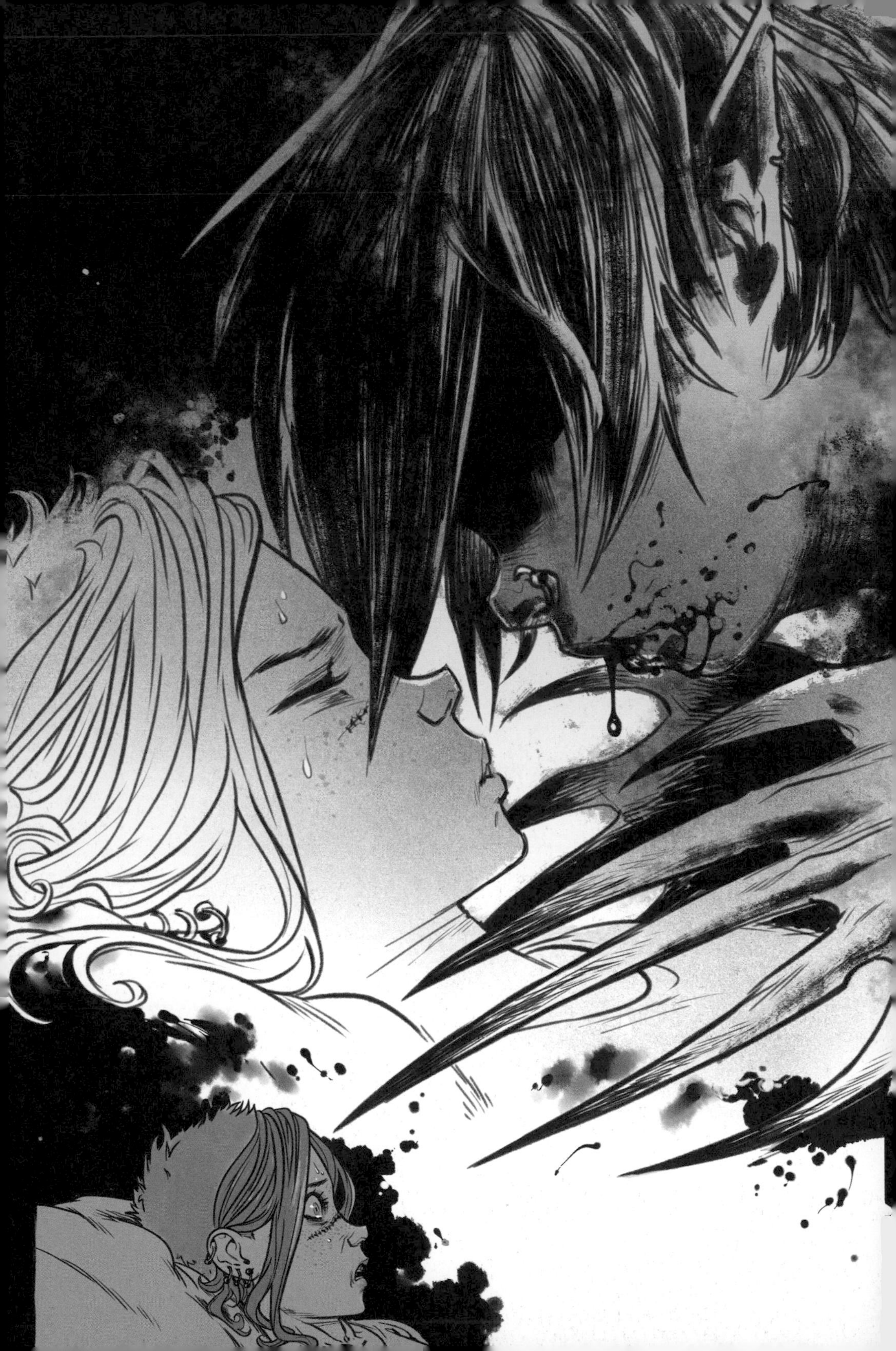

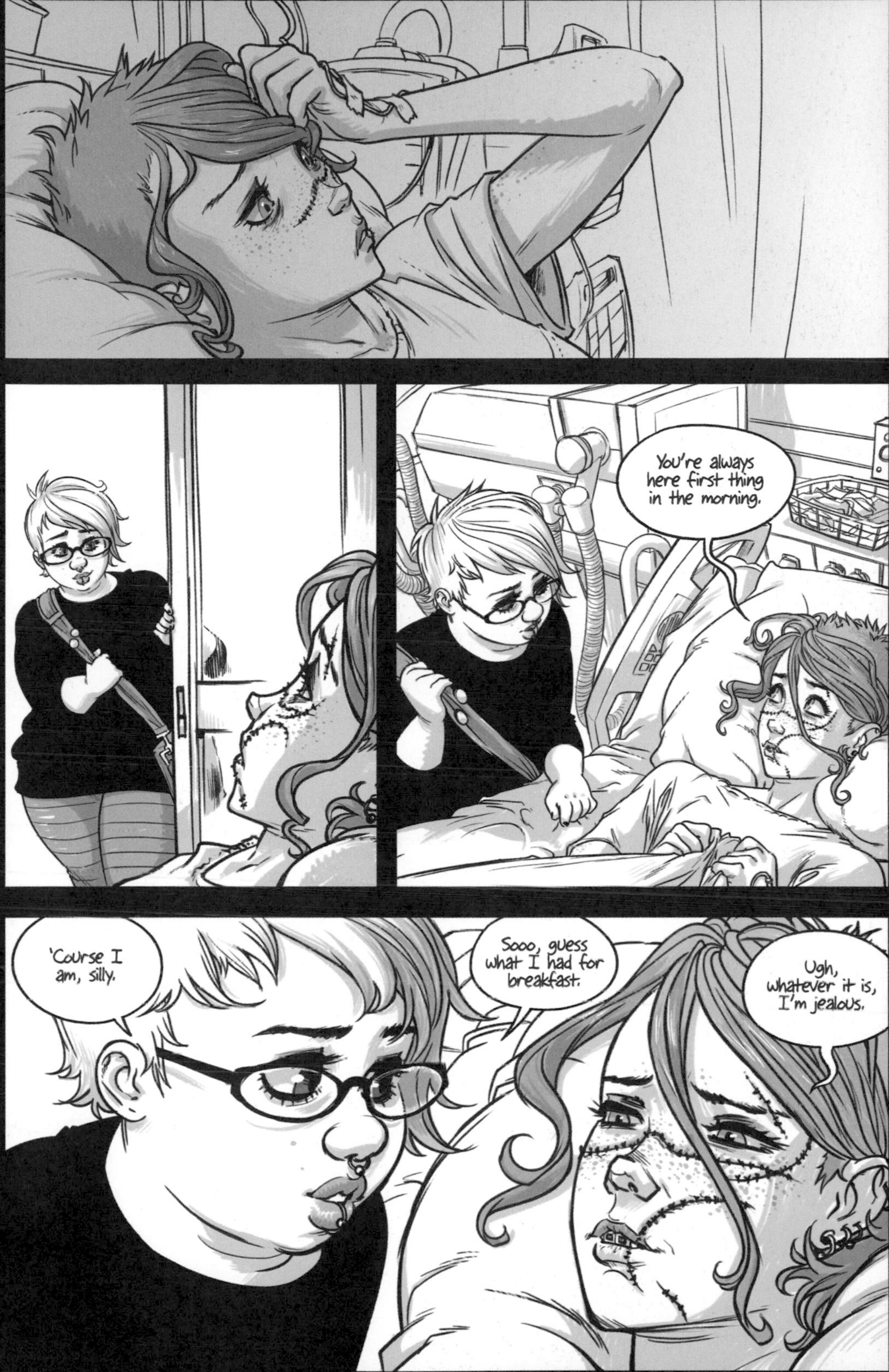
You're always here first thing in the morning.
'Course I am, silly.
Sooo, guess what I had for breakfast.
Ugh, whatever it is, I'm jealous.

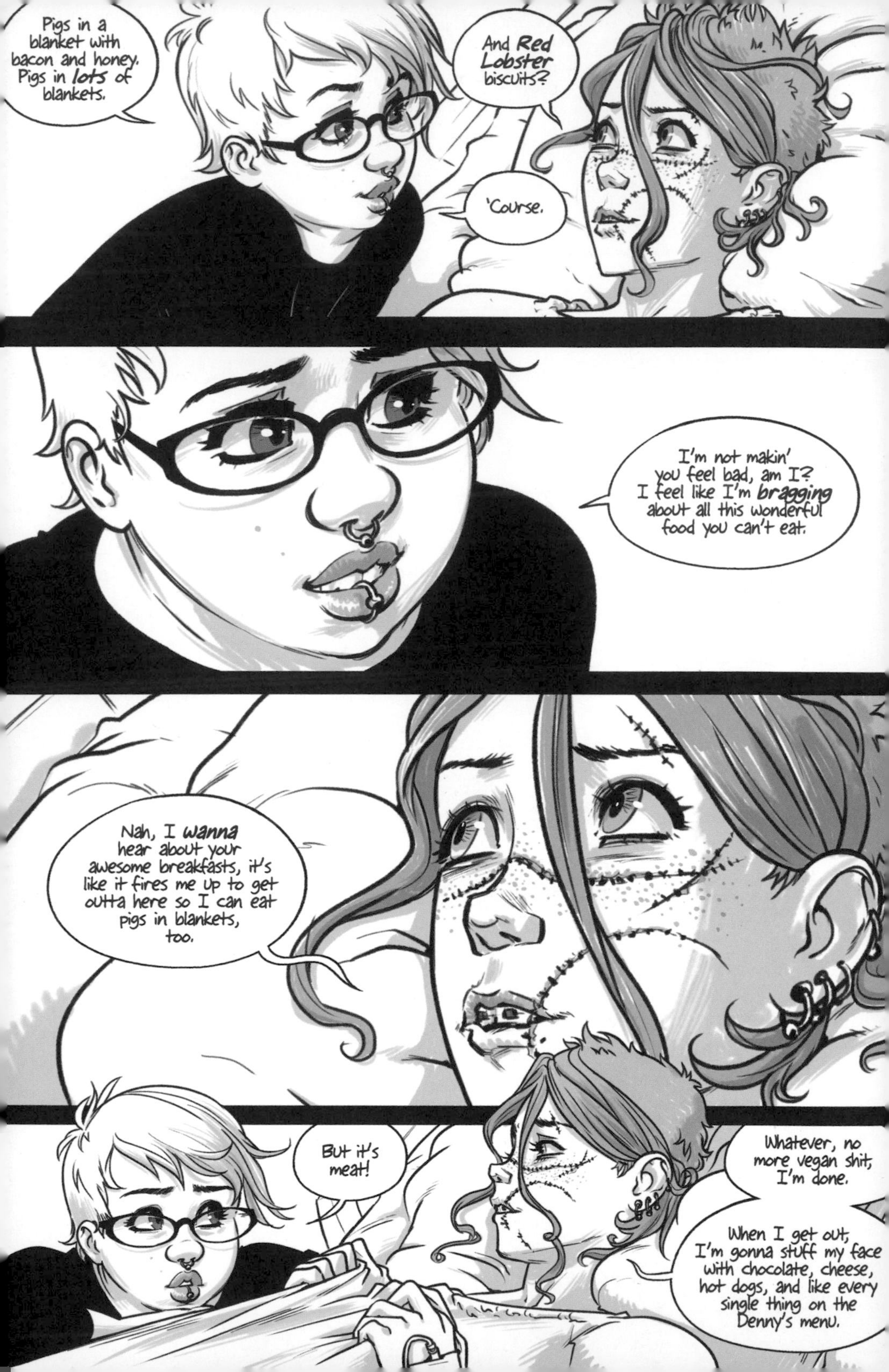
Pigs in a blanket with bacon and honey. Pigs in *lots* of blankets.
And **Red Lobster** biscuits?
'Course.
I'm not makin' you feel bad, am I? I feel like I'm ***bragging*** about all this wonderful food you can't eat.
Nah, I **wanna** hear about your awesome breakfasts, it's like it fires me up to get outta here so I can eat pigs in blankets, too.
But it's meat!
Whatever, no more vegan shit, I'm done.
When I get out, I'm gonna stuff my face with chocolate, cheese, hot dogs, and like every single thing on the Denny's menu.

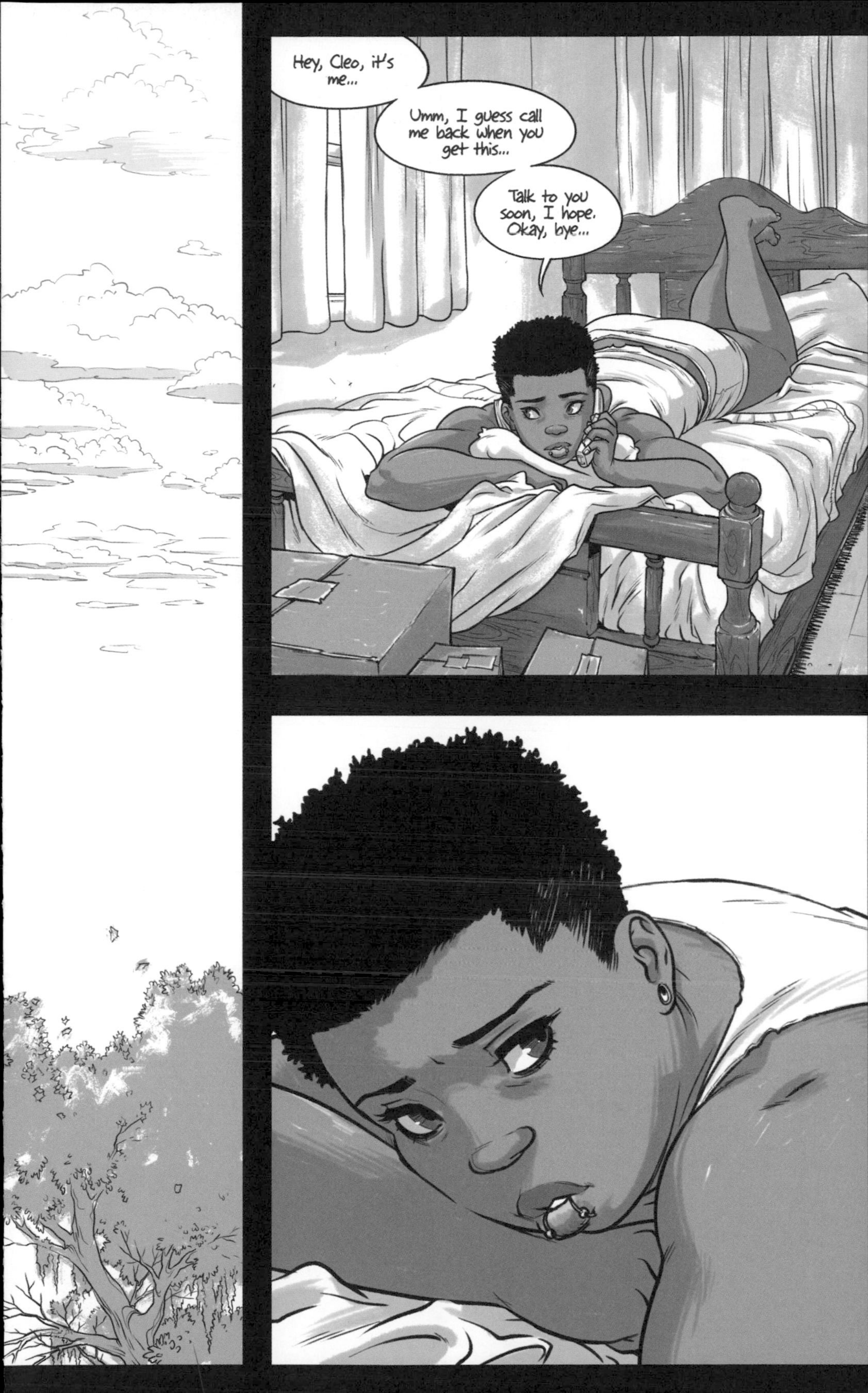
Hey, Cleo, it's me...
Umm, I guess call me back when you get this...
Talk to you soon, I hope. Okay, bye...

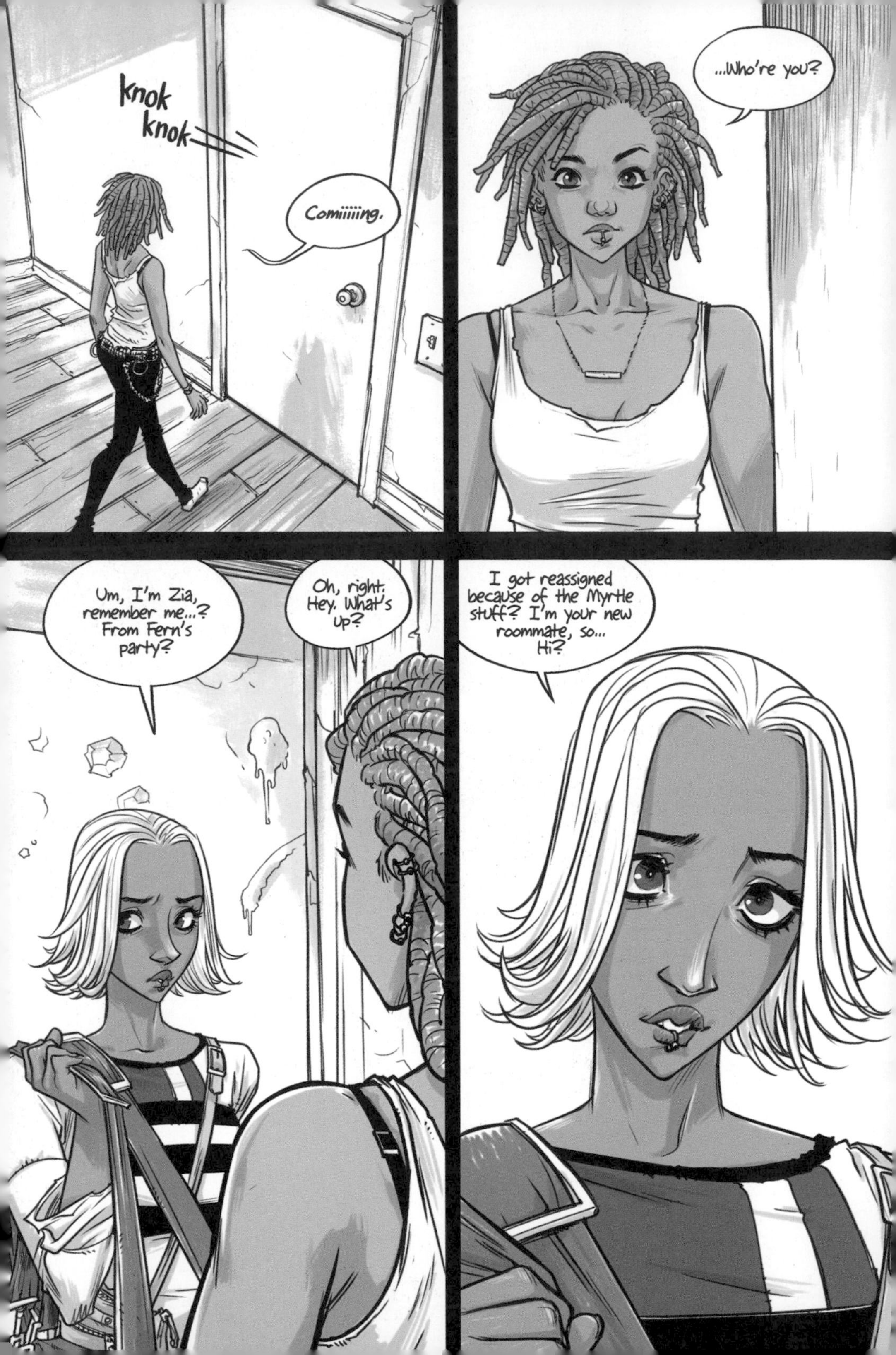
knok knok
Comiiiiing.
...Who're you?
Um, I'm Zia, remember me...? From Fern's party?
Oh, right. Hey. What's up?
I got reassigned because of the Myrtle stuff? I'm your new roommate, so... Hi?

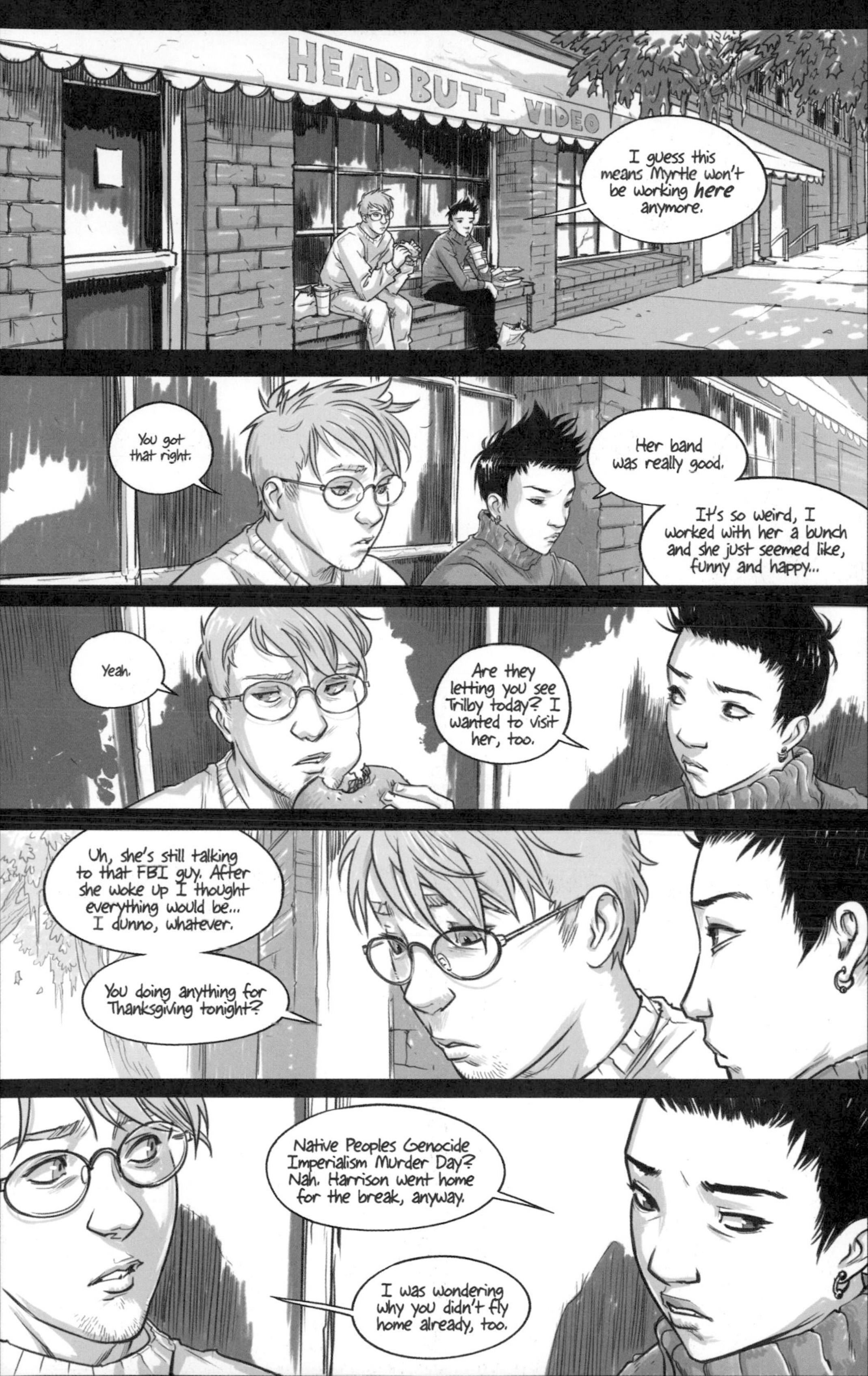
HEAD BUTT VIDEO
I guess this means Myrtle won't be working *here* anymore.
You got that right.
Her band was really good.
It's so weird, I worked with her a bunch and she just seemed like, funny and happy...
Yeah.
Are they letting you see Trilby today? I wanted to visit her, too.
Uh, she's still talking to that FBI guy. After she woke up I thought everything would be... I dunno, whatever.
You doing anything for Thanksgiving tonight?
Native Peoples Genocide Imperialism Murder Day? Nah. Harrison went home for the break, anyway.
I was wondering why you didn't fly home already, too.

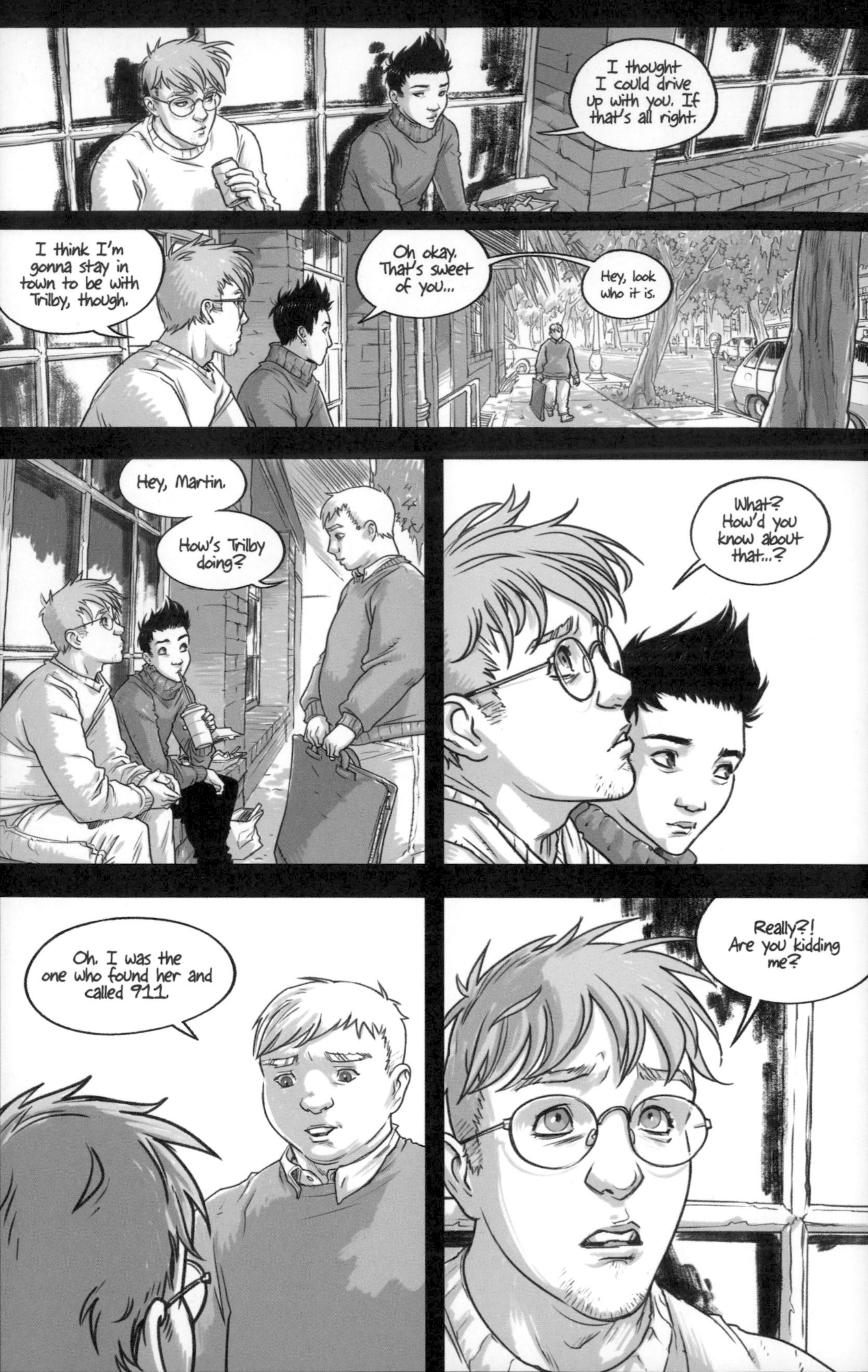

I thought I could drive up with you. If that's all right.
I think I'm gonna stay in town to be with Trilby, though.
Oh okay. That's sweet of you...
Hey, look who it is.
Hey, Martin.
How's Trilby doing?
What? How'd you know about that...?
Oh. I was the one who found her and called 911.
Really?! Are you kidding me?

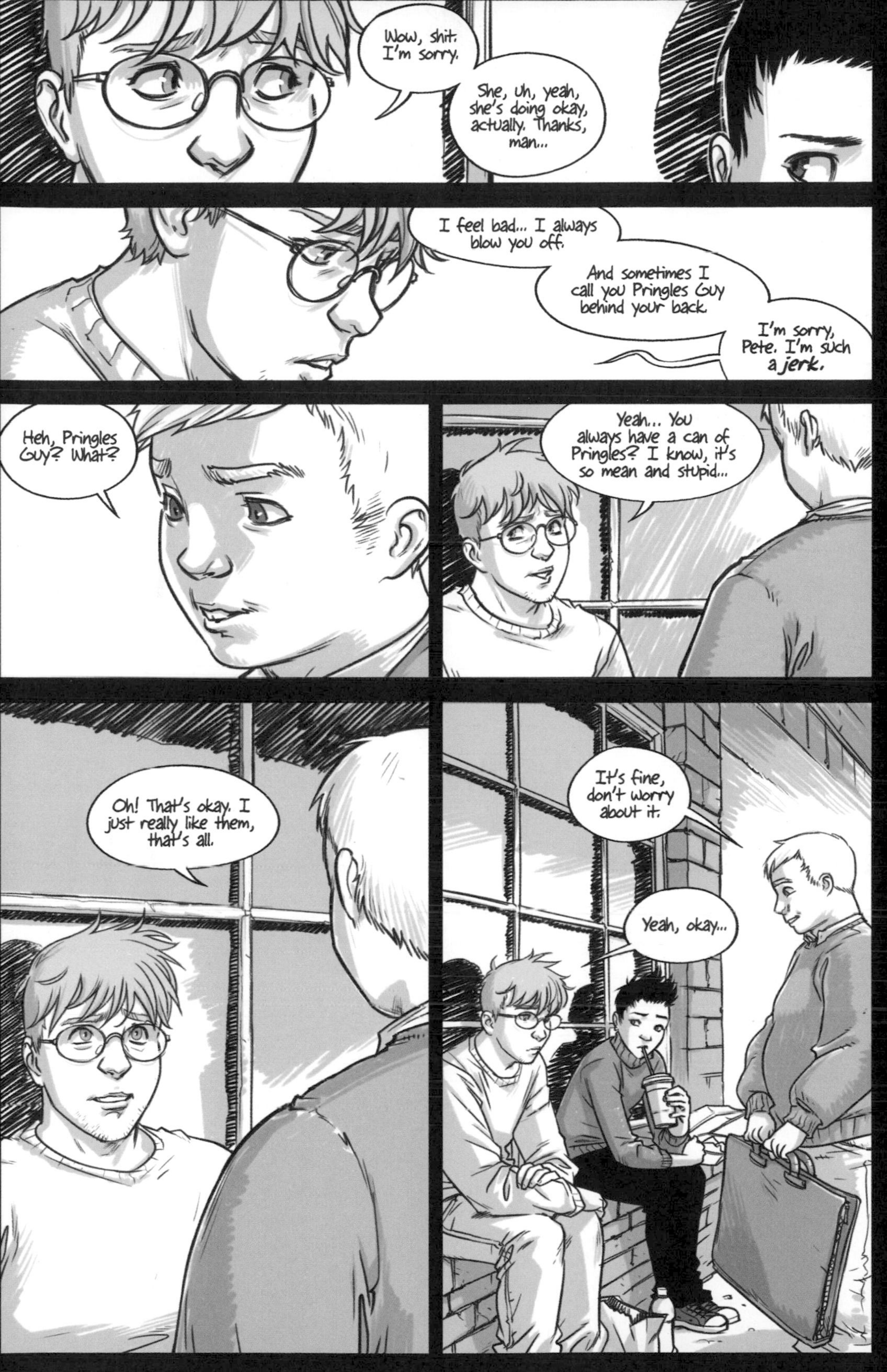
Wow, shit. I'm sorry.
She, uh, yeah, she's doing okay, actually. Thanks, man...
I feel bad... I always blow you off.
And sometimes I call you Pringles Guy behind your back.
I'm sorry, Pete. I'm such a *jerk.*
Heh, Pringles Guy? What?
Yeah... You always have a can of Pringles? I know, it's so mean and stupid...
Oh! That's okay. I just really like them, that's all.
It's fine, don't worry about it.
Yeah, okay...

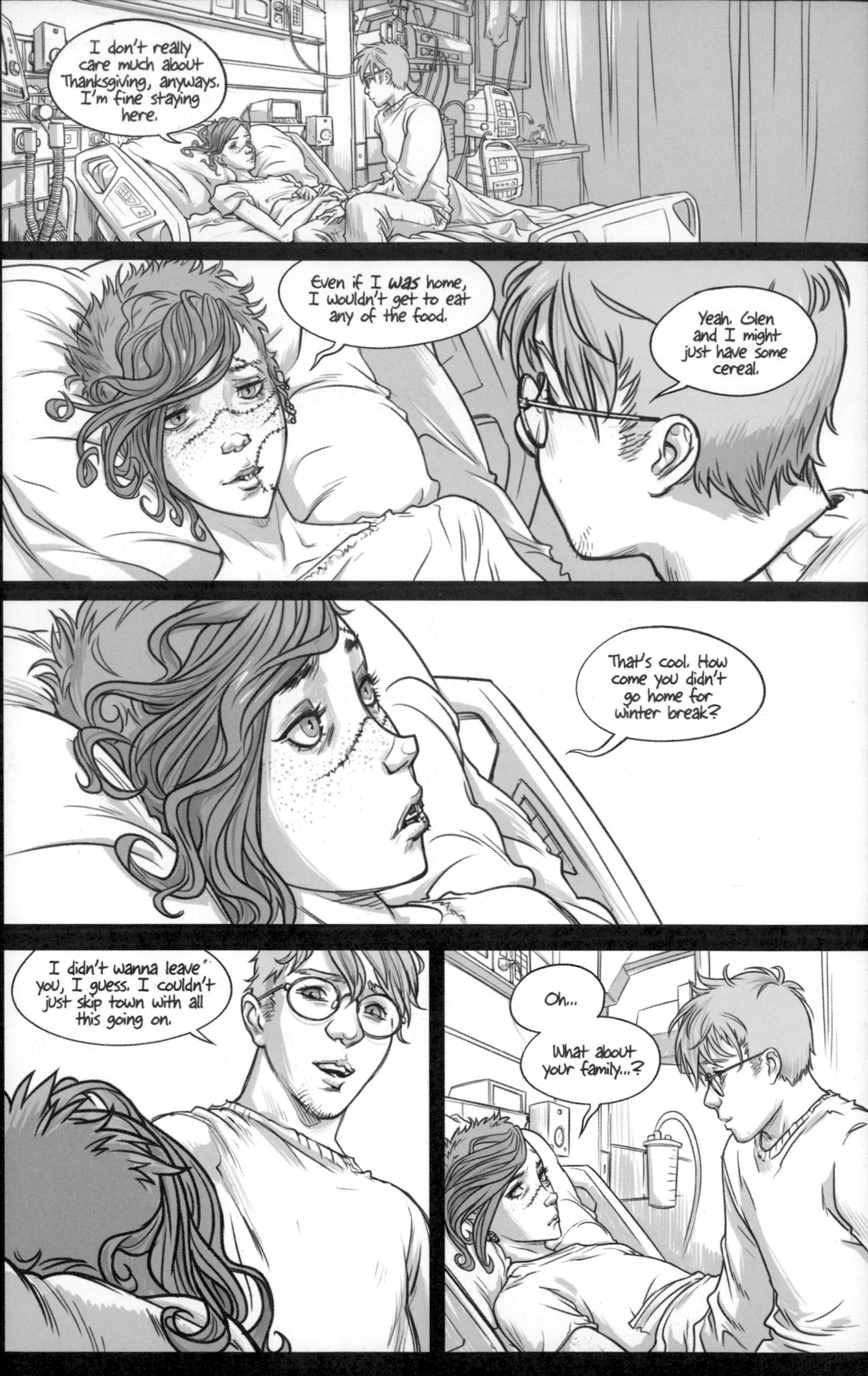
I don't really care much about Thanksgiving, anyways. I'm fine staying here.
Even if I *was* home, I wouldn't get to eat any of the food.
Yeah. Glen and I might just have some cereal.
That's cool. How come you didn't go home for winter break?
I didn't wanna leave you, I guess. I couldn't just skip town with all this going on.
Oh...
What about your family...?

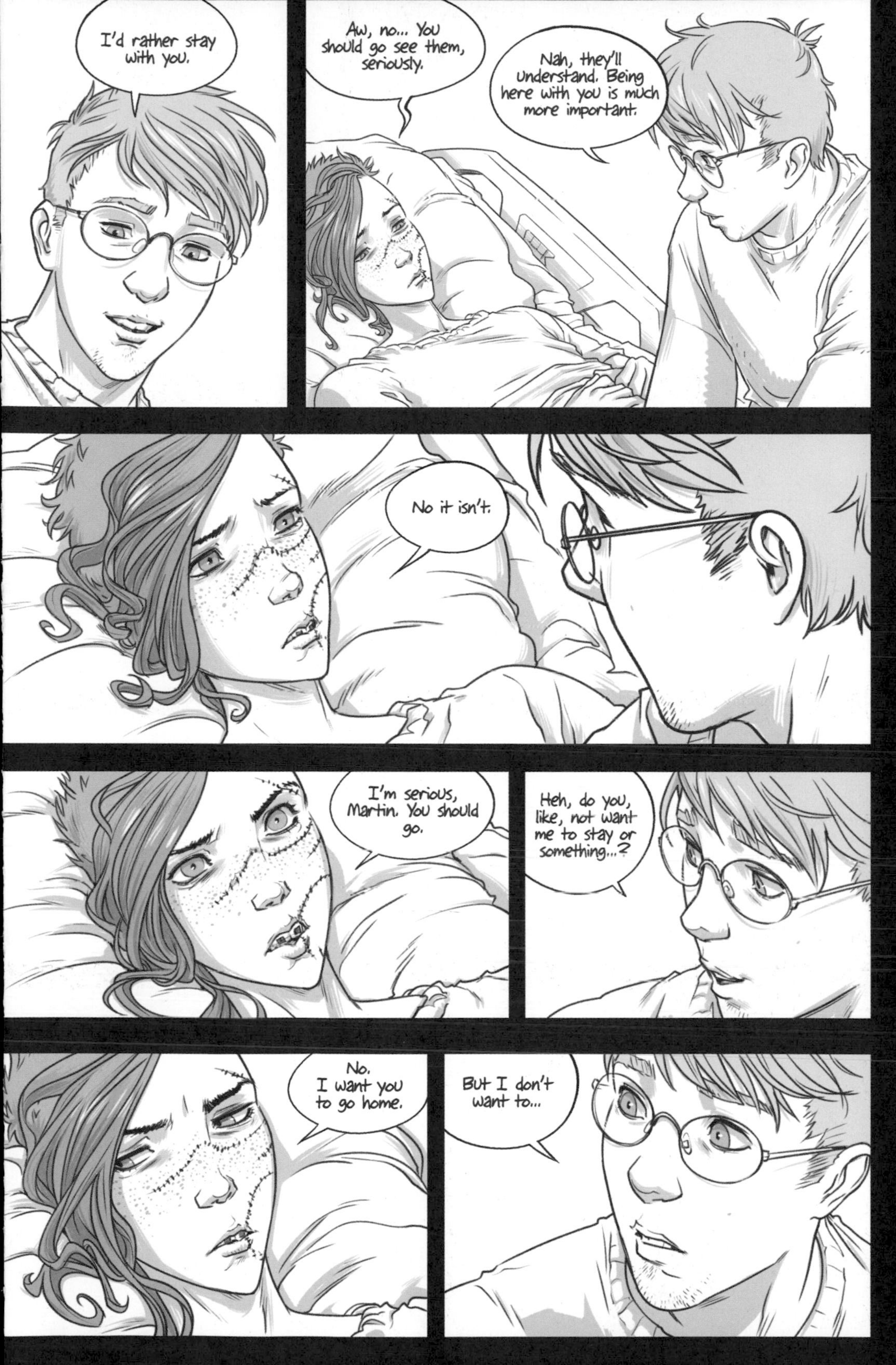
I'd rather stay with you.
Aw, no... You should go see them, seriously.
Nah, they'll understand. Being here with you is much more important.
No it isn't.
I'm serious, Martin. You should go.
Heh, do you, like, not want me to stay or something...?
No. I want you to go home.
But I don't want to...

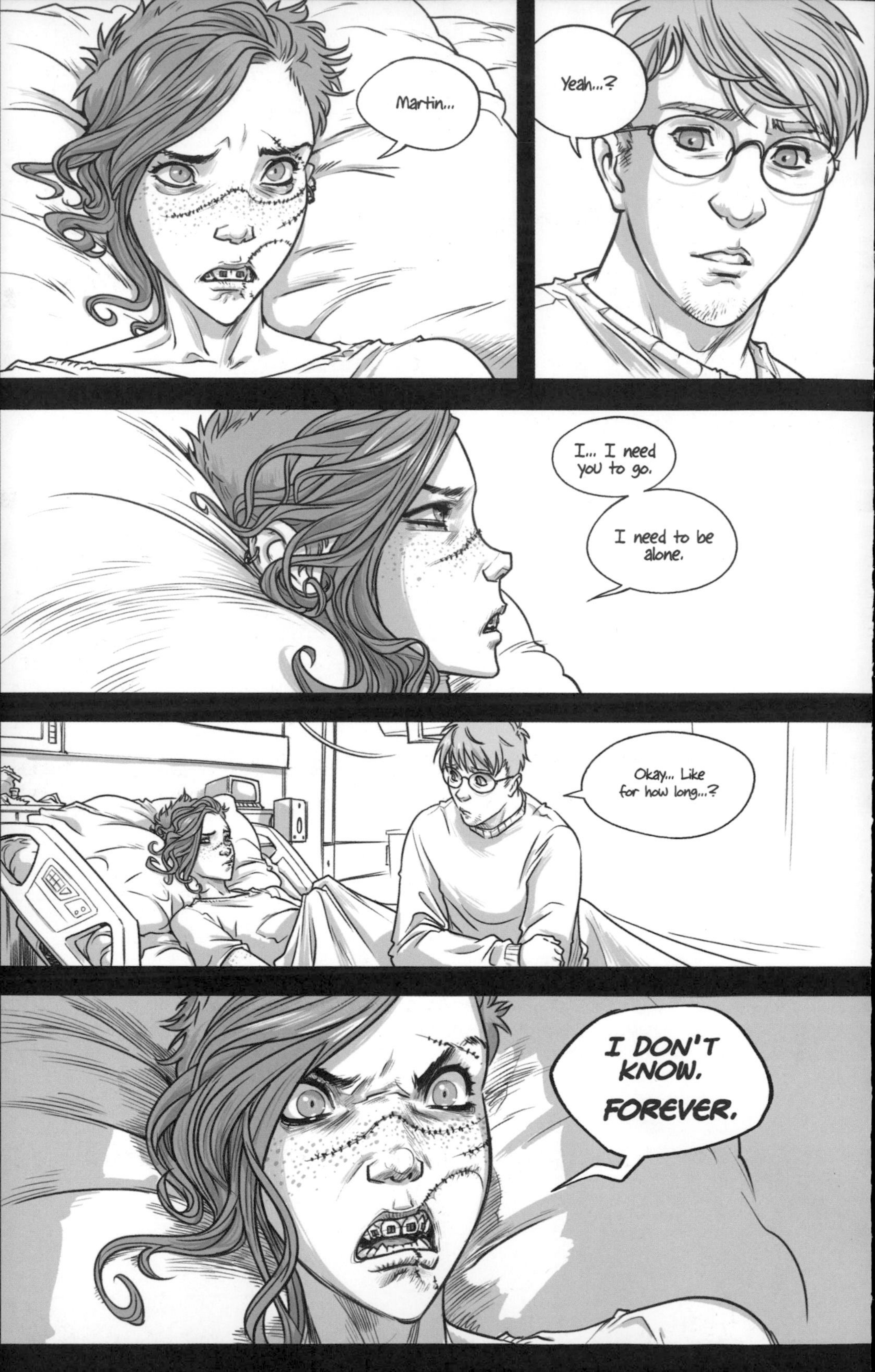

Martin...
Yeah...?
I... I need you to go.
I need to be alone.
Okay... Like for how long...?
I DON'T KNOW.
FOREVER.

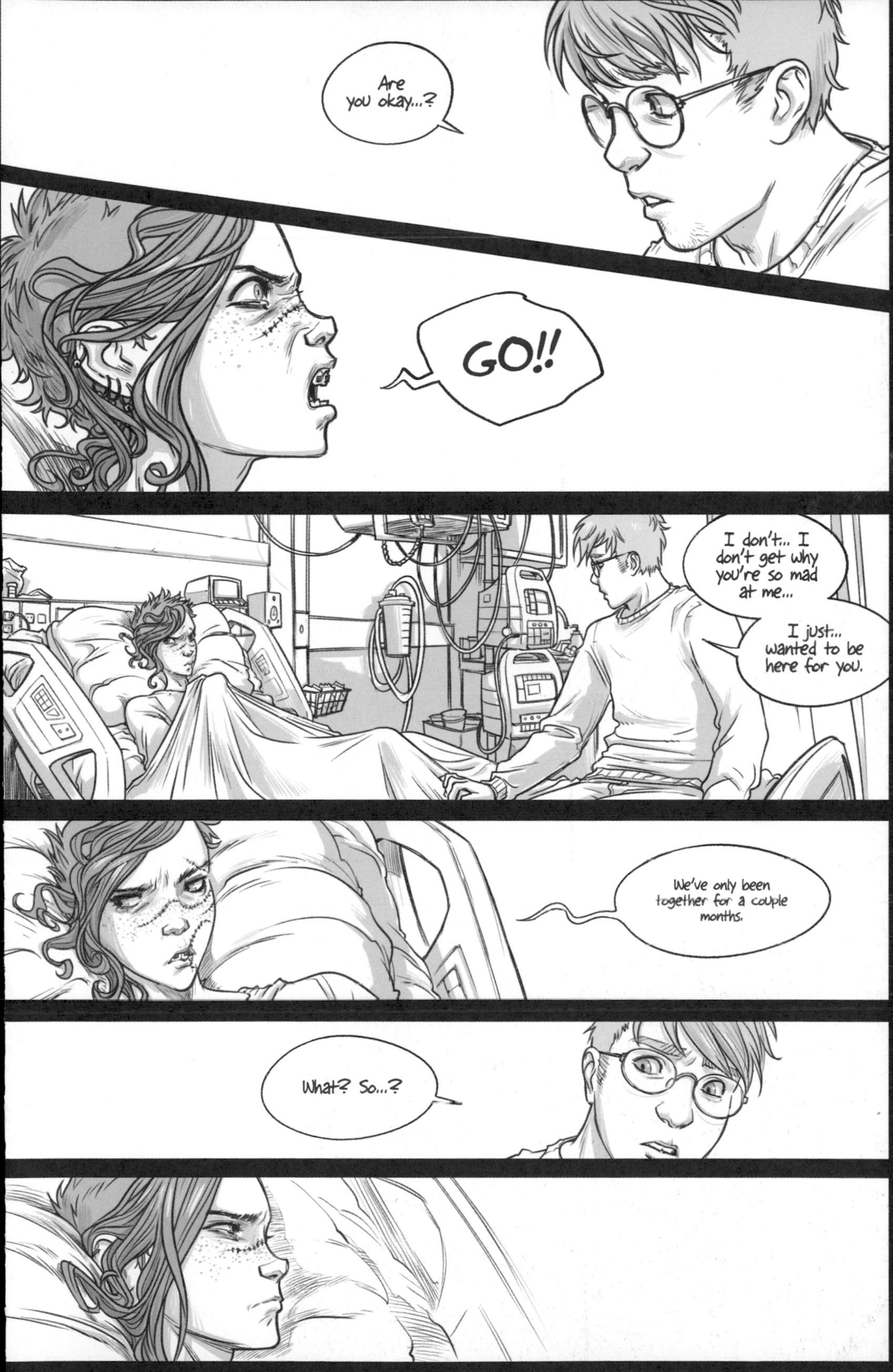
Are you okay...?
GO!!
I don't... I don't get why you're so mad at me...
I just... wanted to be here for you.
We've only been together for a couple months.
What? So...?

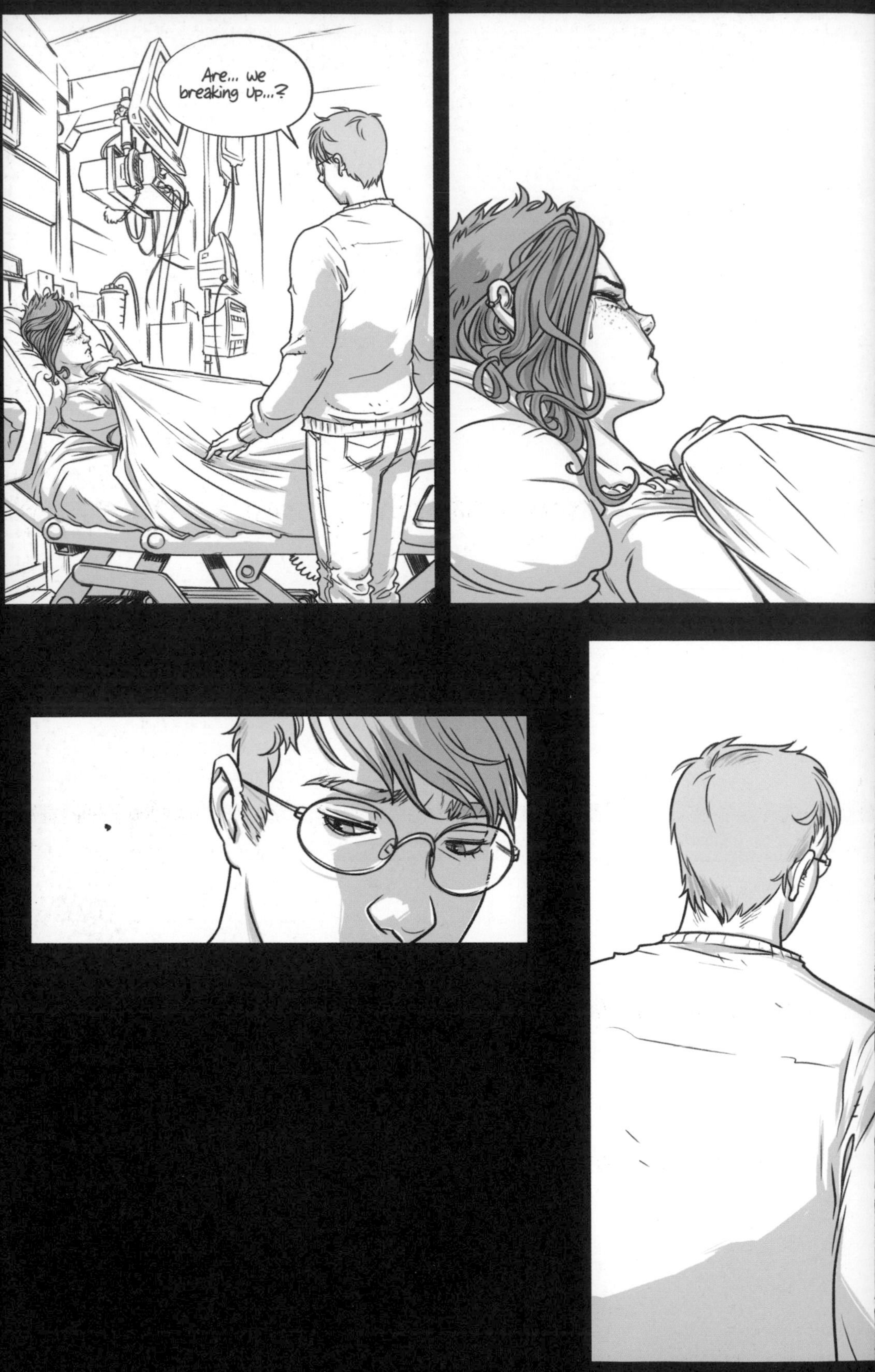
Are... we breaking up...?

32

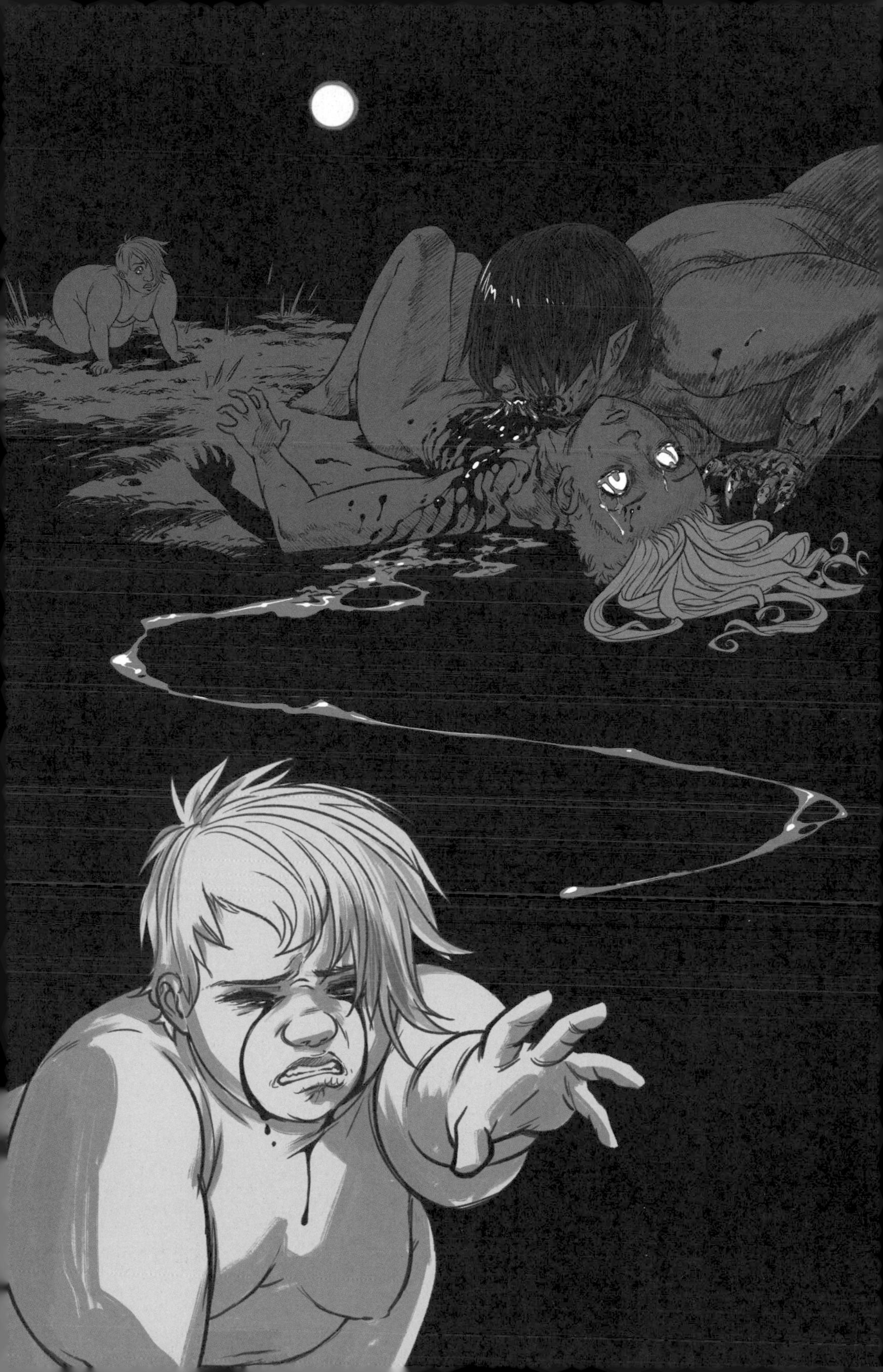

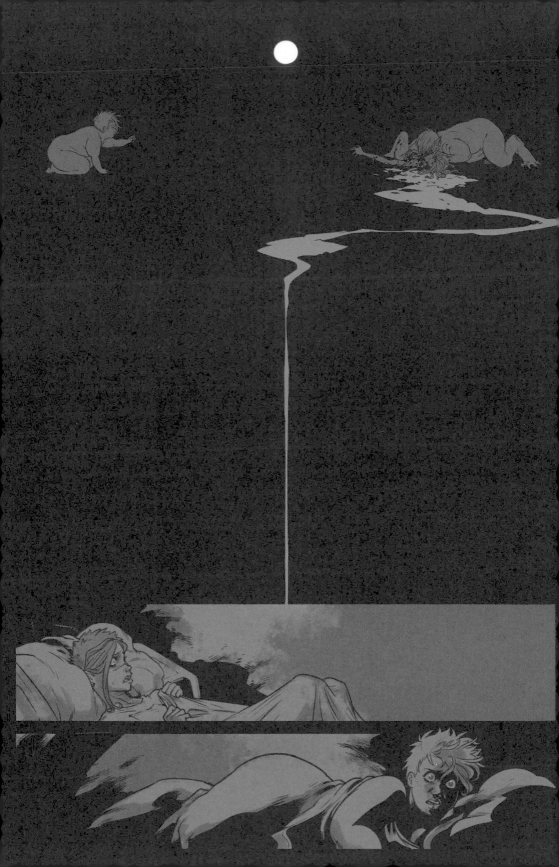

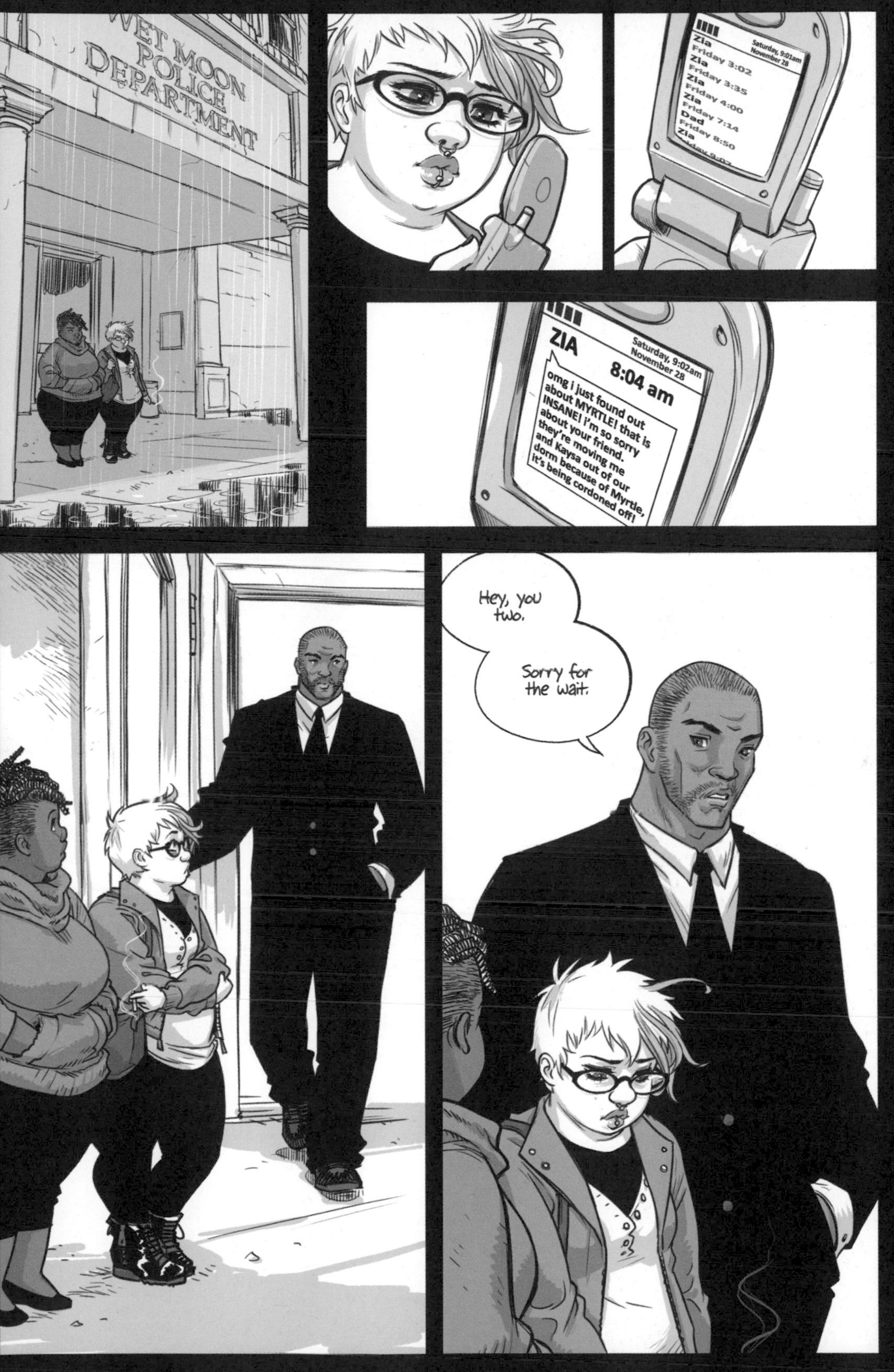
WET MOON POLICE DEPARTMENT
Saturday, 9:01am November 28
Zia
Friday 3:02
Zia
Friday 3:35
Zia
Friday 4:00
Zia
Friday 7:14
Dad
Friday 8:50
Zia
ZIA
Saturday, 9:02am November 28
8:04 am
omg i just found out about MYRTLE! that is INSANE! i'm so sorry about your friend. they're moving me and Kaysa out of our dorm because of Myrtle, it's being cordoned off!
Hey, you two.
Sorry for the wait.

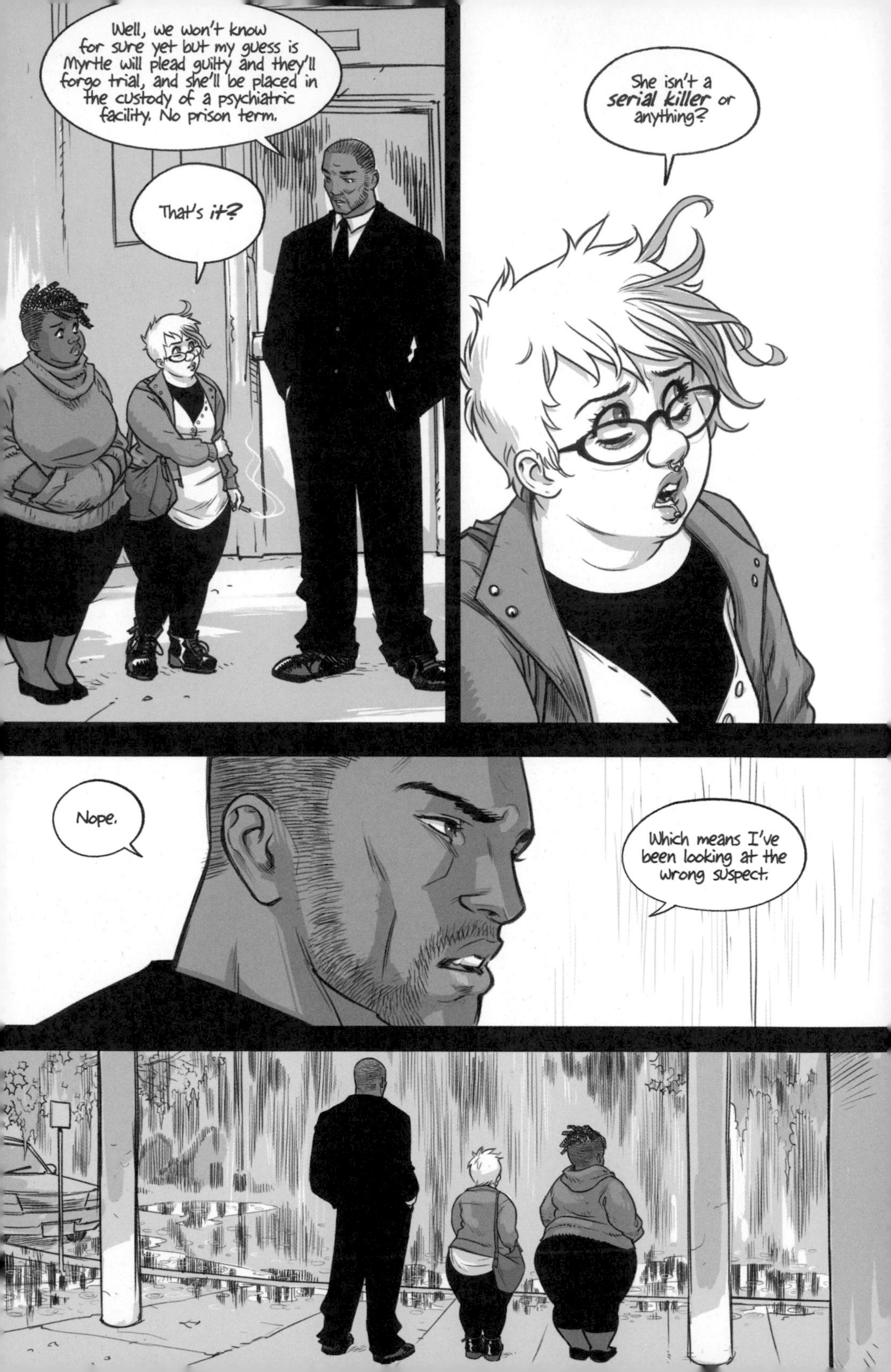
Well, we won't know for sure yet but my guess is Myrtle will plead guilty and they'll forgo trial, and she'll be placed in the custody of a psychiatric facility. No prison term.
That's *it?*
She isn't a ***serial killer*** or anything?
Nope.
Which means I've been looking at the wrong suspect.

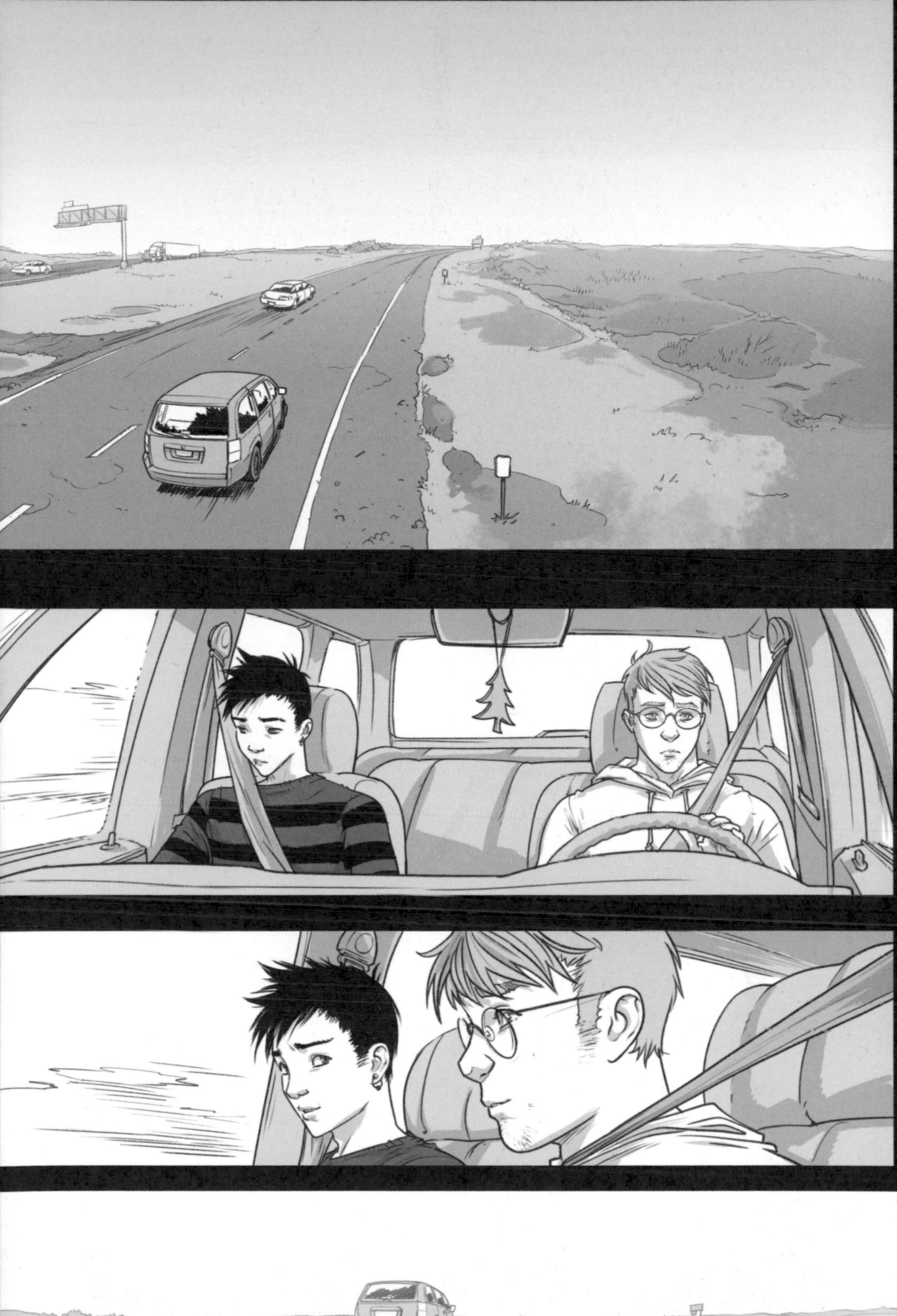

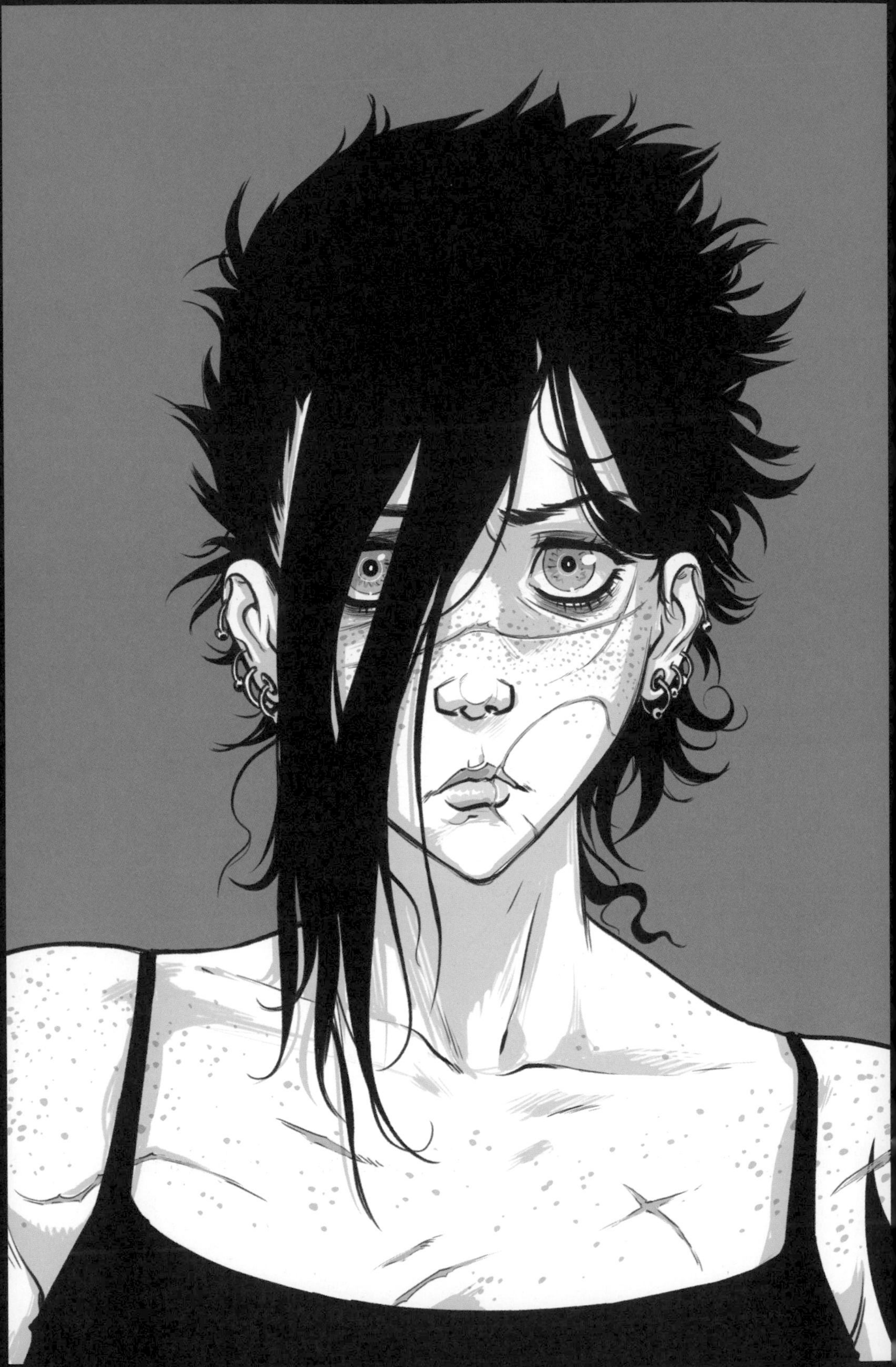

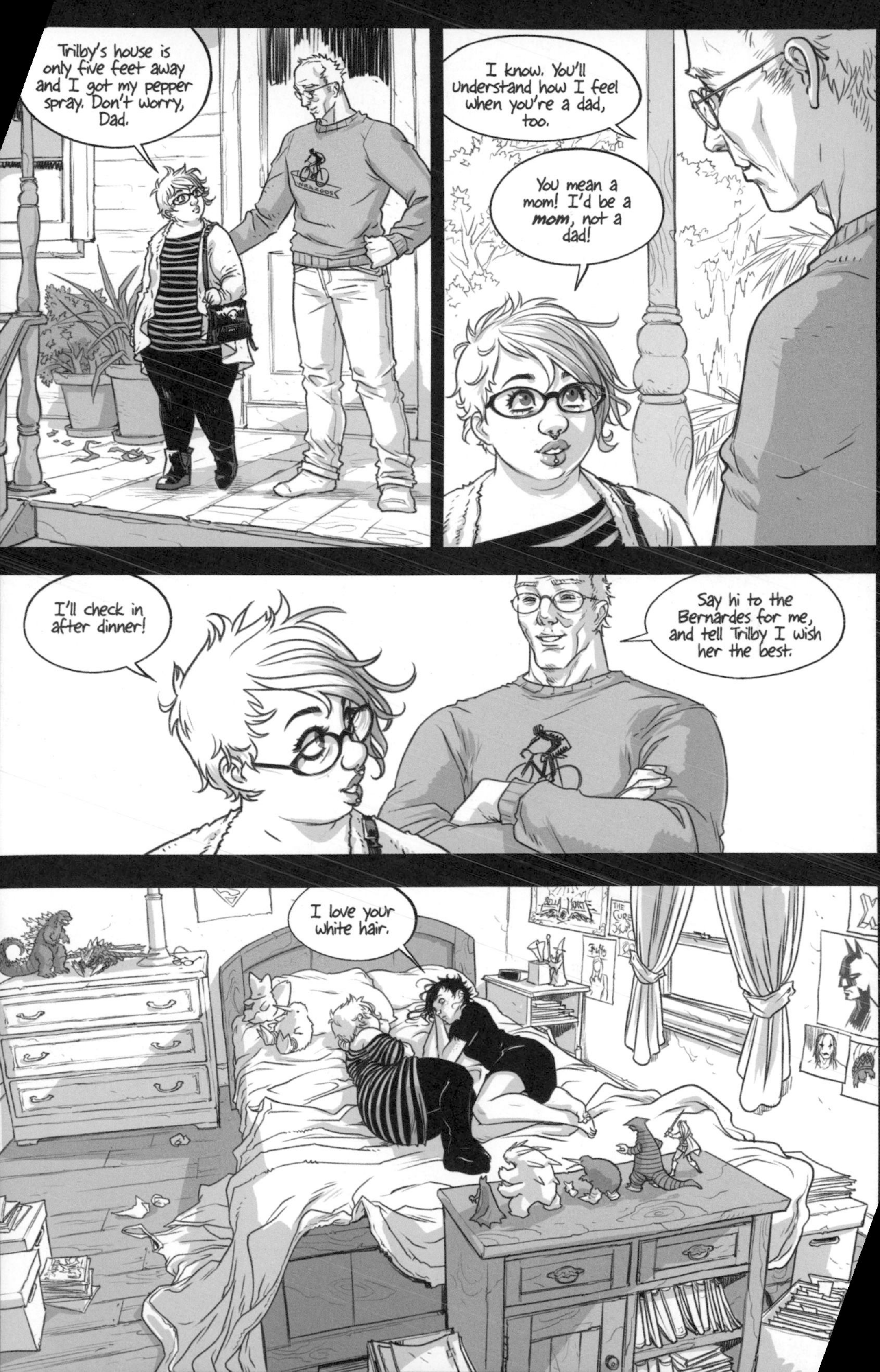
Trilby's house is only five feet away and I got my pepper spray. Don't worry, Dad.
I know. You'll understand how I feel when you're a dad, too.
You mean a mom! I'd be a **mom**, not a dad!
I'll check in after dinner!
Say hi to the Bernardes for me, and tell Trilby I wish her the best.
I love your white hair.

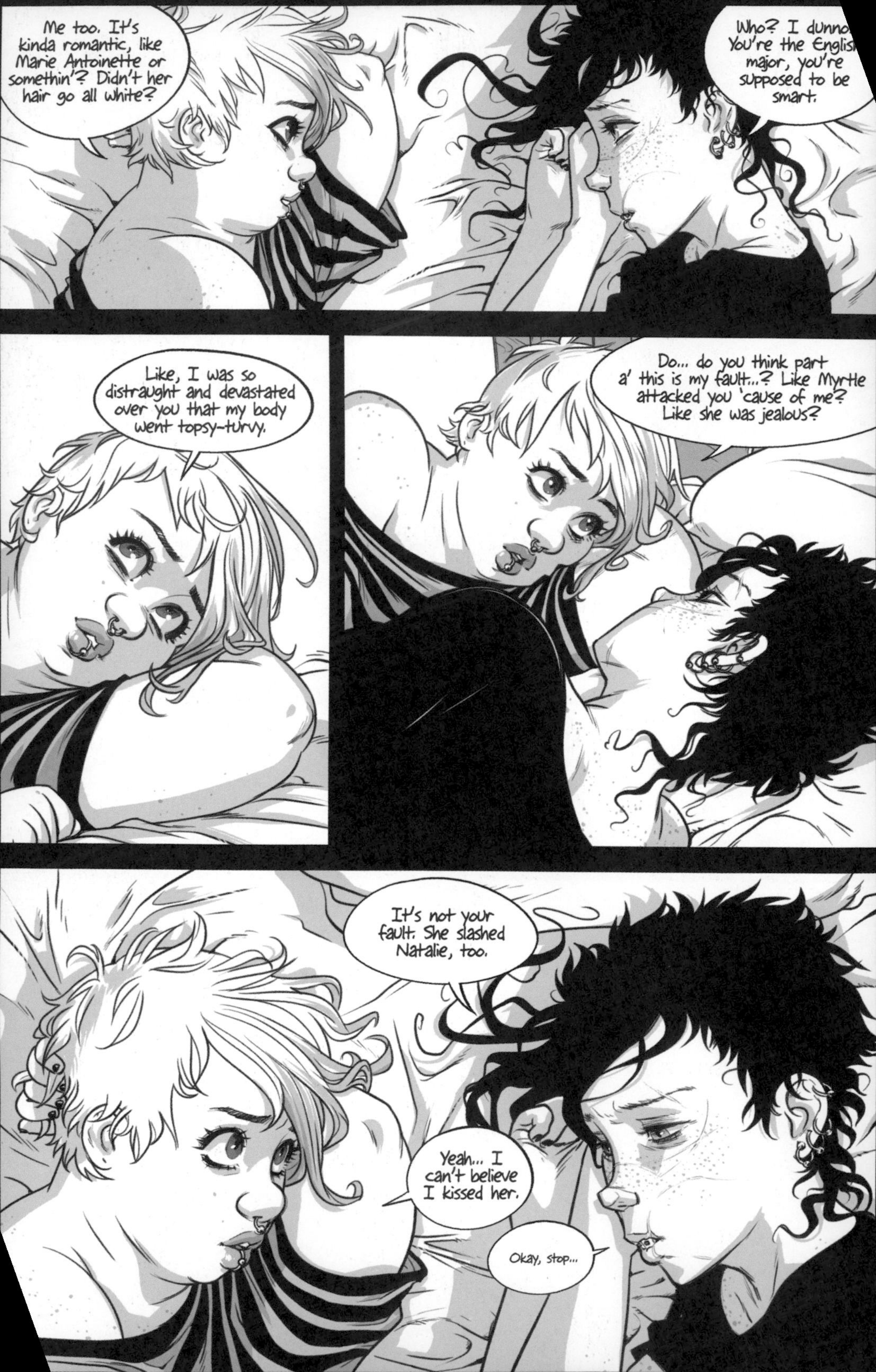
Me too. It's kinda romantic, like Marie Antoinette or somethin'? Didn't her hair go all white?
Who? I dunno. You're the English major, you're supposed to be smart.
Like, I was so distraught and devastated over you that my body went topsy-turvy.
Do... do you think part a' this is my fault...? Like Myrtle attacked you 'cause of me? Like she was jealous?
It's not your fault. She slashed Natalie, too.
Yeah... I can't believe I kissed her.
Okay, stop...

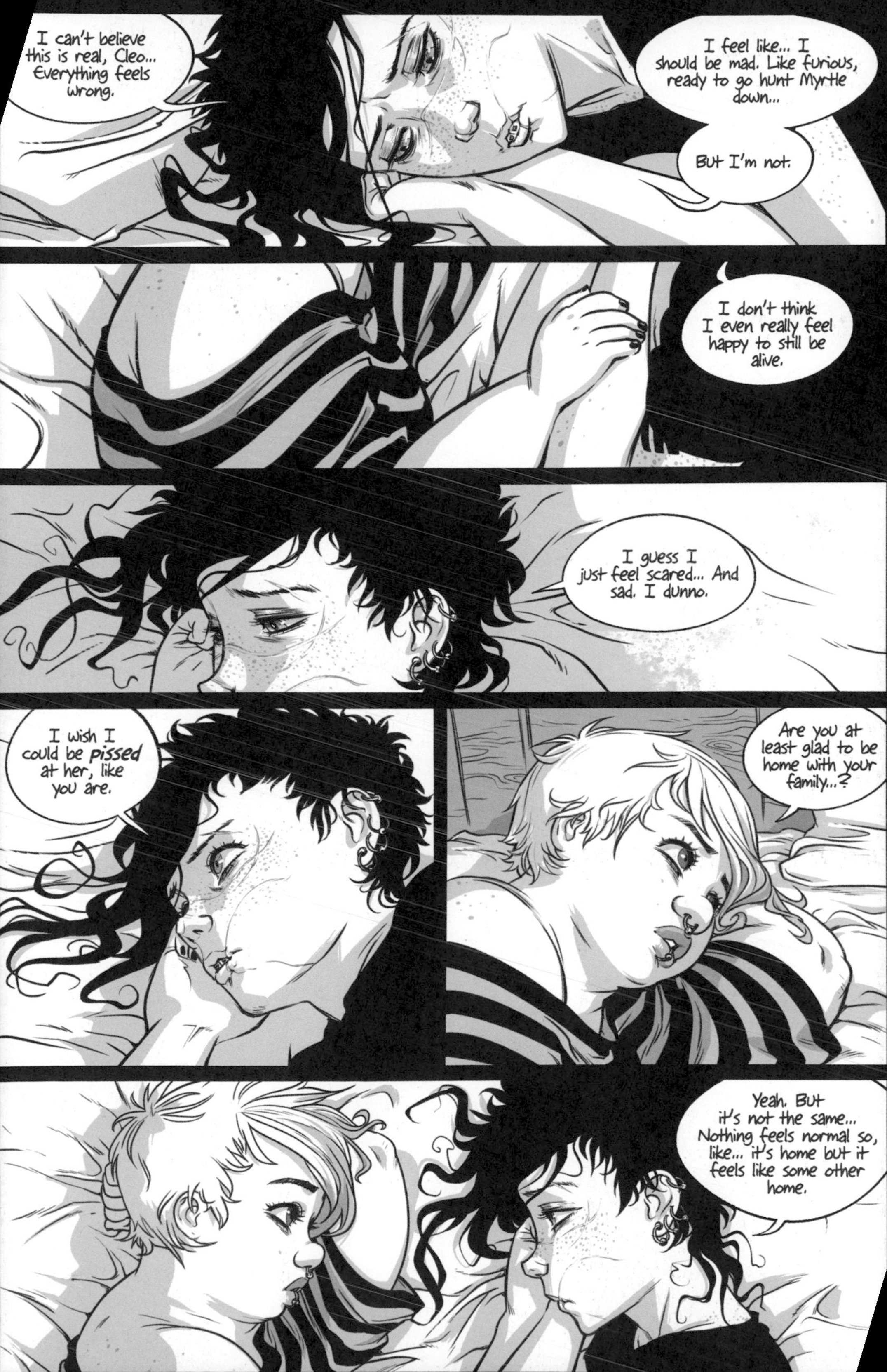
I can't believe this is real, Cleo... Everything feels wrong.
I feel like... I should be mad. Like furious, ready to go hunt Myrtle down...
But I'm not.
I don't think I even really feel happy to still be alive.
I guess I just feel scared... And sad. I dunno.
I wish I could be ***pissed*** at her, like you are.
Are you at least glad to be home with your family...?
Yeah. But it's not the same... Nothing feels normal so, like... it's home but it feels like some other home.

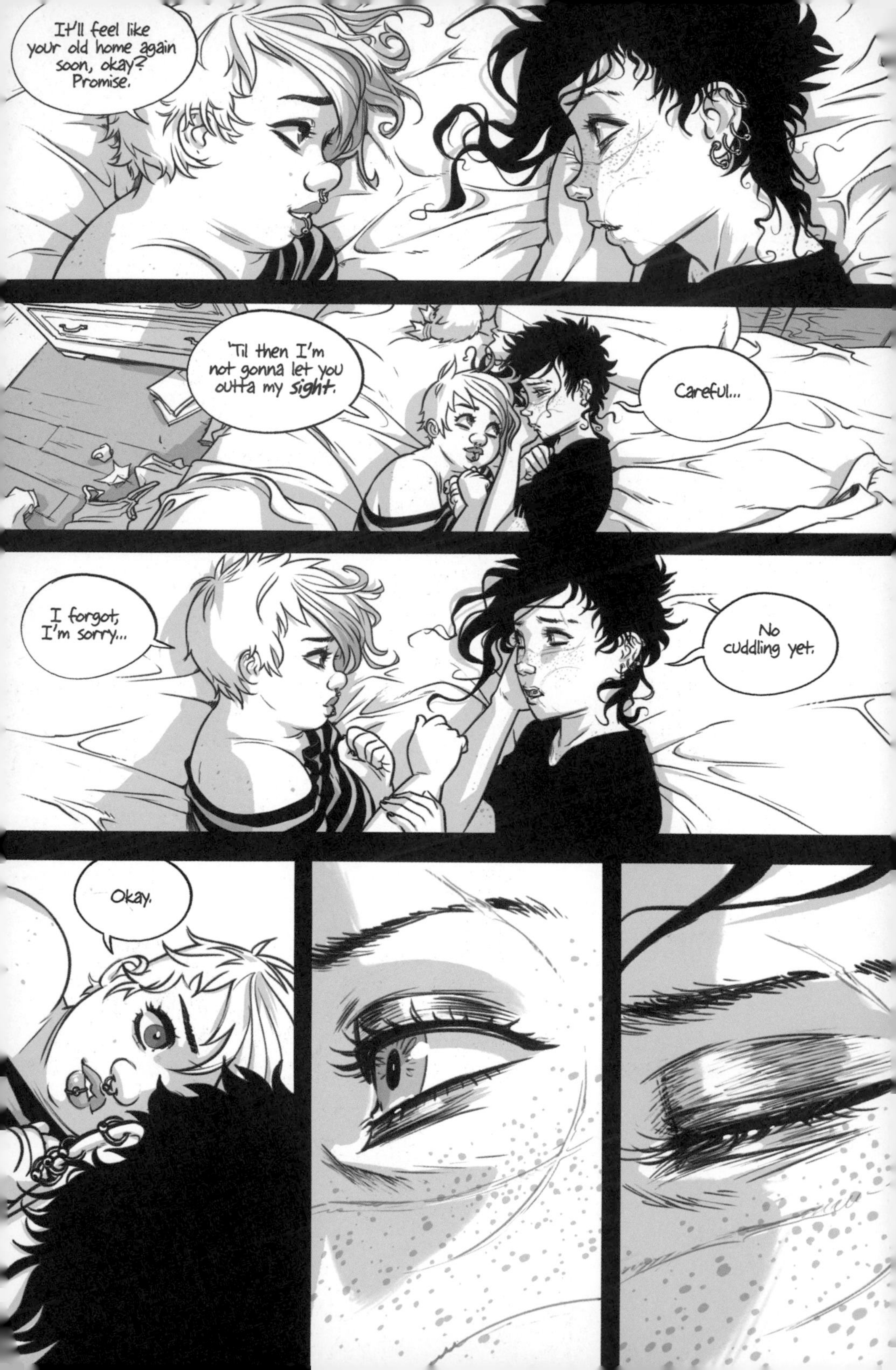
It'll feel like your old home again soon, okay? Promise.
'Til then I'm not gonna let you outta my *sight*.
Careful...
I forgot, I'm sorry...
No cuddling yet.
Okay.

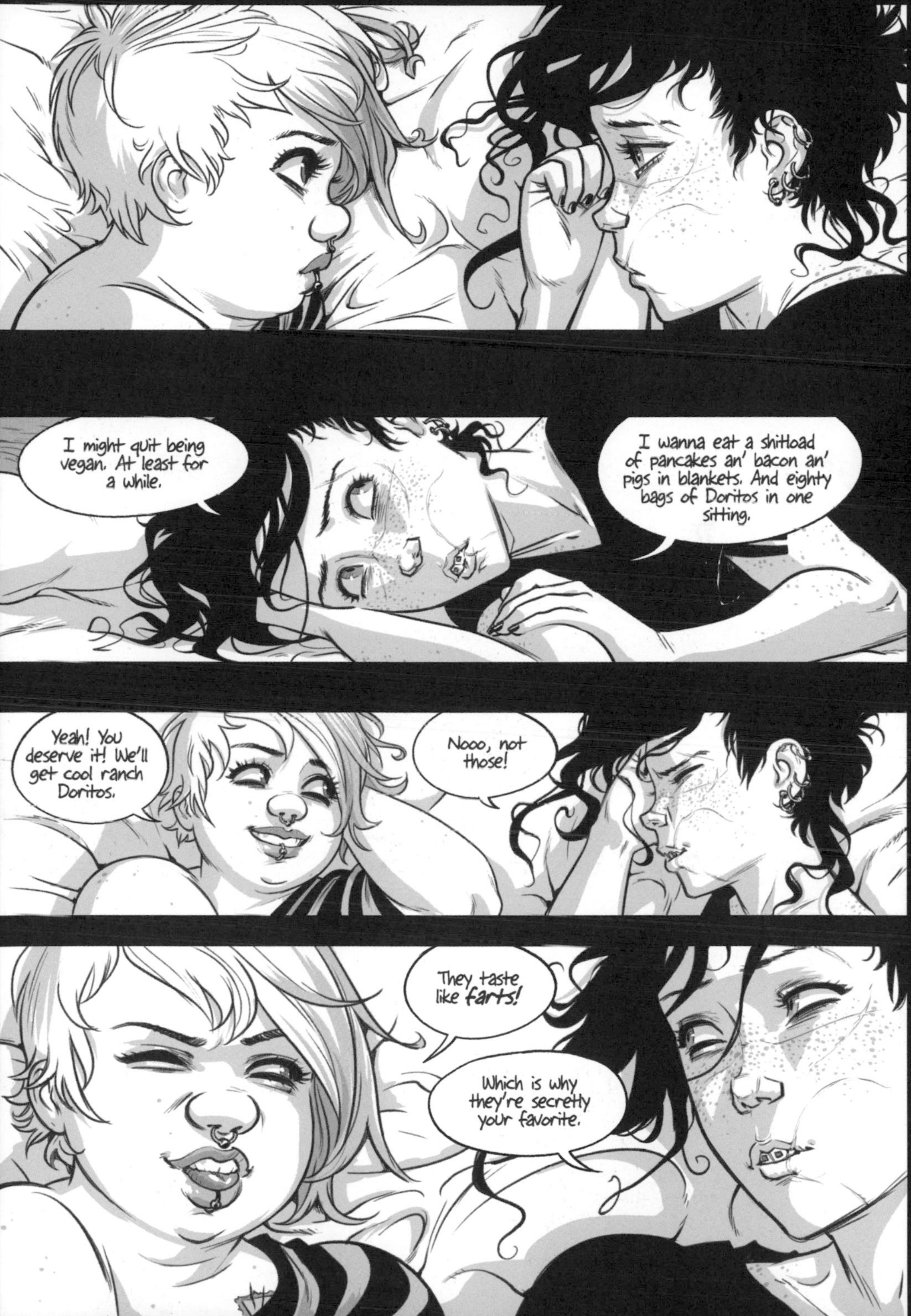
I might quit being vegan. At least for a while.
I wanna eat a shitload of pancakes an' bacon an' pigs in blankets. And eighty bags of Doritos in one sitting.
Yeah! You deserve it! We'll get cool ranch Doritos.
Nooo, not those!
They taste like farts!
Which is why they're secretly your favorite.

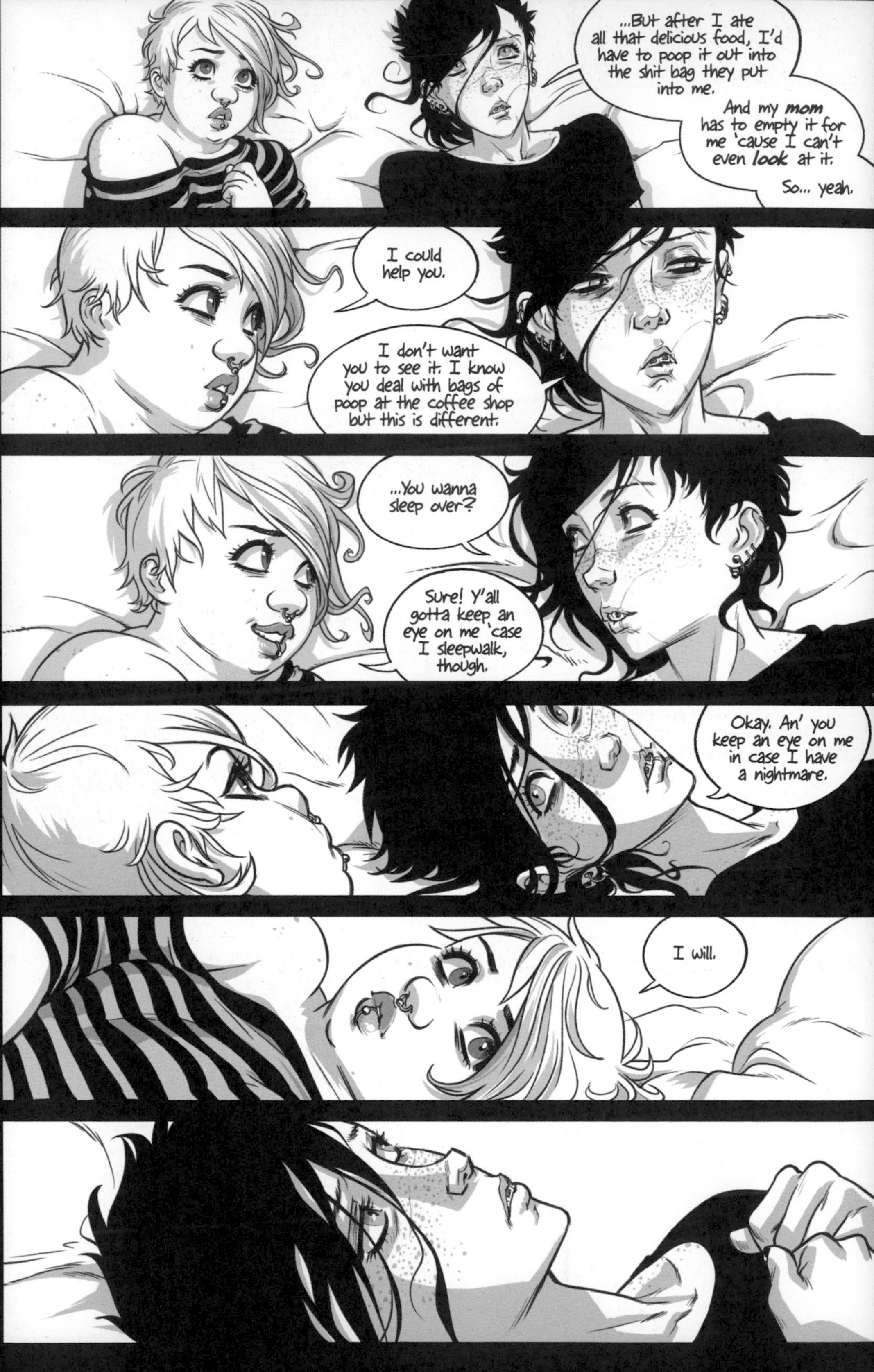
...But after I ate all that delicious food, I'd have to poop it out into the shit bag they put into me.
And my **mom** has to empty it for me 'cause I can't even **look** at it.
So... yeah.
I could help you.
I don't want you to see it. I know you deal with bags of poop at the coffee shop but this is different.
...You wanna sleep over?
Sure! Y'all gotta keep an eye on me 'case I sleepwalk, though.
Okay. An' you keep an eye on me in case I have a nightmare.
I will.

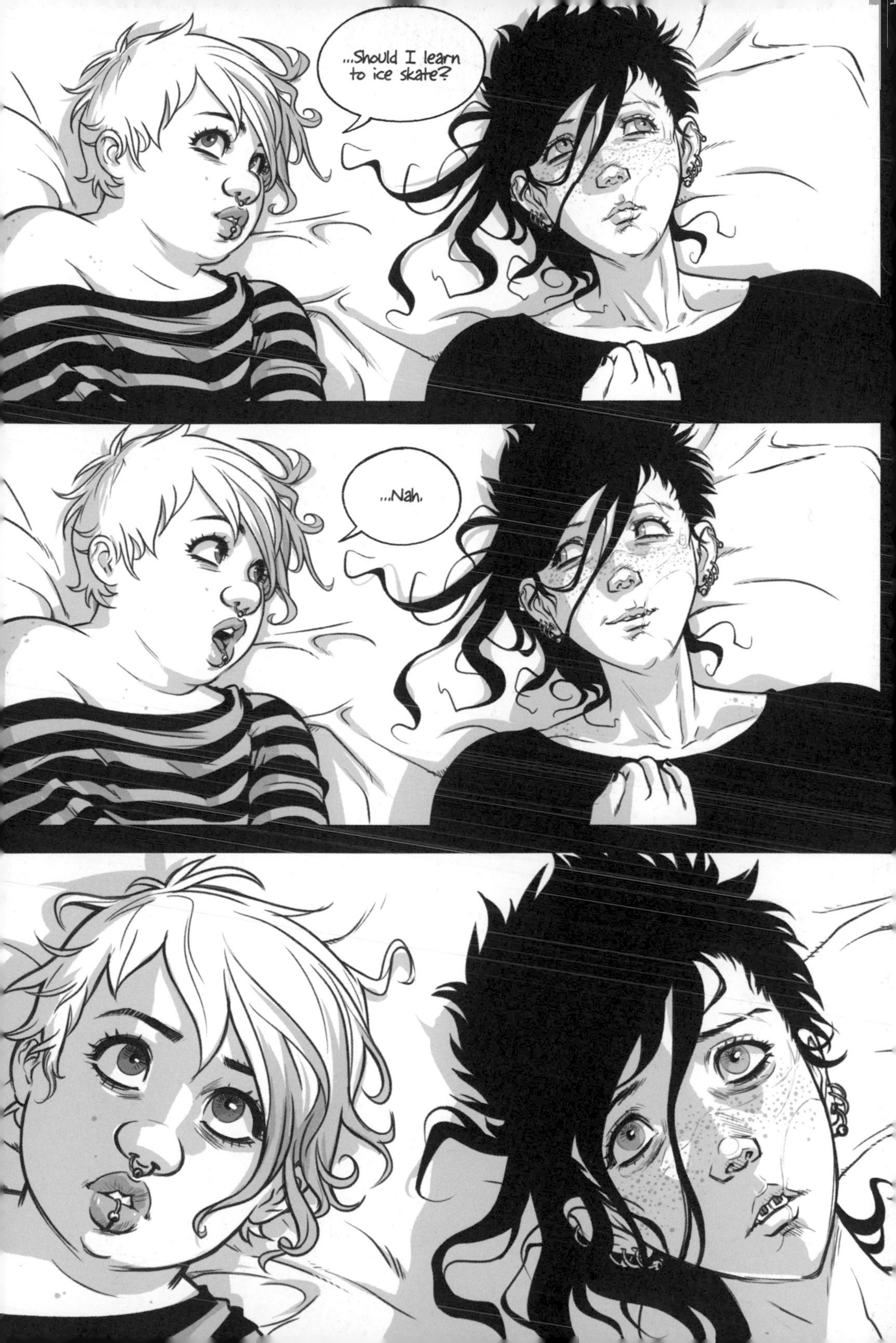
...Should I learn to ice skate?
...Nah.

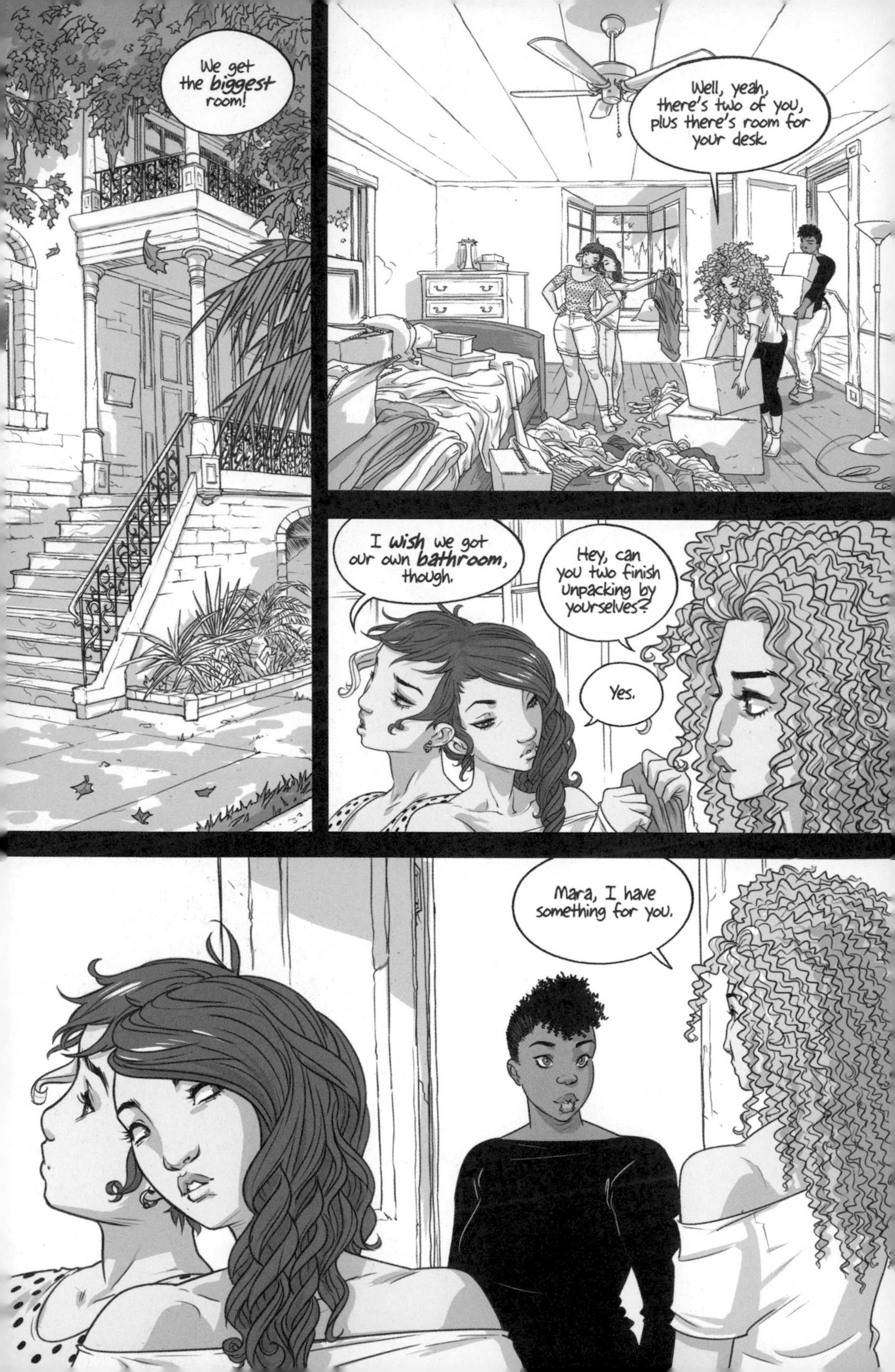
We get the biggest room!
Well, yeah, there's two of you, plus there's room for your desk.
I wish we got our own bathroom, though.
Hey, can you two finish unpacking by yourselves?
Yes.
Mara, I have something for you.

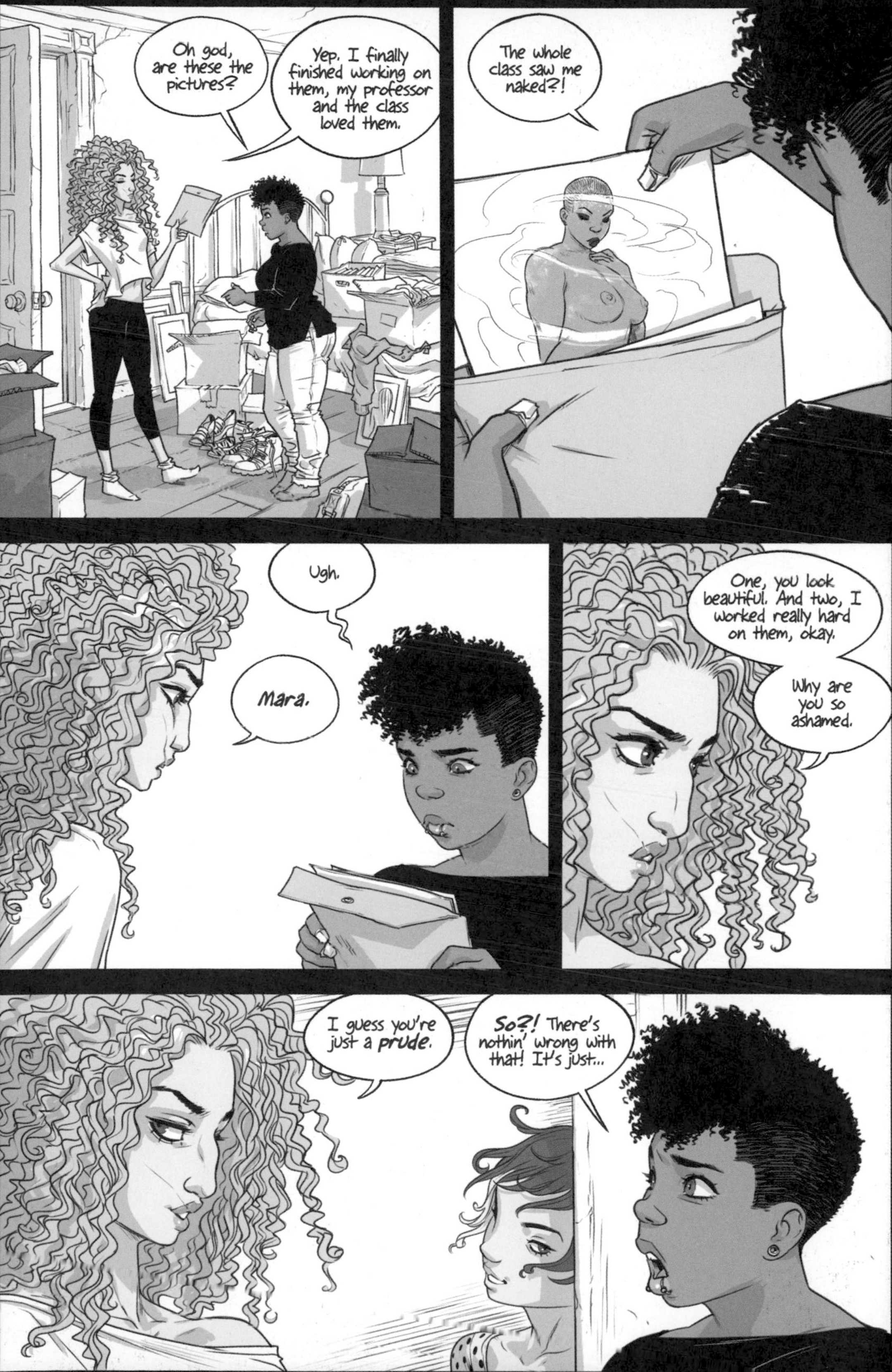
Oh god, are these the pictures?
Yep. I finally finished working on them, my professor and the class loved them.
The whole class saw me naked?!
Ugh.
Mara.
One, you look beautiful. And two, I worked really hard on them, okay.
Why are you so ashamed.
I guess you're just a **prude**.
So?! There's nothin' wrong with that! It's just...

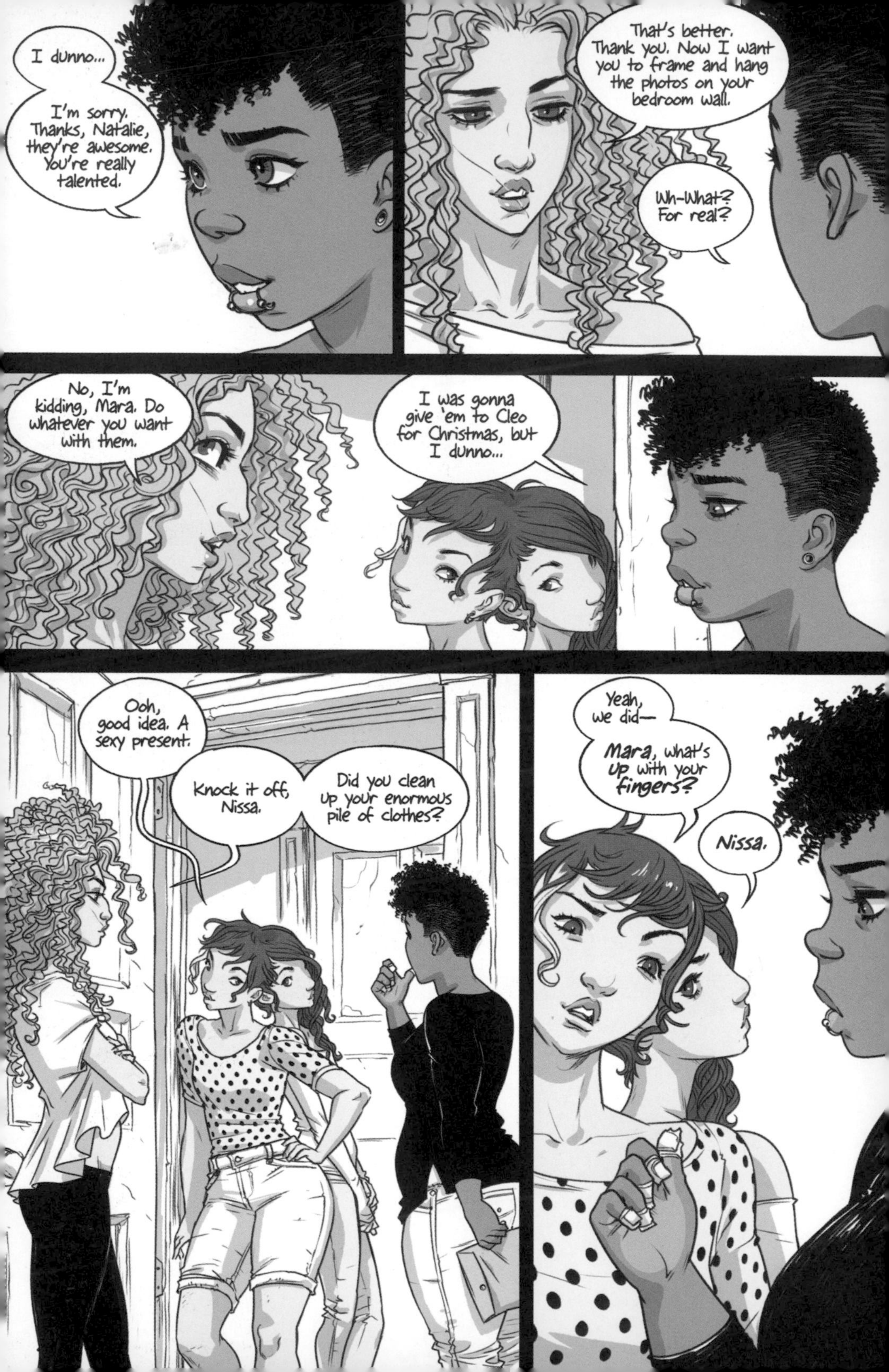

I dunno...
I'm sorry. Thanks, Natalie, they're awesome. You're really talented.
That's better. Thank you. Now I want you to frame and hang the photos on your bedroom wall.
Wh-What? For real?
No, I'm kidding, Mara. Do whatever you want with them.
I was gonna give 'em to Cleo for Christmas, but I dunno...
Ooh, good idea. A sexy present.
Knock it off, Nissa.
Did you clean up your enormous pile of clothes?
Yeah, we did—
Mara, what's up with your fingers?
Nissa.

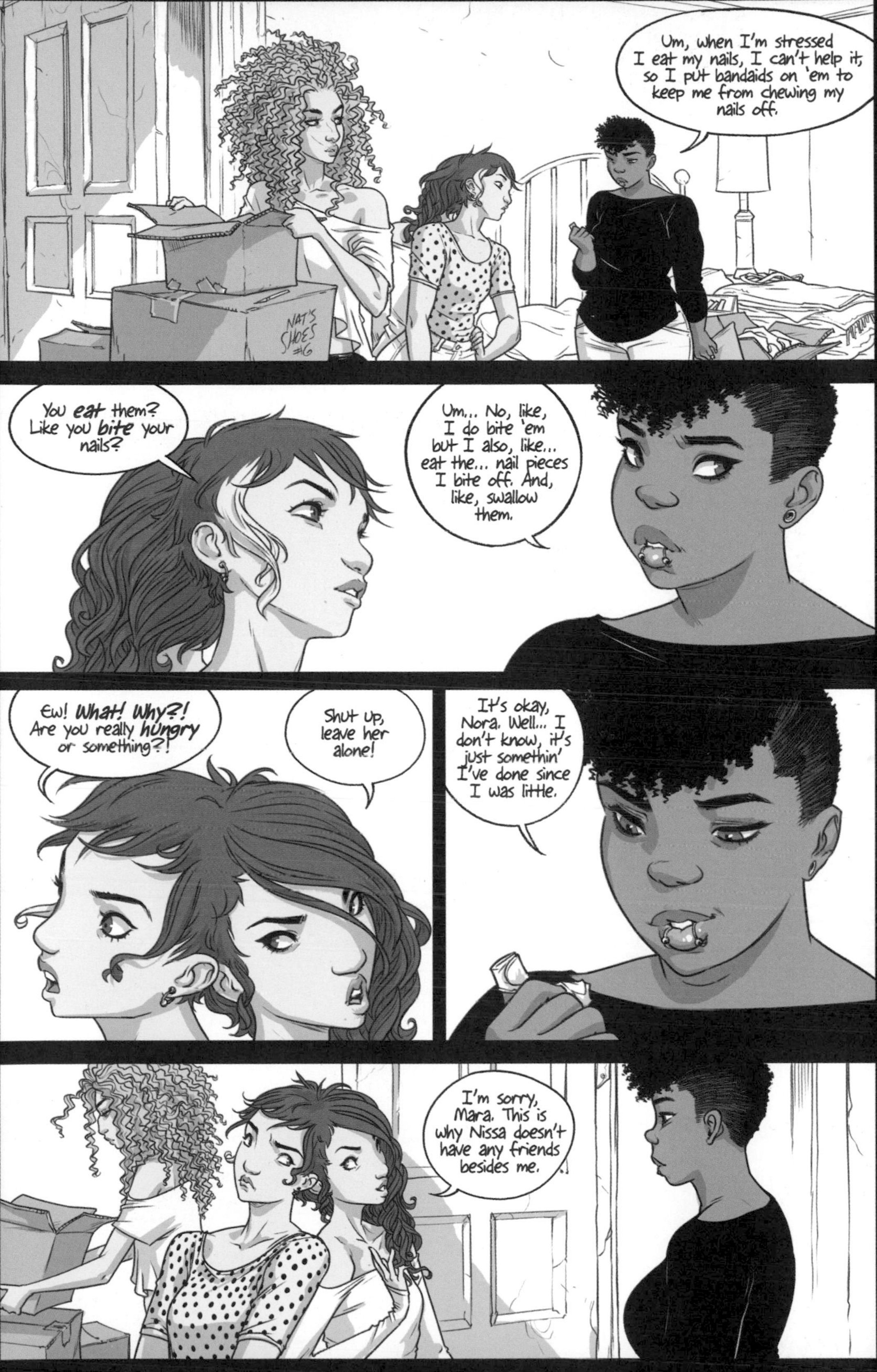
Um, when I'm stressed I eat my nails, I can't help it, so I put bandaids on 'em to keep me from chewing my nails off.
NAT'S SHOES #6
You eat them? Like you bite your nails?
Um... No, like, I do bite 'em but I also, like... eat the... nail pieces I bite off. And, like, swallow them.
Ew! What! Why?! Are you really hungry or something?!
Shut up, leave her alone!
It's okay, Nora. Well... I don't know, it's just somethin' I've done since I was little.
I'm sorry, Mara. This is why Nissa doesn't have any friends besides me.

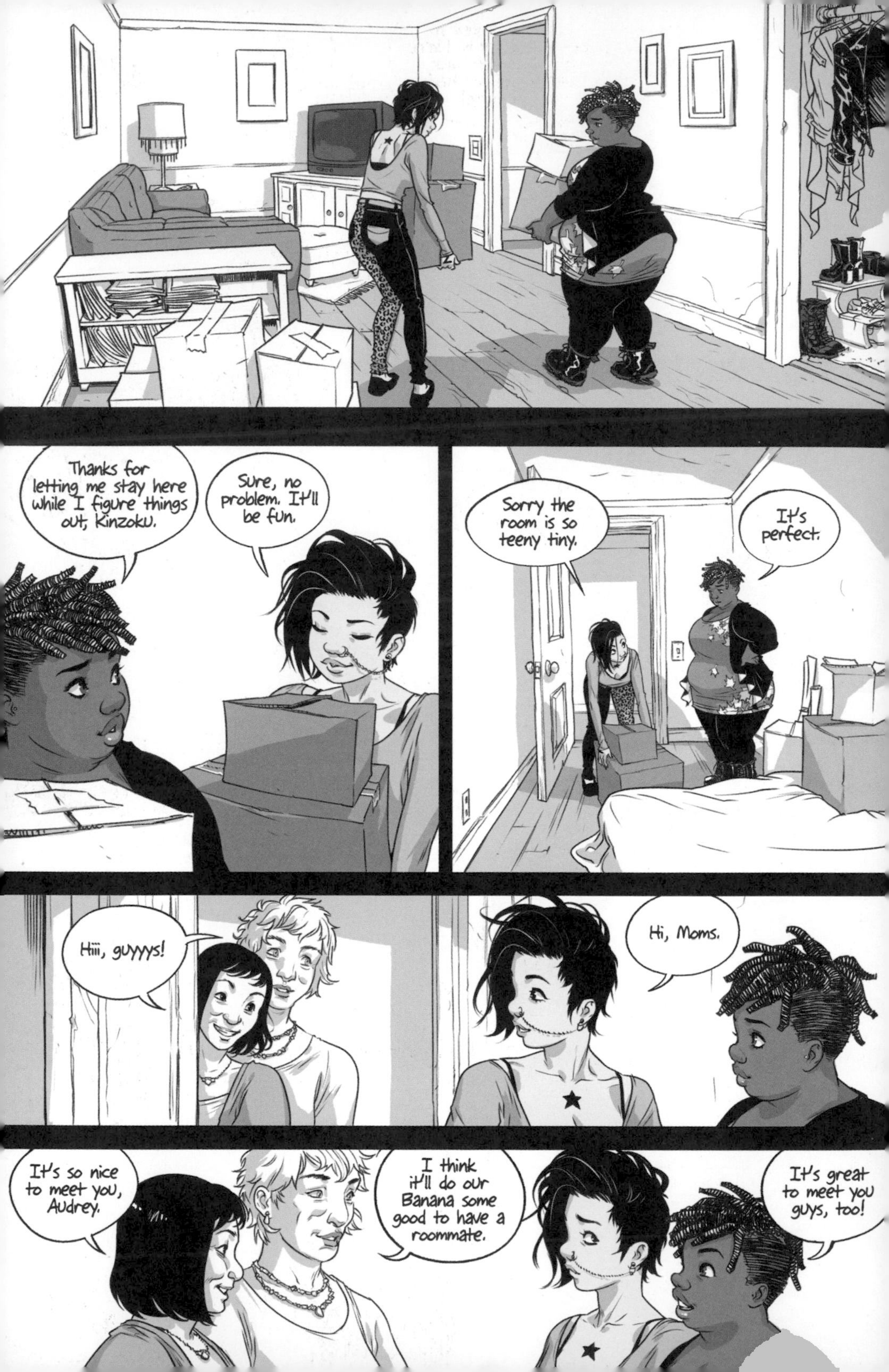

Thanks for letting me stay here while I figure things out, Kinzoku.
Sure, no problem. It'll be fun.
Sorry the room is so teeny tiny.
It's perfect.
Hiii, guyyys!
Hi, Moms.
It's so nice to meet you, Audrey.
I think it'll do our Banana some good to have a roommate.
It's great to meet you guys, too!

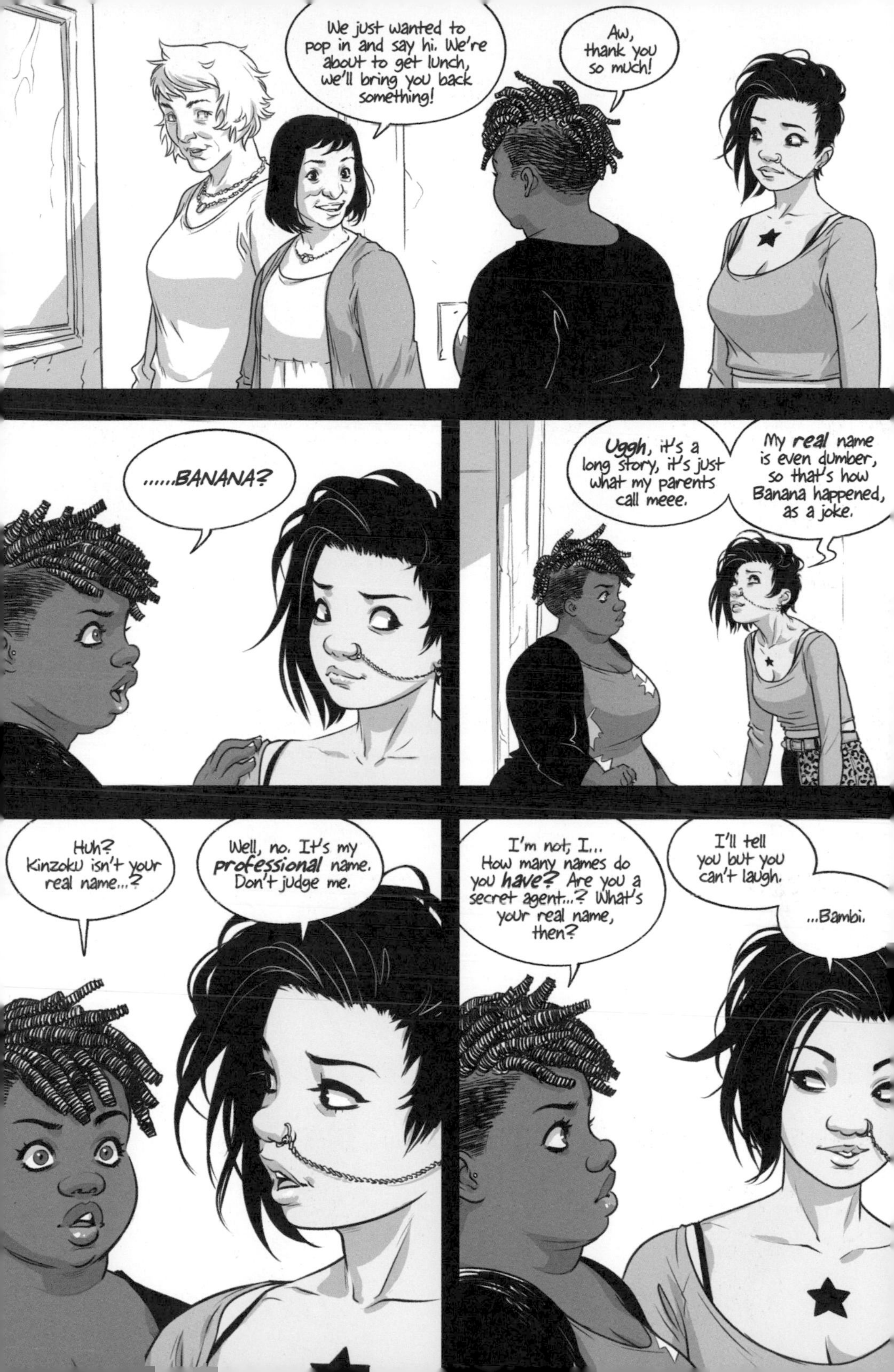
We just wanted to pop in and say hi. We're about to get lunch, we'll bring you back something!
Aw, thank you so much!
......BANANA?
Uggh, it's a long story, it's just what my parents call meee.
My real name is even dumber, so that's how Banana happened, as a joke.
Huh? Kinzoku isn't your real name...?
Well, no. It's my professional name. Don't judge me.
I'm not, I... How many names do you have? Are you a secret agent...? What's your real name, then?
I'll tell you but you can't laugh.
...Bambi.

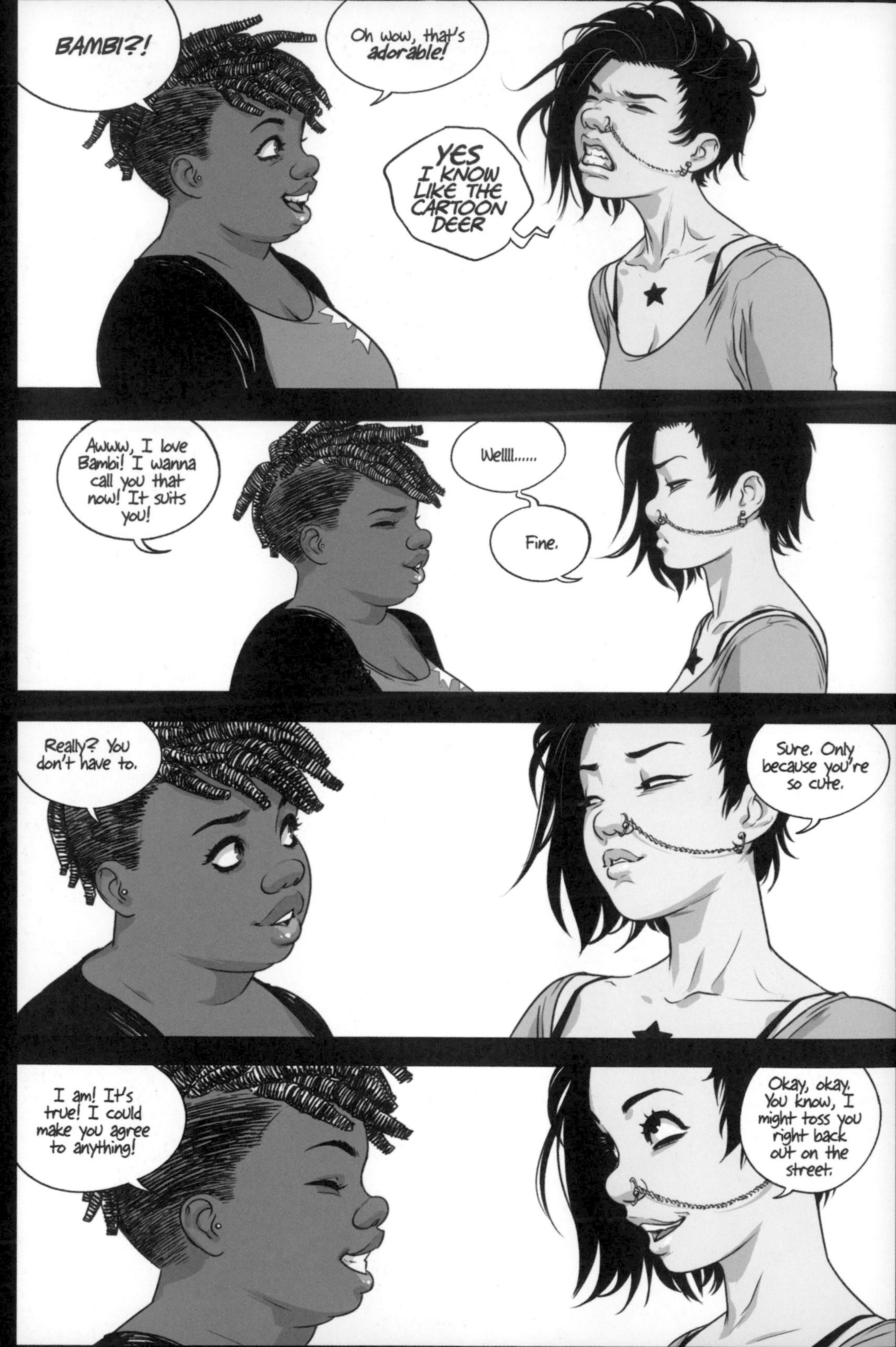

BAMBI?!
Oh wow, that's adorable!
YES I KNOW LIKE THE CARTOON DEER
Awww, I love Bambi! I wanna call you that now! It suits you!
Wellll......
Fine.
Really? You don't have to.
Sure. Only because you're so cute.
I am! It's true! I could make you agree to anything!
Okay, okay. You know, I might toss you right back out on the street.

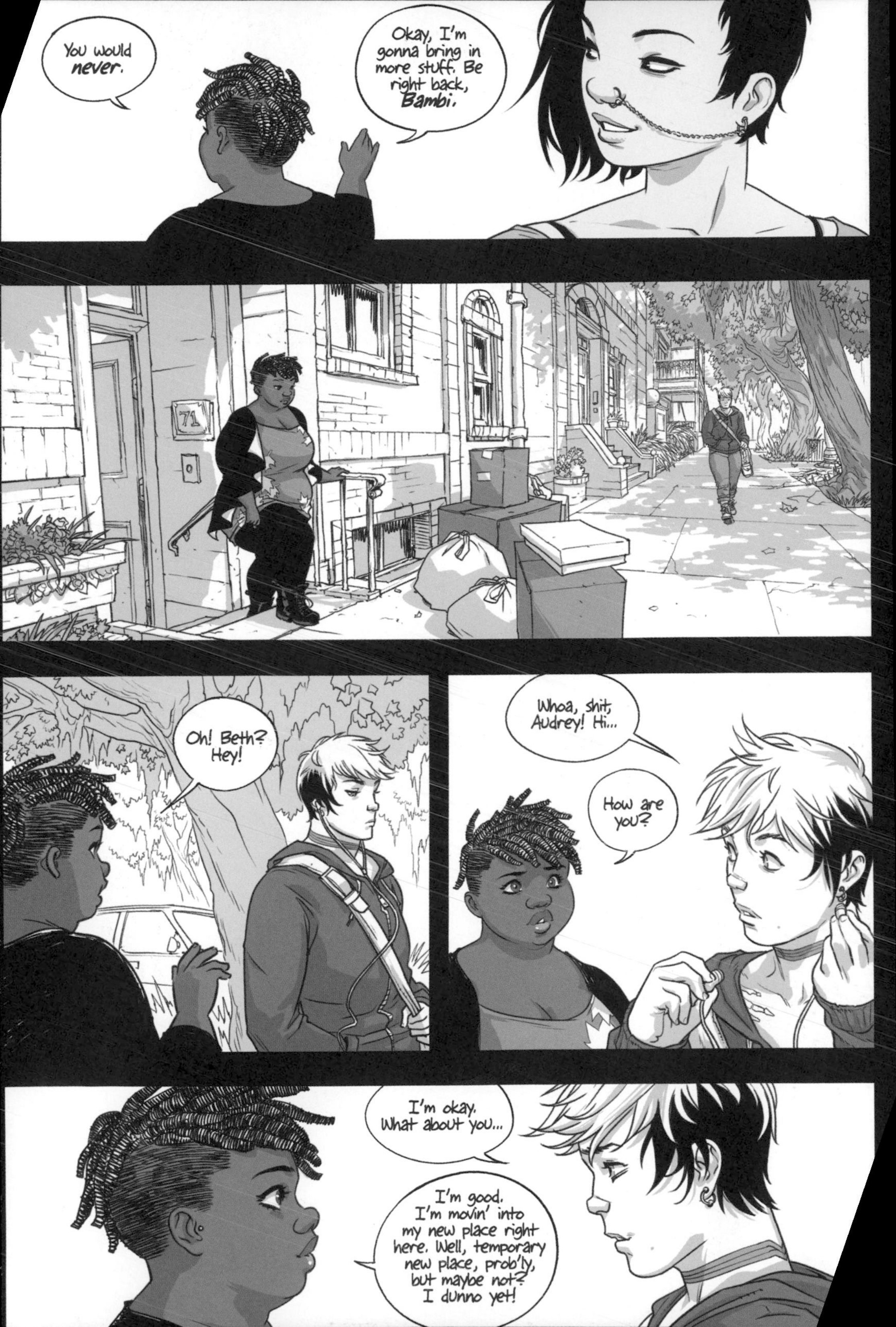
You would *never*.
Okay, I'm gonna bring in more stuff. Be right back, ***Bambi.***
Oh! Beth? Hey!
Whoa, shit, Audrey! Hi...
How are you?
I'm okay. What about you...
I'm good. I'm movin' into my new place right here. Well, temporary new place, prob'ly, but maybe not? I dunno yet!

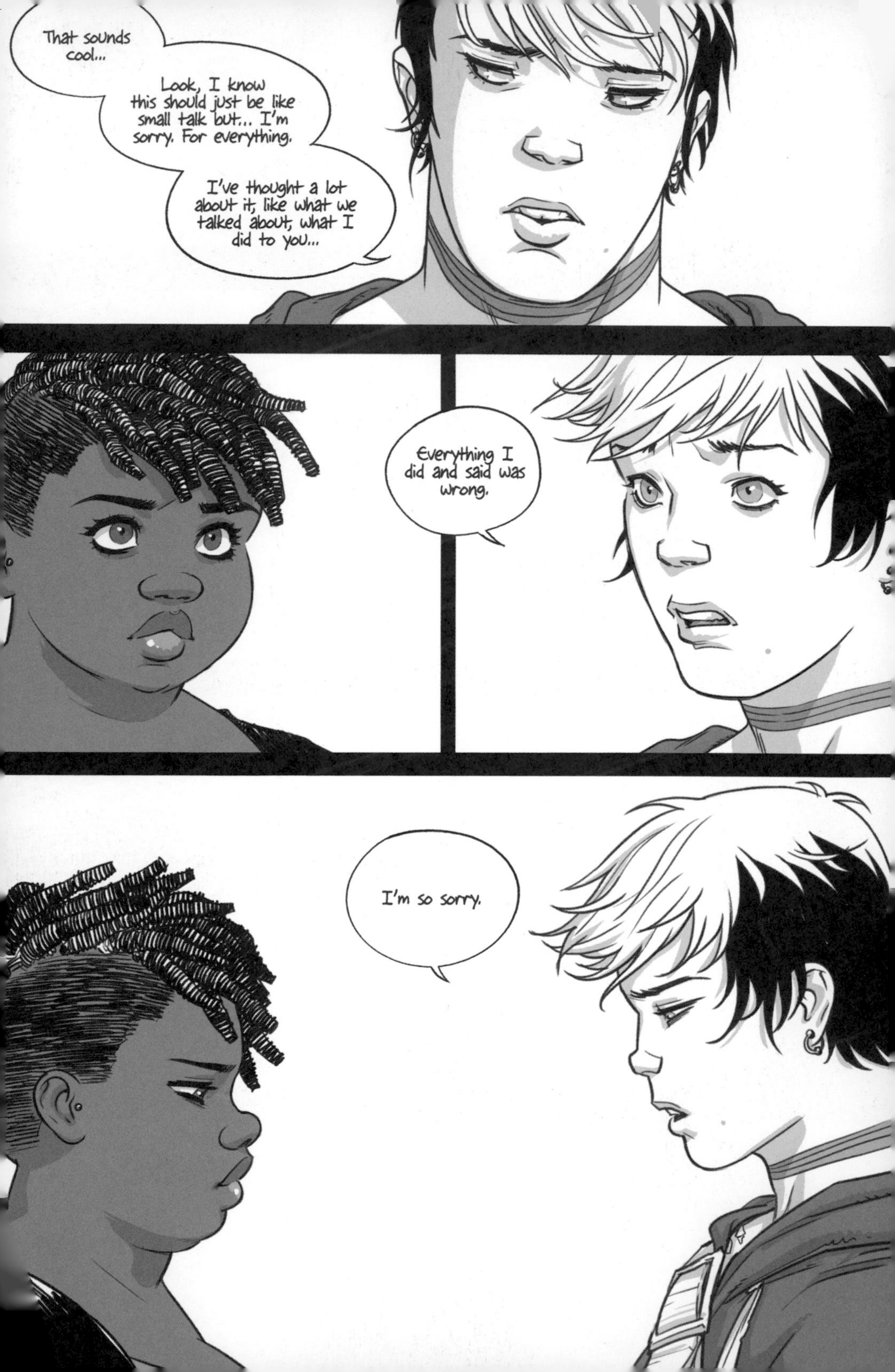
That sounds cool...
Look, I know this should just be like small talk but... I'm sorry. For everything.
I've thought a lot about it, like what we talked about, what I did to you...
Everything I did and said was wrong.
I'm so sorry.

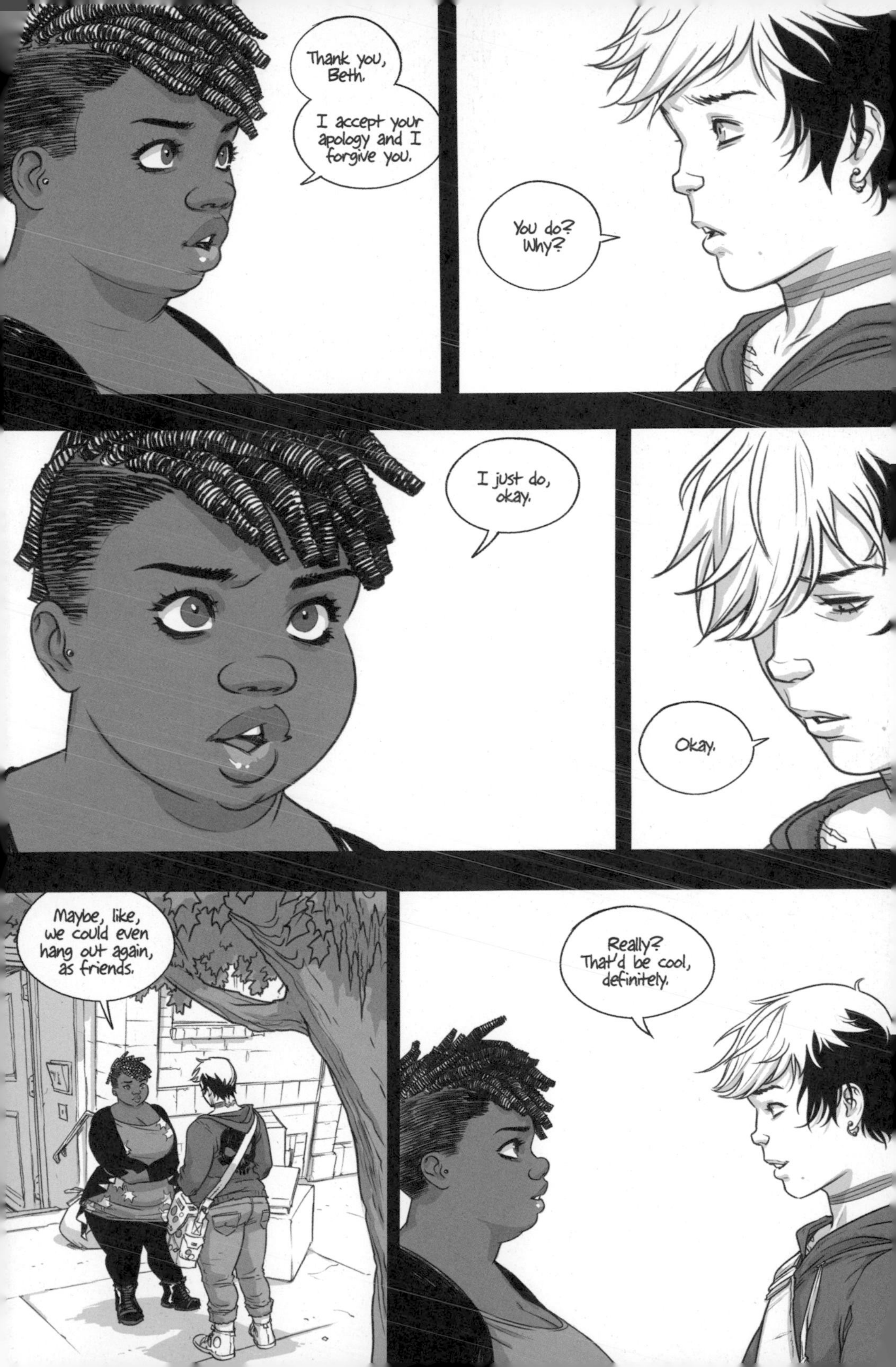
Thank you, Beth.
I accept your apology and I forgive you.
You do? Why?
I just do, okay.
Okay.
Maybe, like, we could even hang out again, as friends.
Really? That'd be cool, definitely.

33

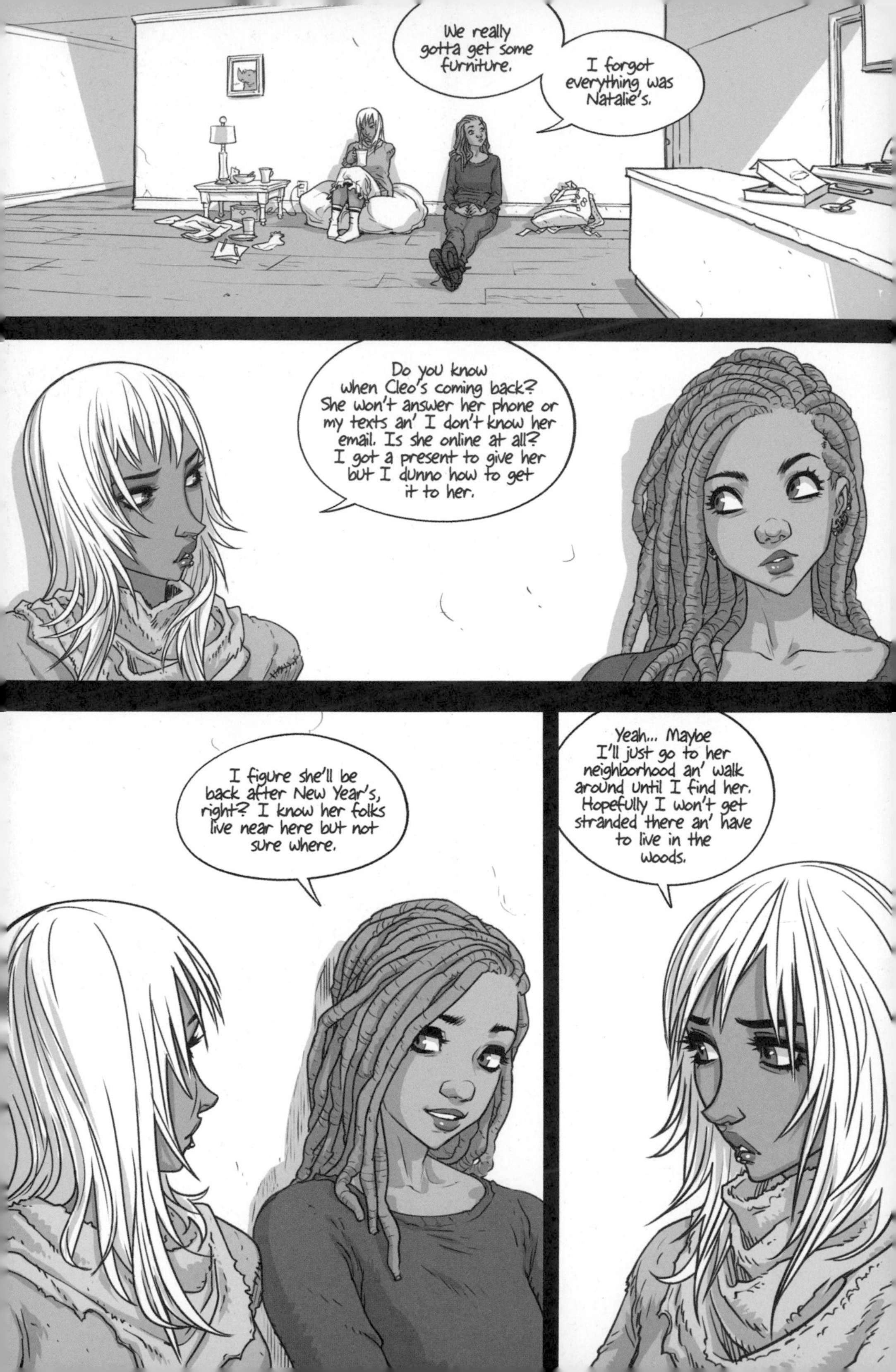
We really gotta get some furniture.
I forgot everything was Natalie's.
Do you know when Cleo's coming back? She won't answer her phone or my texts an' I don't know her email. Is she online at all? I got a present to give her but I dunno how to get it to her.
I figure she'll be back after New Year's, right? I know her folks live near here but not sure where.
Yeah... Maybe I'll just go to her neighborhood an' walk around until I find her. Hopefully I won't get stranded there an' have to live in the woods.

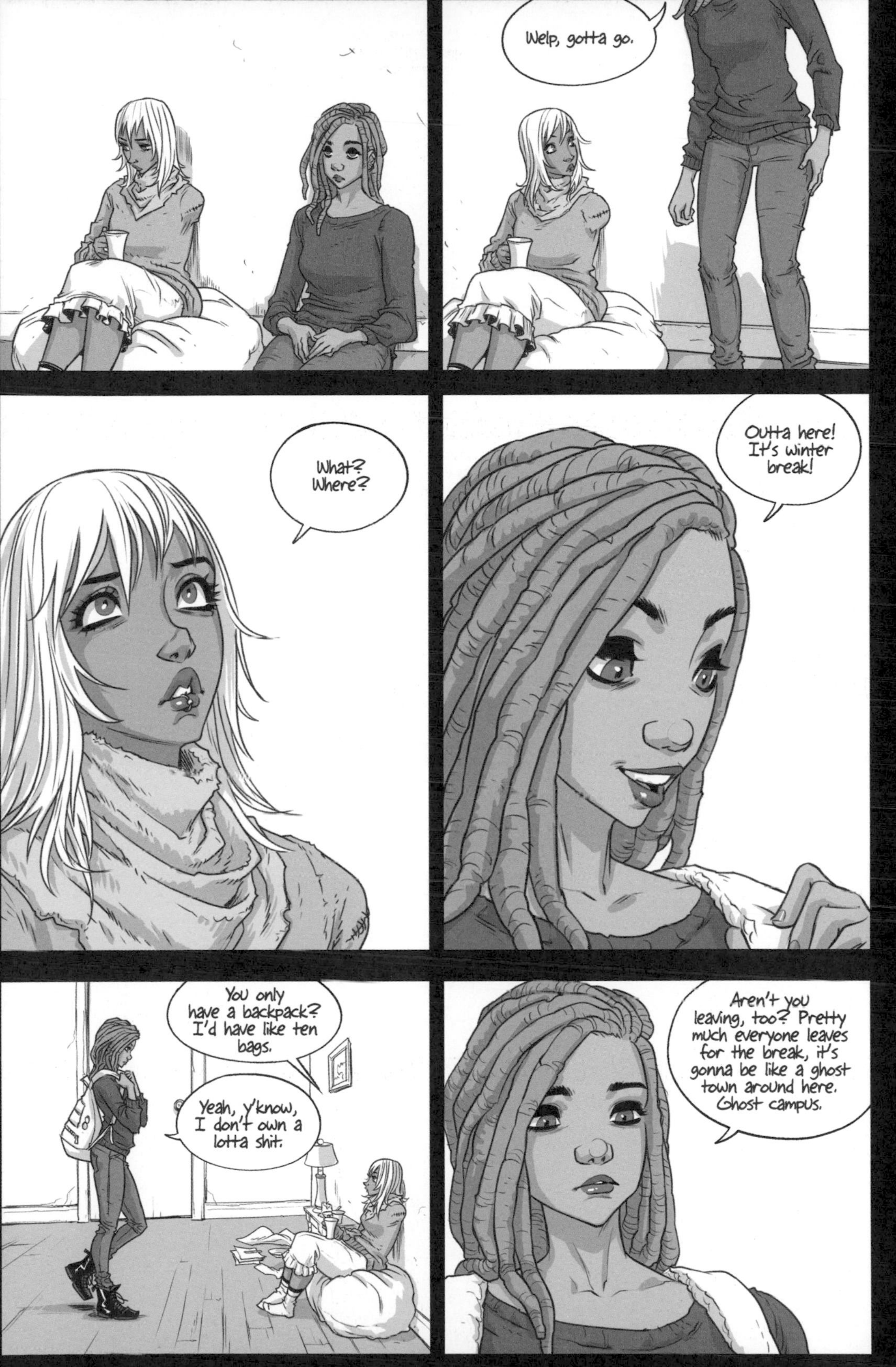
Welp, gotta go.
What? Where?
Outta here! It's winter break!
You only have a backpack? I'd have like ten bags.
Yeah, y'know, I don't own a lotta shit.
Aren't you leaving, too? Pretty much everyone leaves for the break, it's gonna be like a ghost town around here. Ghost campus.

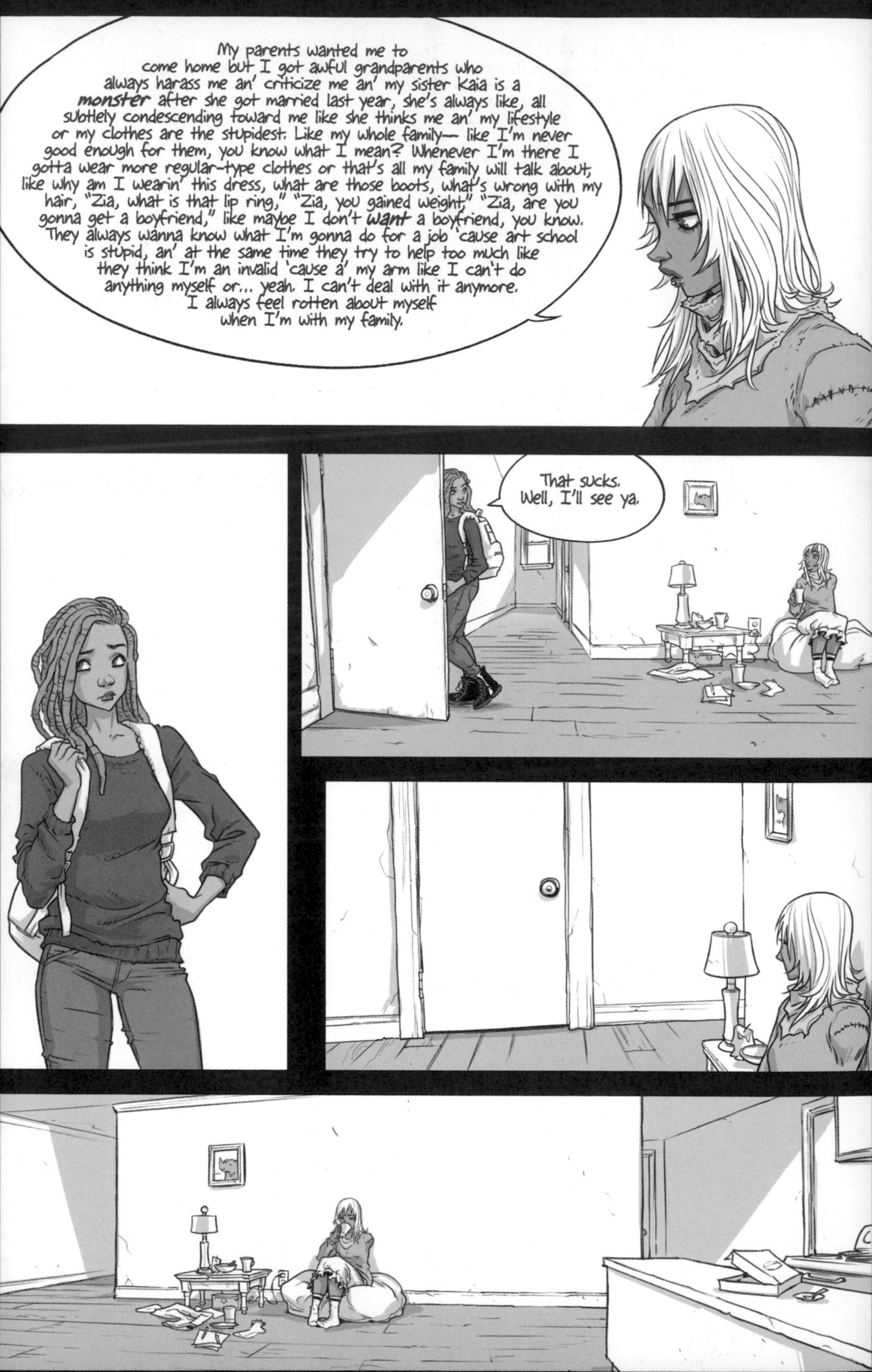
My parents wanted me to come home but I got awful grandparents who always harass me an' criticize me an' my sister Kaia is a **monster** after she got married last year, she's always like, all subtletly condescending toward me like she thinks me an' my lifestyle or my clothes are the stupidest. Like my whole family— like I'm never good enough for them, you know what I mean? Whenever I'm there I gotta wear more regular-type clothes or that's all my family will talk about, like why am I wearin' this dress, what are those boots, what's wrong with my hair, "Zia, what is that lip ring," "Zia, you gained weight," "Zia, are you gonna get a boyfriend," like maybe I don't **want** a boyfriend, you know. They always wanna know what I'm gonna do for a job 'cause art school is stupid, an' at the same time they try to help too much like they think I'm an invalid 'cause a' my arm like I can't do anything myself or... yeah. I can't deal with it anymore. I always feel rotten about myself when I'm with my family.
That sucks. Well, I'll see ya.

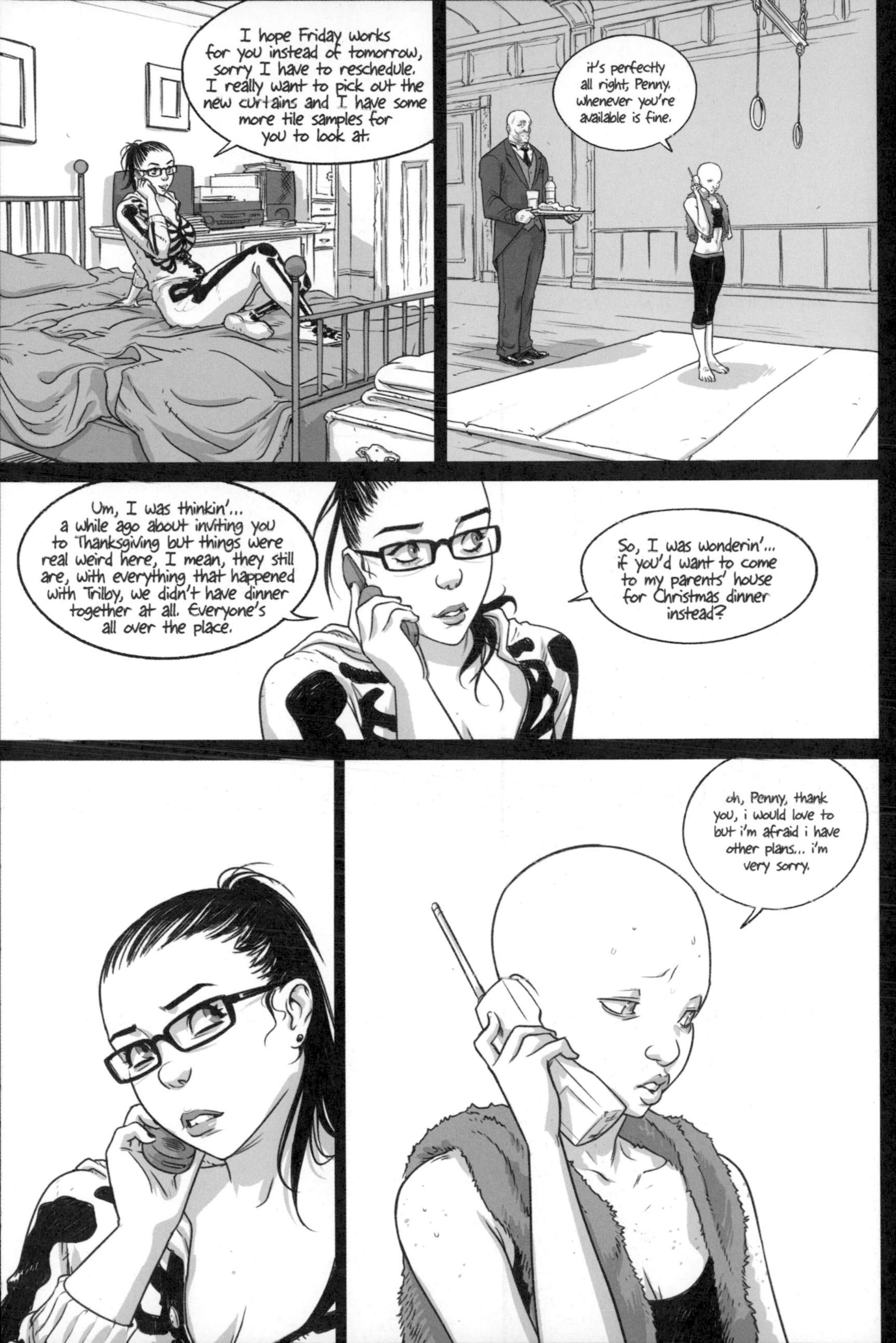
I hope Friday works for you instead of tomorrow, sorry I have to reschedule. I really want to pick out the new curtains and I have some more tile samples for you to look at.
it's perfectly all right, Penny. whenever you're available is fine.
Um, I was thinkin'... a while ago about inviting you to Thanksgiving but things were real weird here, I mean, they still are, with everything that happened with Trilby, we didn't have dinner together at all. Everyone's all over the place.
So, I was wonderin'... if you'd want to come to my parents' house for Christmas dinner instead?
oh, Penny, thank you, i would love to but i'm afraid i have other plans... i'm very sorry.

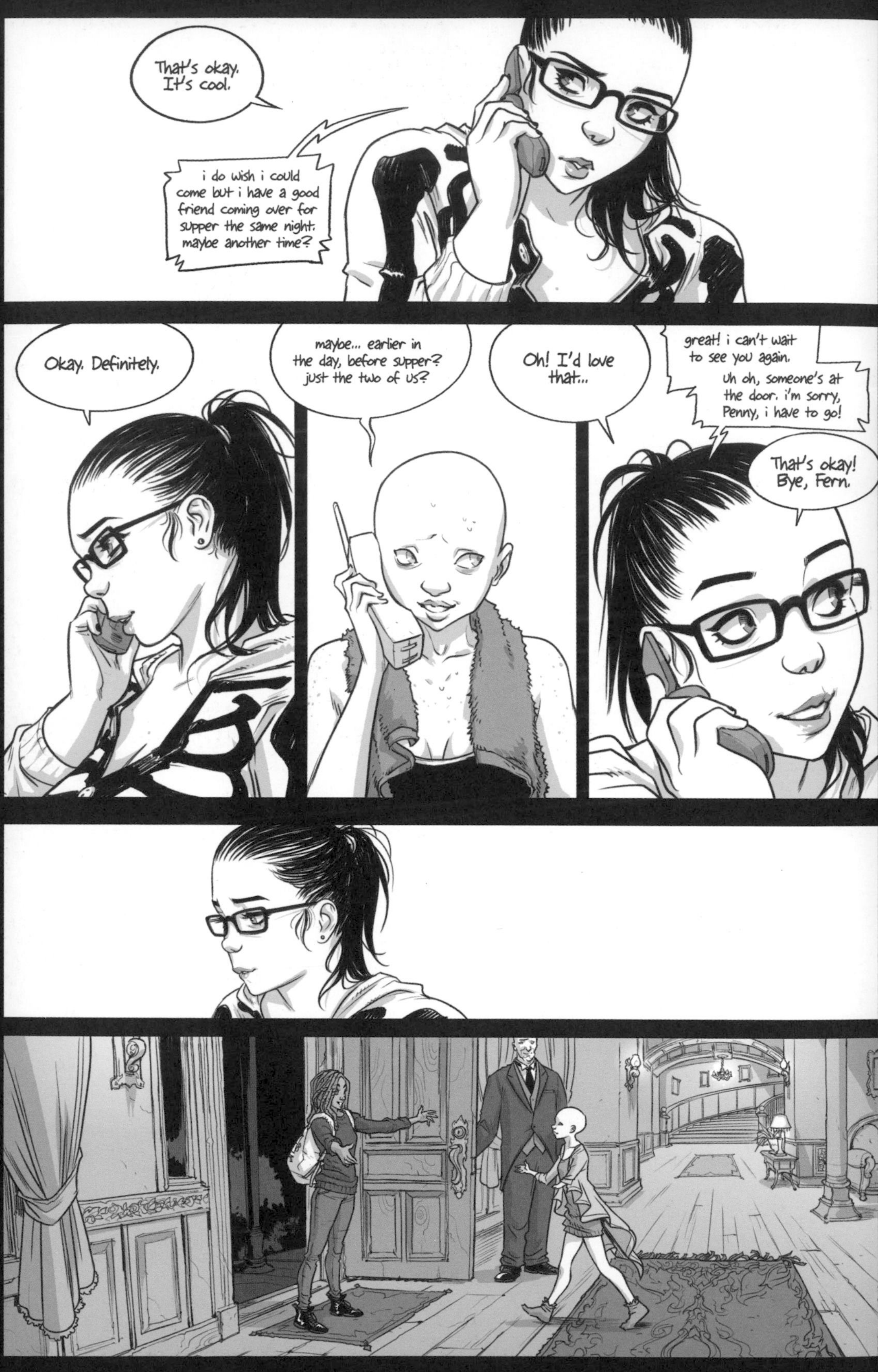
That's okay. It's cool.
i do wish i could come but i have a good friend coming over for supper the same night. maybe another time?
Okay. Definitely.
maybe... earlier in the day, before supper? just the two of us?
Oh! I'd love that...
great! i can't wait to see you again.
Uh oh, someone's at the door. i'm sorry, Penny, i have to go!
That's okay! Bye, Fern.

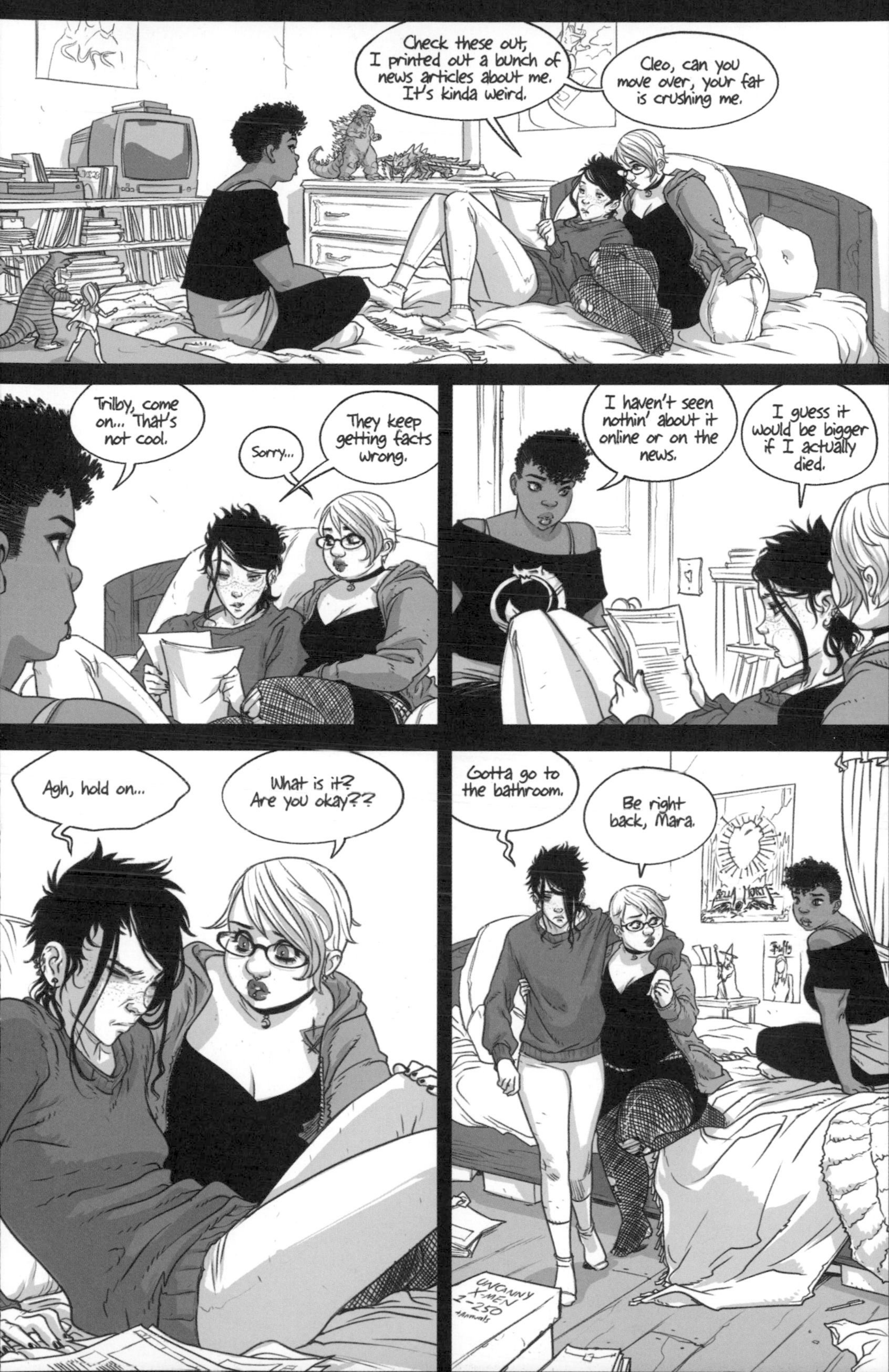
Check these out, I printed out a bunch of news articles about me. It's kinda weird.
Cleo, can you move over, your fat is crushing me.
Trilby, come on... That's not cool.
Sorry...
They keep getting facts wrong.
I haven't seen nothin' about it online or on the news.
I guess it would be bigger if I actually died.
Agh, hold on...
What is it? Are you okay??
Gotta go to the bathroom.
Be right back, Mara.
UNCANNY X-MEN 1-250 +Annuals

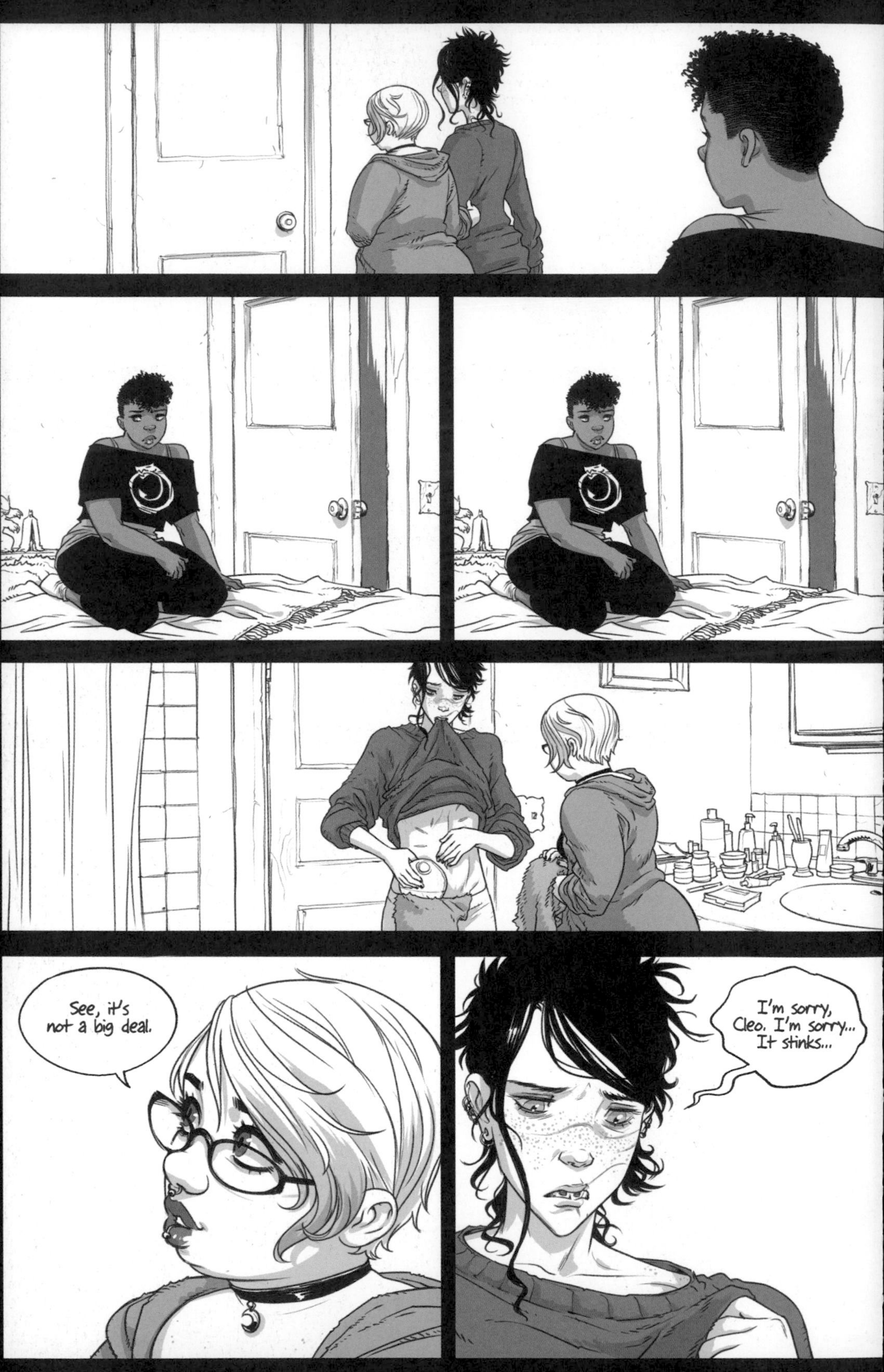

See, it's not a big deal.
I'm sorry, Cleo. I'm sorry... It stinks...

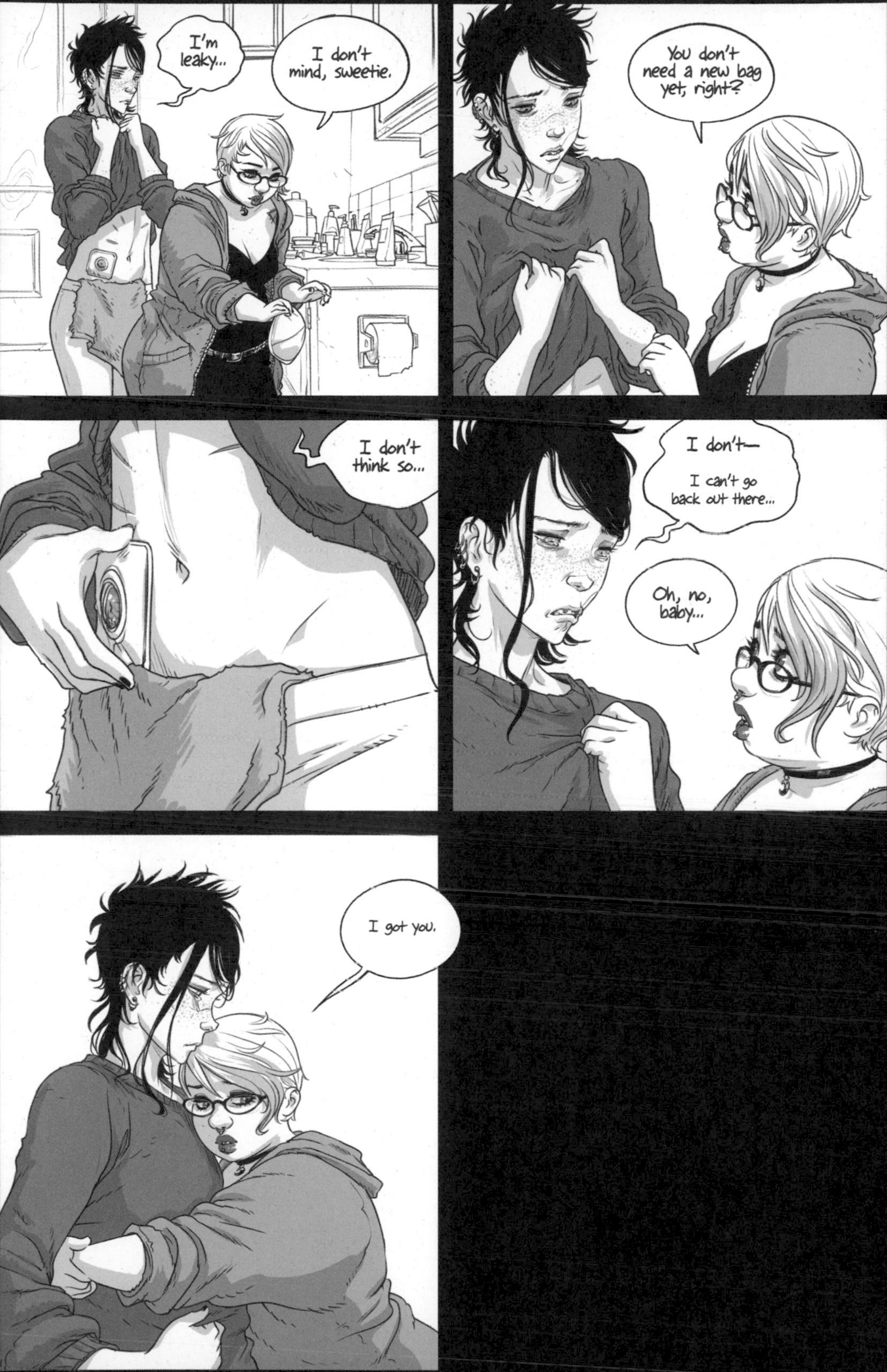
I'm leaky...
I don't mind, sweetie.
You don't need a new bag yet, right?
I don't think so...
I don't—
I can't go back out there...
Oh, no, baby...
I got you.

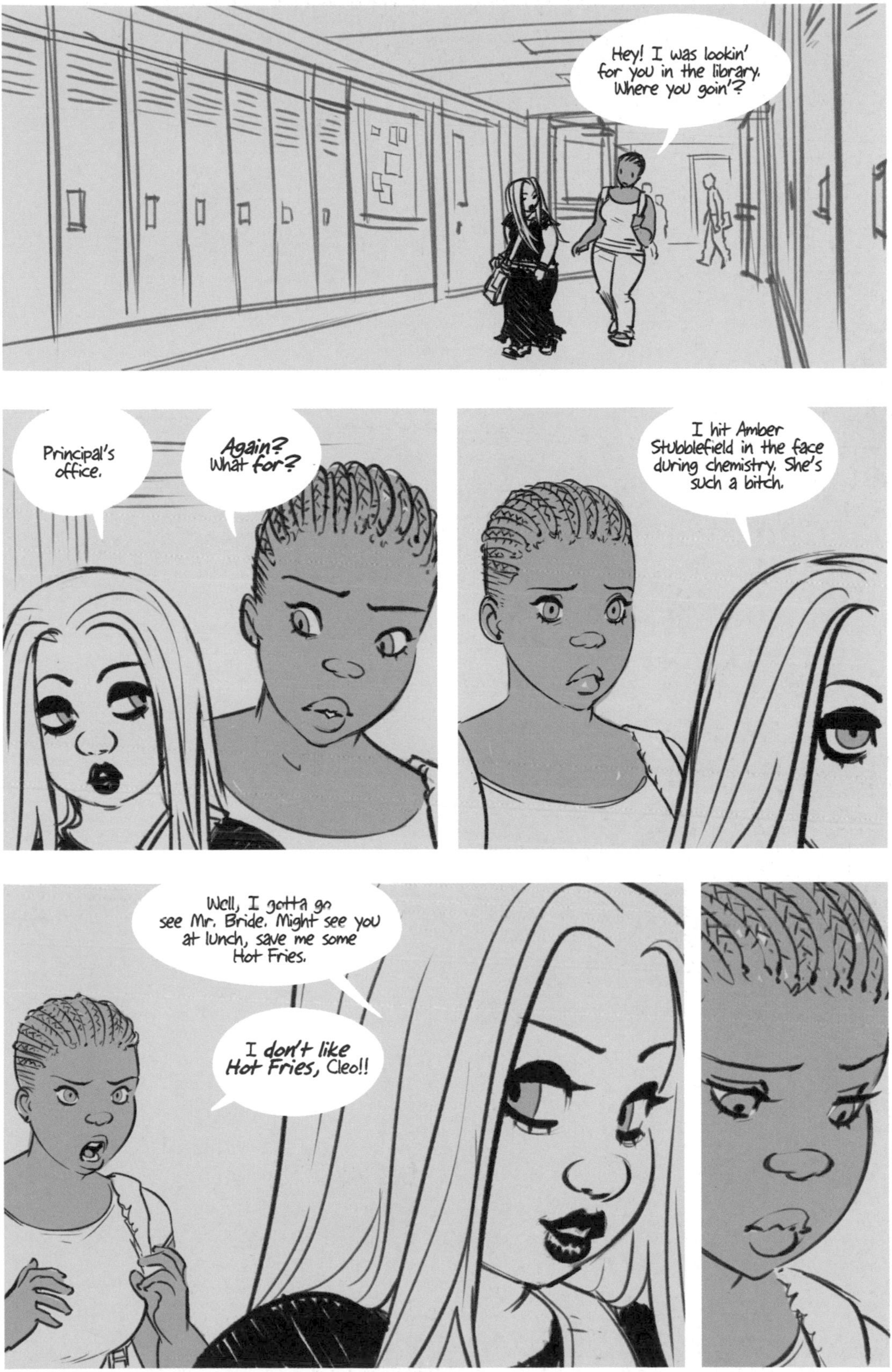
Hey! I was lookin' for you in the library. Where you goin'?
Principal's office.
Again? What for?
I hit Amber Stubblefield in the face during chemistry. She's such a bitch.
Well, I gotta go see Mr. Bride. Might see you at lunch, save me some Hot Fries.
I don't like Hot Fries, Cleo!!

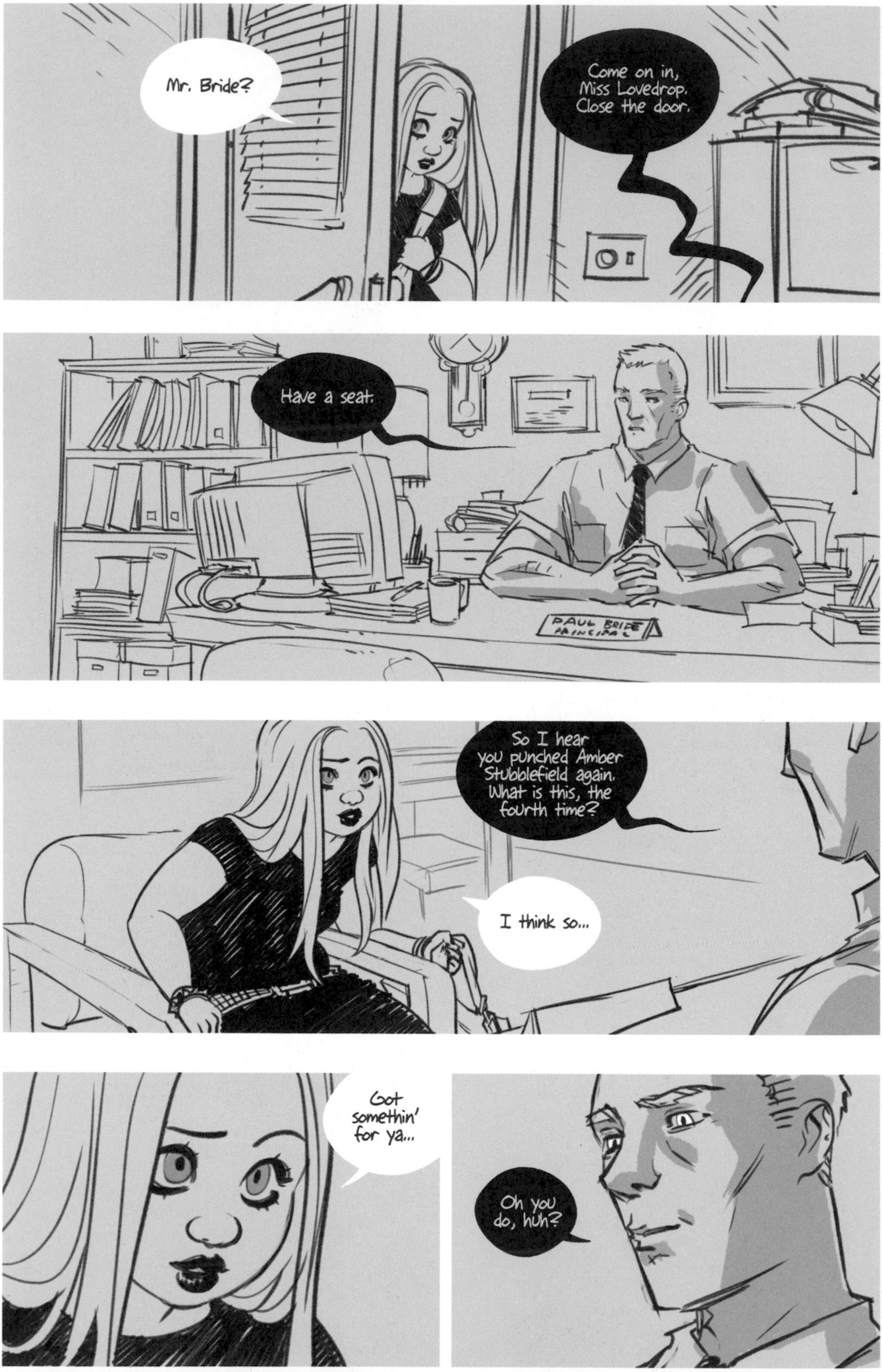

Mr. Bride?
Come on in, Miss Lovedrop. Close the door.
Have a seat.
PAUL BRIDE PRINCIPAL
So I hear you punched Amber Stubblefield again. What is this, the fourth time?
I think so...
Got somethin' for ya...
Oh you do, huh?

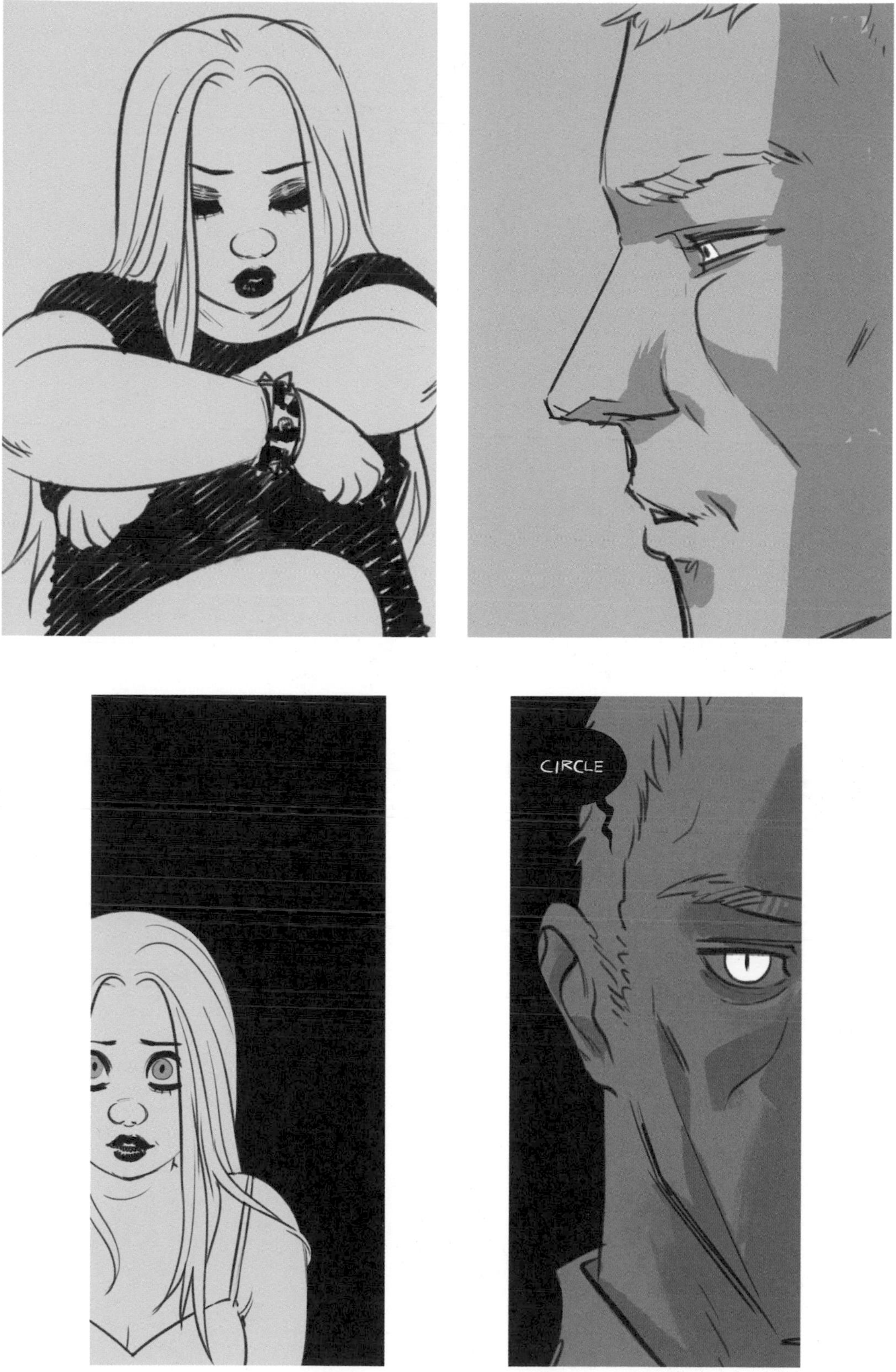
CIRCLE

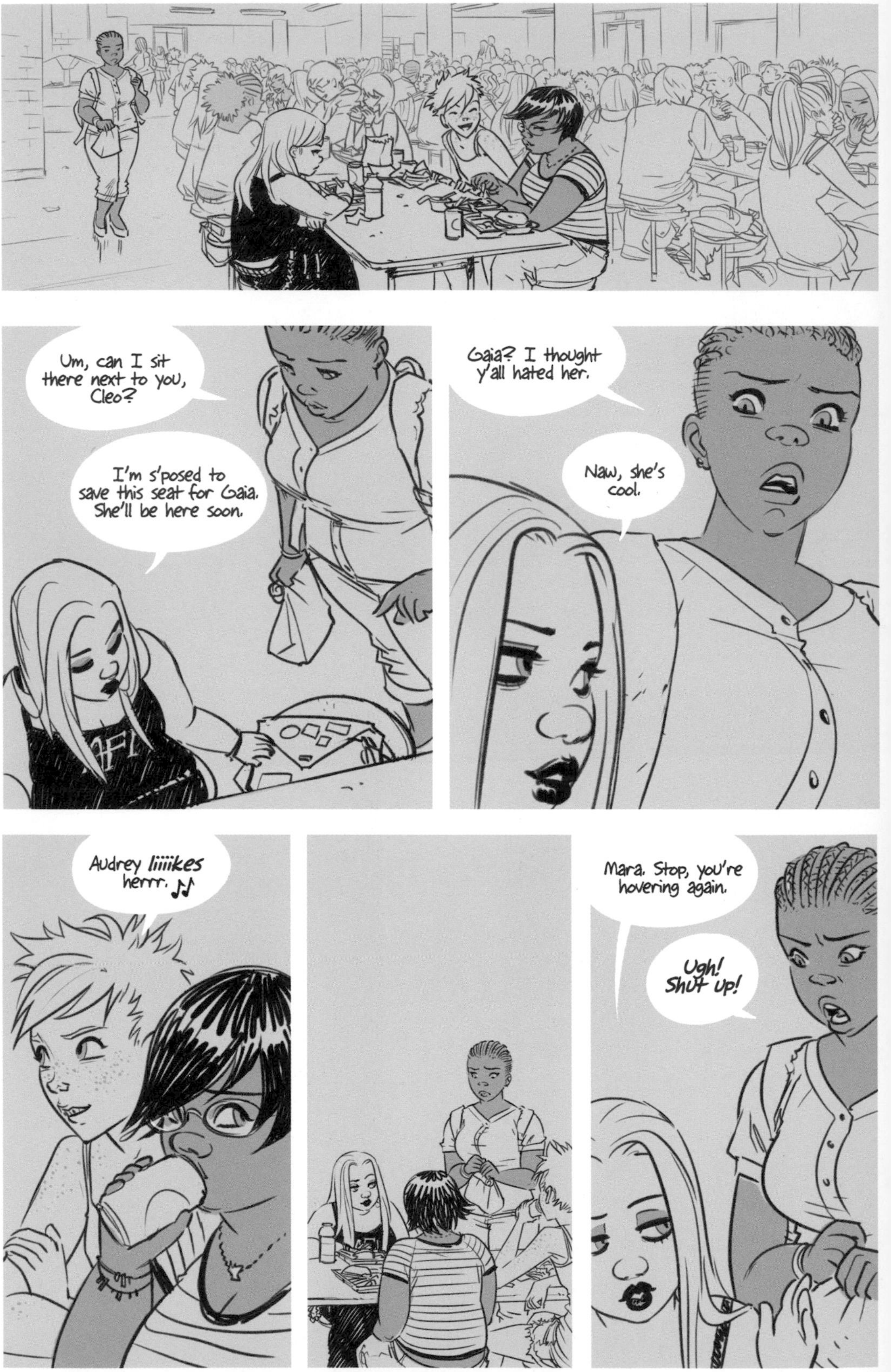
Um, can I sit there next to you, Cleo?
I'm s'posed to save this seat for Gaia. She'll be here soon.
Gaia? I thought y'all hated her.
Naw, she's cool.
Audrey liiiikes herrr. ♫
Mara. Stop, you're hovering again.
Ugh! Shut up!

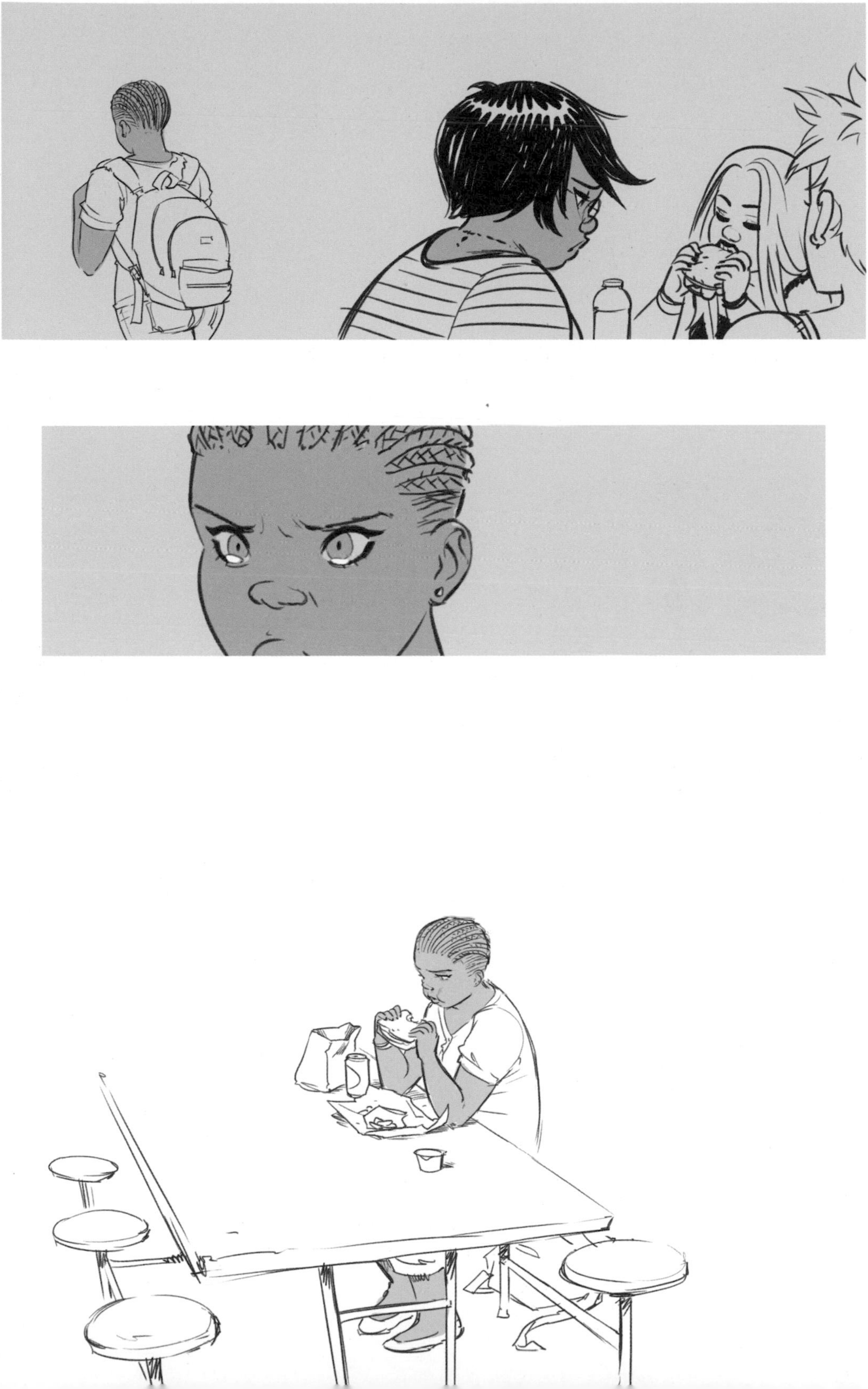

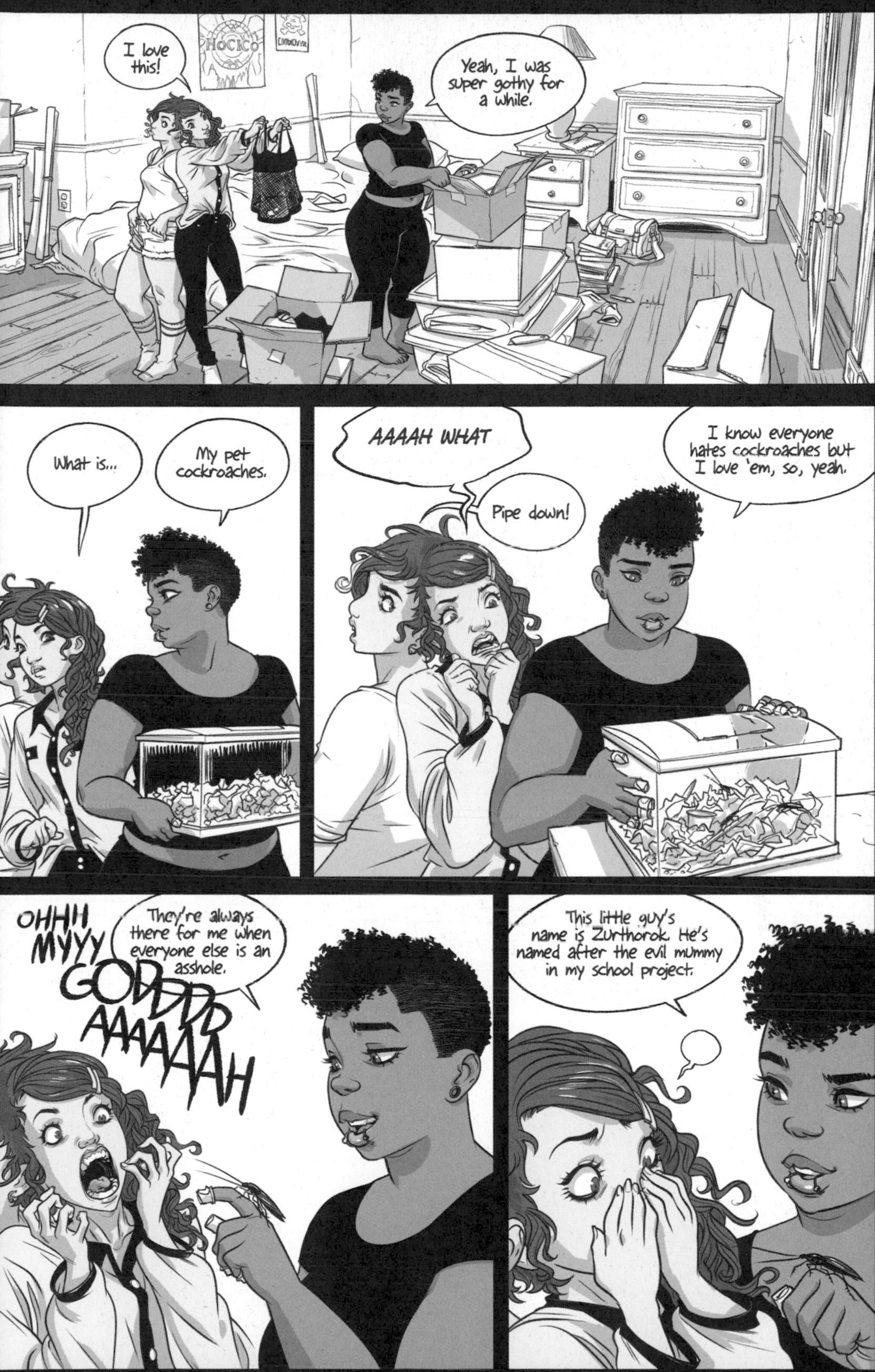

I love this!
Yeah, I was super gothy for a while.
What is...
My pet cockroaches.
AAAAH WHAT
Pipe down!
I know everyone hates cockroaches but I love 'em, so, yeah.
OHHH MYYY GODDDD AAAAAAH
They're always there for me when everyone else is an asshole.
This little guy's name is Zurthorok. He's named after the evil mummy in my school project.

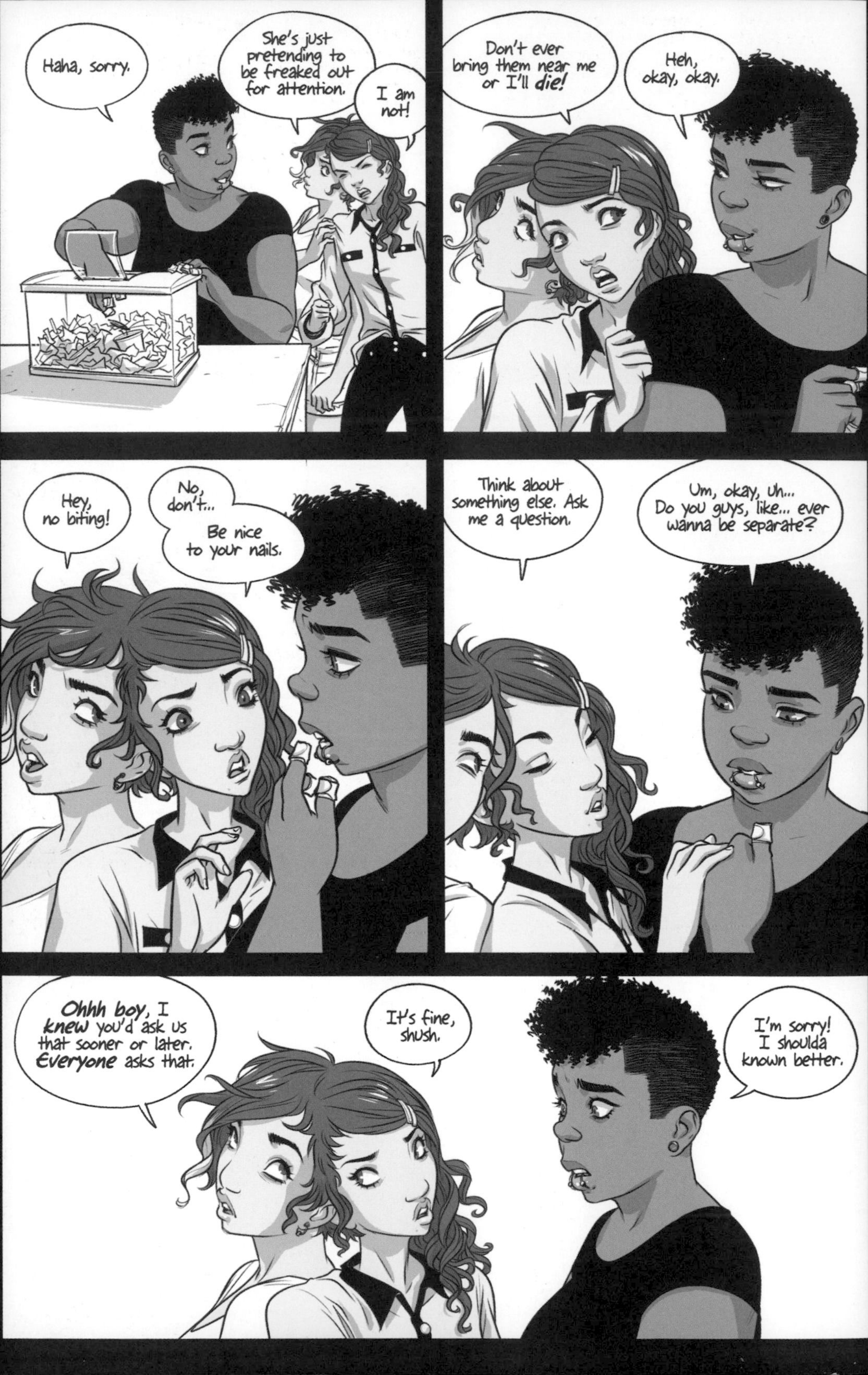

Haha, sorry.
She's just pretending to be freaked out for attention.
I am not!
Don't ever bring them near me or I'll *die!*
Heh, okay, okay.
Hey, no biting!
No, don't...
Be nice to your nails.
Think about something else. Ask me a question.
Um, okay, uh... Do you guys, like... ever wanna be separate?
Ohhh boy, I ***knew*** you'd ask us that sooner or later. ***Everyone*** asks that.
It's fine, shush.
I'm sorry! I shoulda known better.

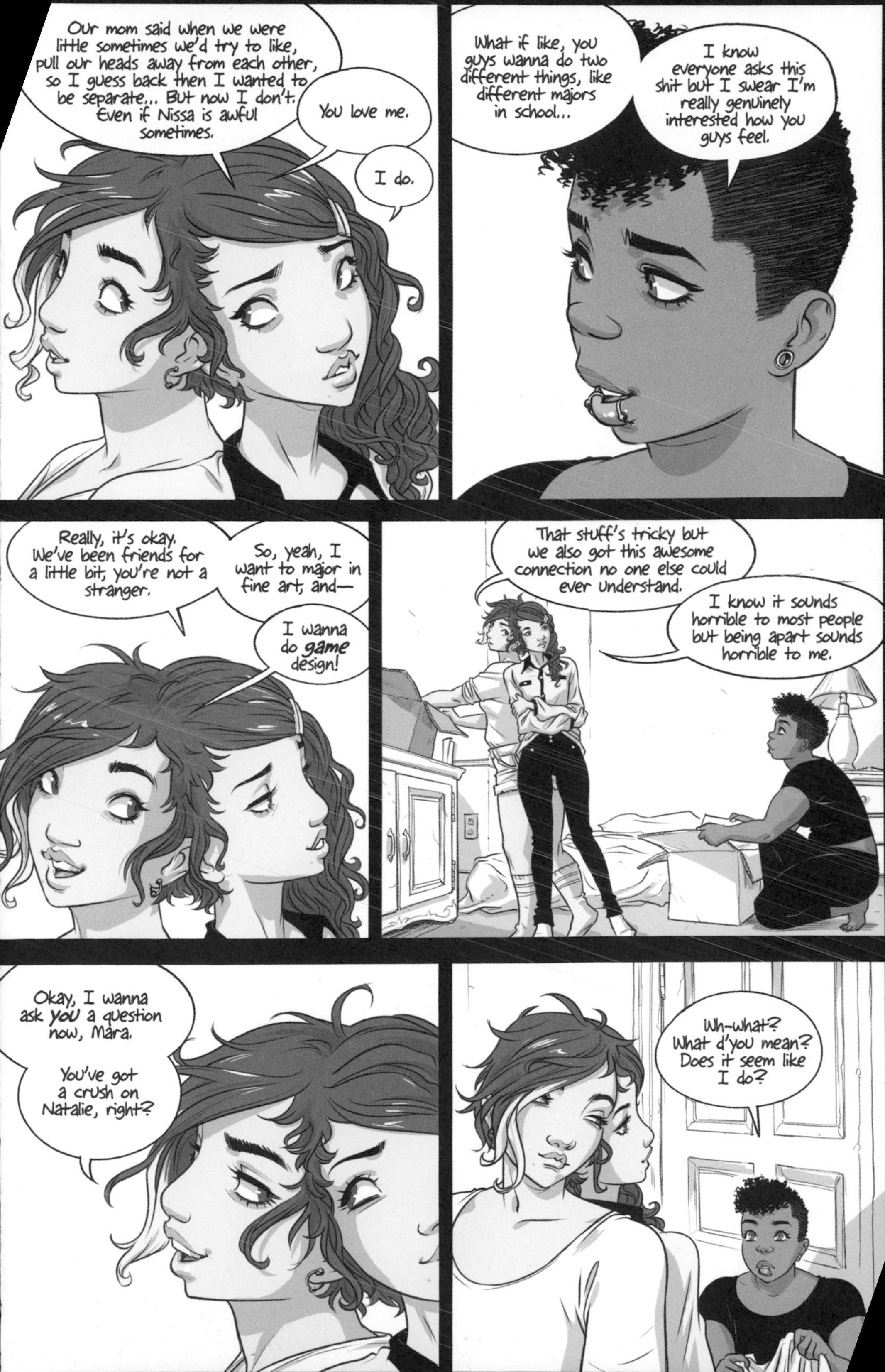
Our mom said when we were little sometimes we'd try to like, pull our heads away from each other, so I guess back then I wanted to be separate... But now I don't. Even if Nissa is awful sometimes.
You love me.
I do.
What if like, you guys wanna do two different things, like different majors in school...
I know everyone asks this shit but I swear I'm really genuinely interested how you guys feel.
Really, it's okay. We've been friends for a little bit, you're not a stranger.
So, yeah, I want to major in fine art, and—
I wanna do game design!
That stuff's tricky but we also got this awesome connection no one else could ever understand.
I know it sounds horrible to most people but being apart sounds horrible to me.
Okay, I wanna ask YOU a question now, Mara.
You've got a crush on Natalie, right?
Wh-what? What d'you mean? Does it seem like I do?

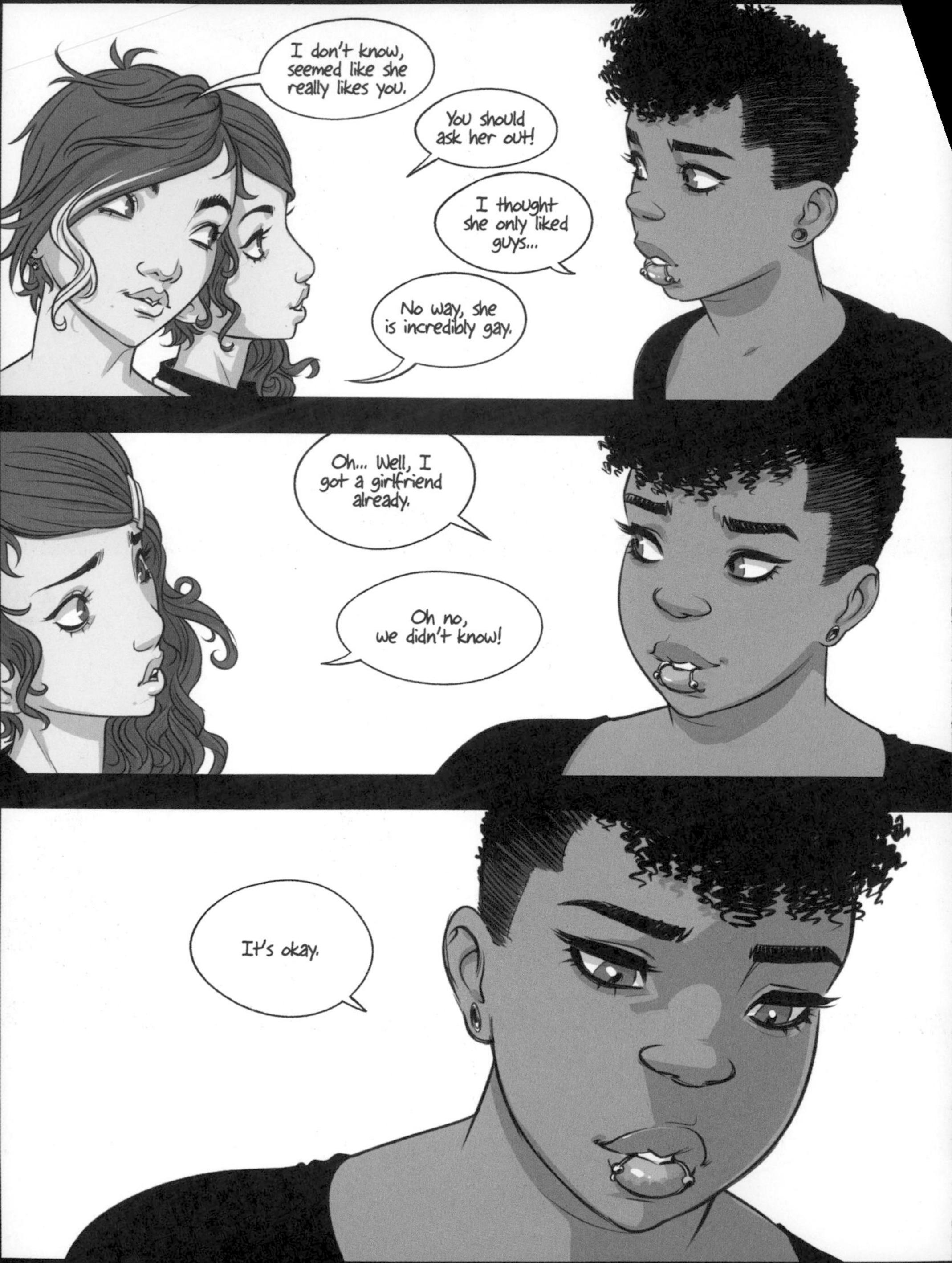
I don't know, seemed like she really likes you.
You should ask her out!
I thought she only liked guys...
No way, she is incredibly gay.
Oh... Well, I got a girlfriend already.
Oh no, we didn't know!
It's okay.

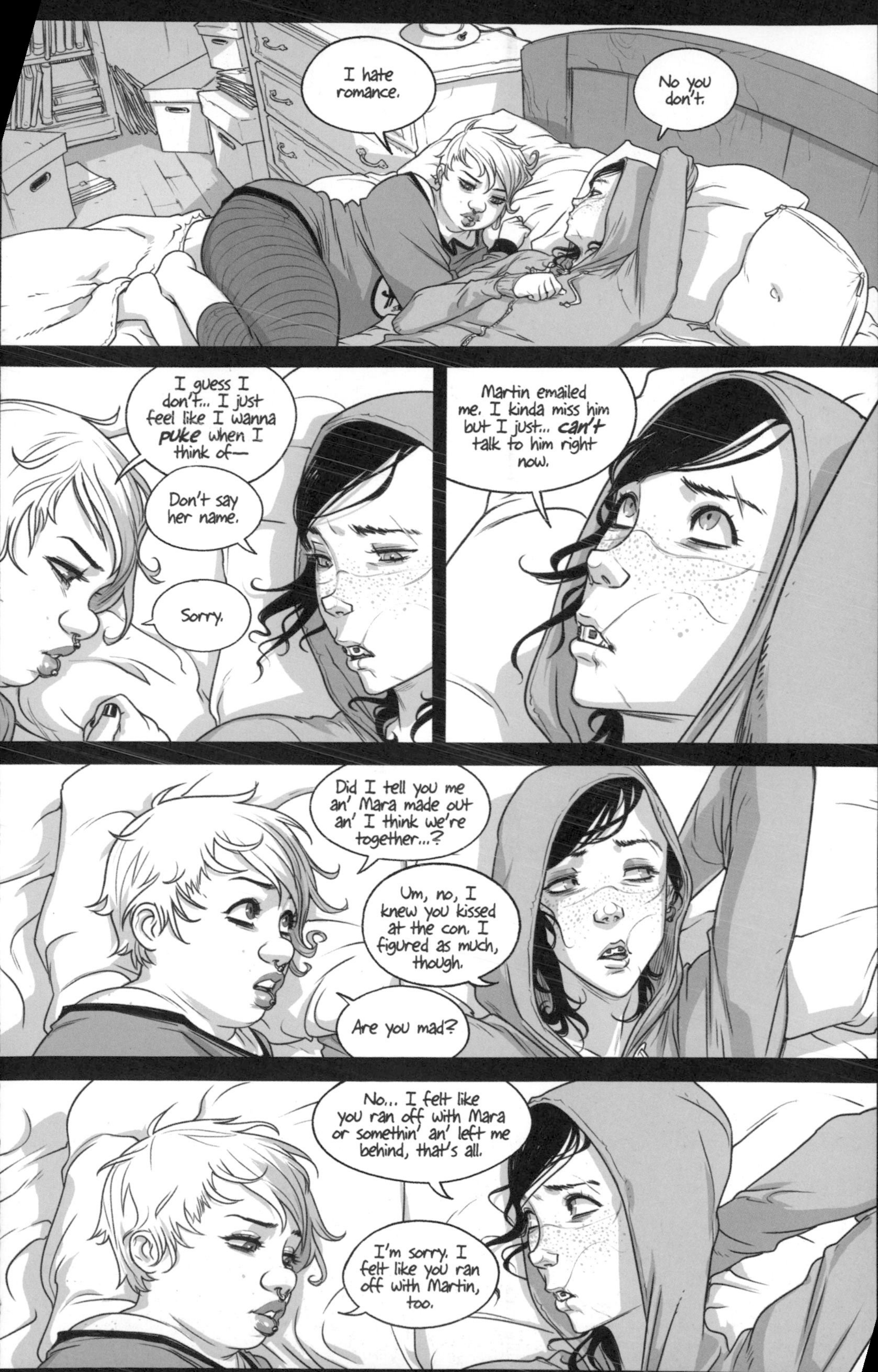

I hate romance.
No you don't.
I guess I don't... I just feel like I wanna PUKE when I think of—
Don't say her name.
Sorry.
Martin emailed me. I kinda miss him but I just... can't talk to him right now.
Did I tell you me an' Mara made out an' I think we're together...?
Um, no, I knew you kissed at the con. I figured as much, though.
Are you mad?
No... I felt like you ran off with Mara or somethin' an' left me behind, that's all.
I'm sorry. I felt like you ran off with Martin, too.

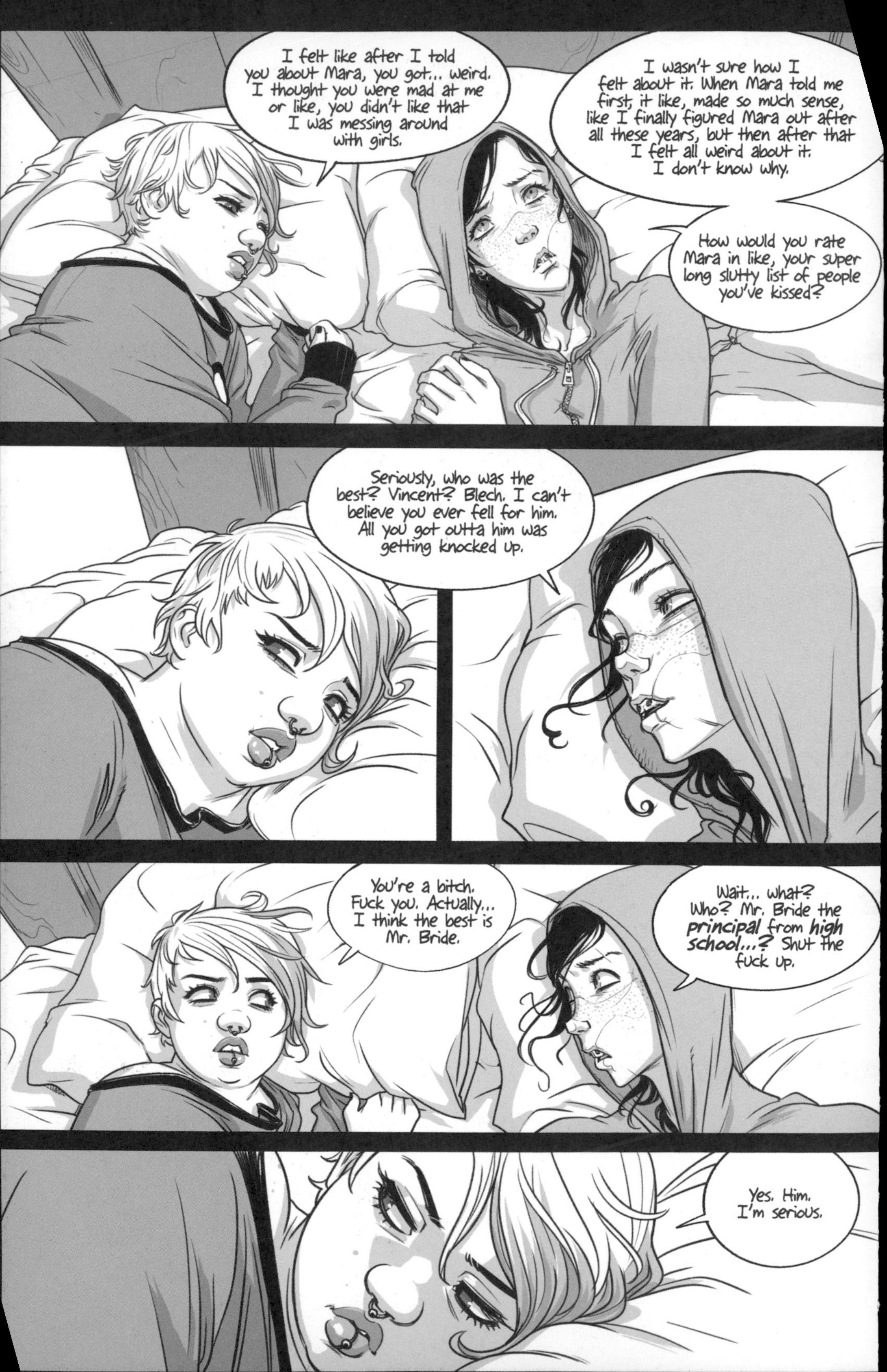
I felt like after I told you about Mara, you got... weird. I thought you were mad at me or like, you didn't like that I was messing around with girls.
I wasn't sure how I felt about it. When Mara told me first, it like, made so much sense, like I finally figured Mara out after all these years, but then after that I felt all weird about it. I don't know why.
How would you rate Mara in like, your super long slutty list of people you've kissed?
Seriously, who was the best? Vincent? Blech. I can't believe you ever fell for him. All you got outta him was getting knocked up.
You're a bitch. Fuck you. Actually... I think the best is Mr. Bride.
Wait... what? Who? Mr. Bride the **principal** from **high school...?** Shut the fuck up.
Yes. Him. I'm serious.

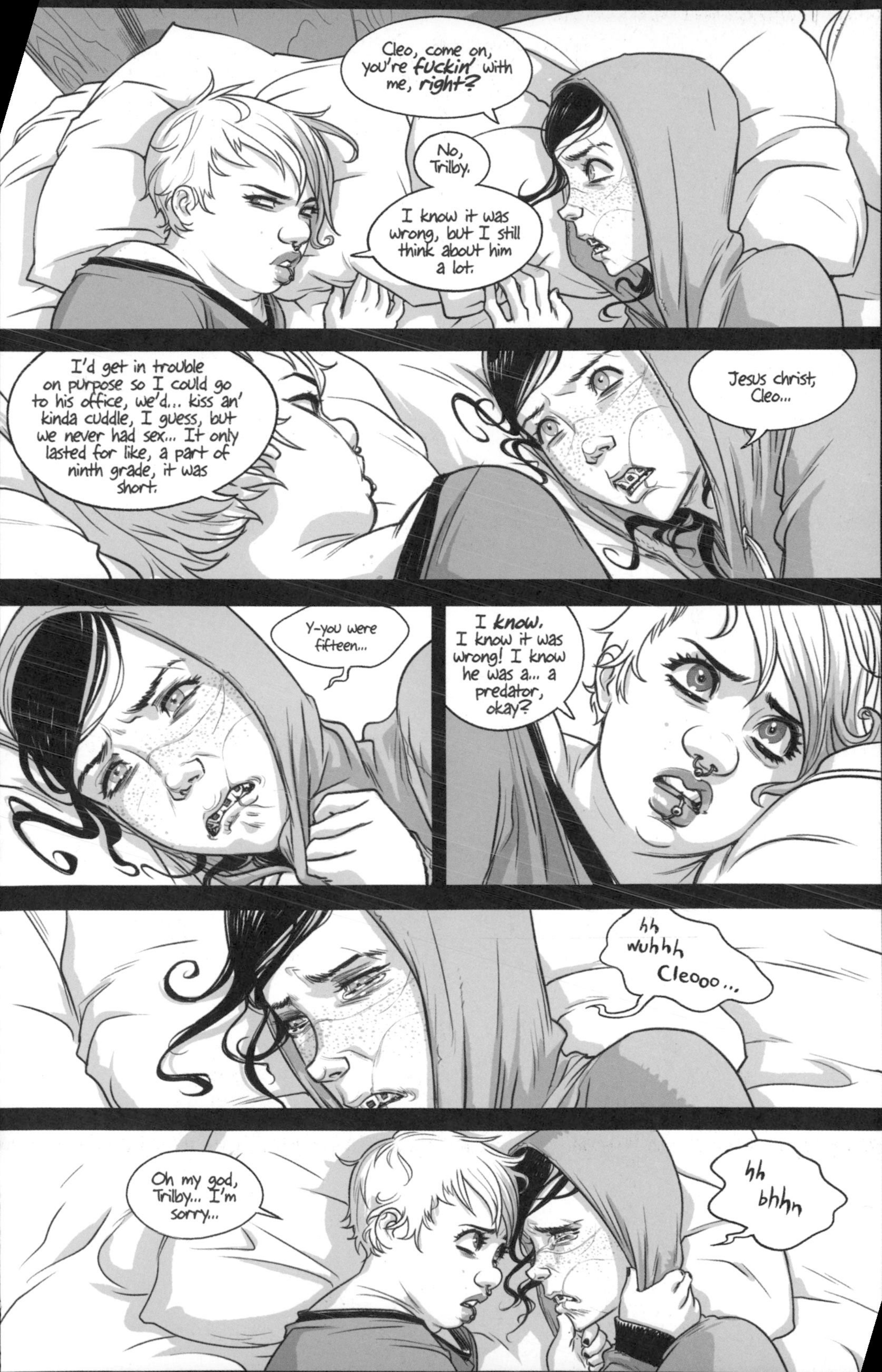
Cleo, come on, you're fuckin' with me, right?
No, Trilby.
I know it was wrong, but I still think about him a lot.
I'd get in trouble on purpose so I could go to his office, we'd... kiss an' kinda cuddle, I guess, but we never had sex... It only lasted for like, a part of ninth grade, it was short.
Jesus christ, Cleo...
Y-you were fifteen...
I know. I know it was wrong! I know he was a... a predator, okay?
hh wuhhh Cleooo...
Oh my god, Trilby... I'm sorry...
hh bhhn

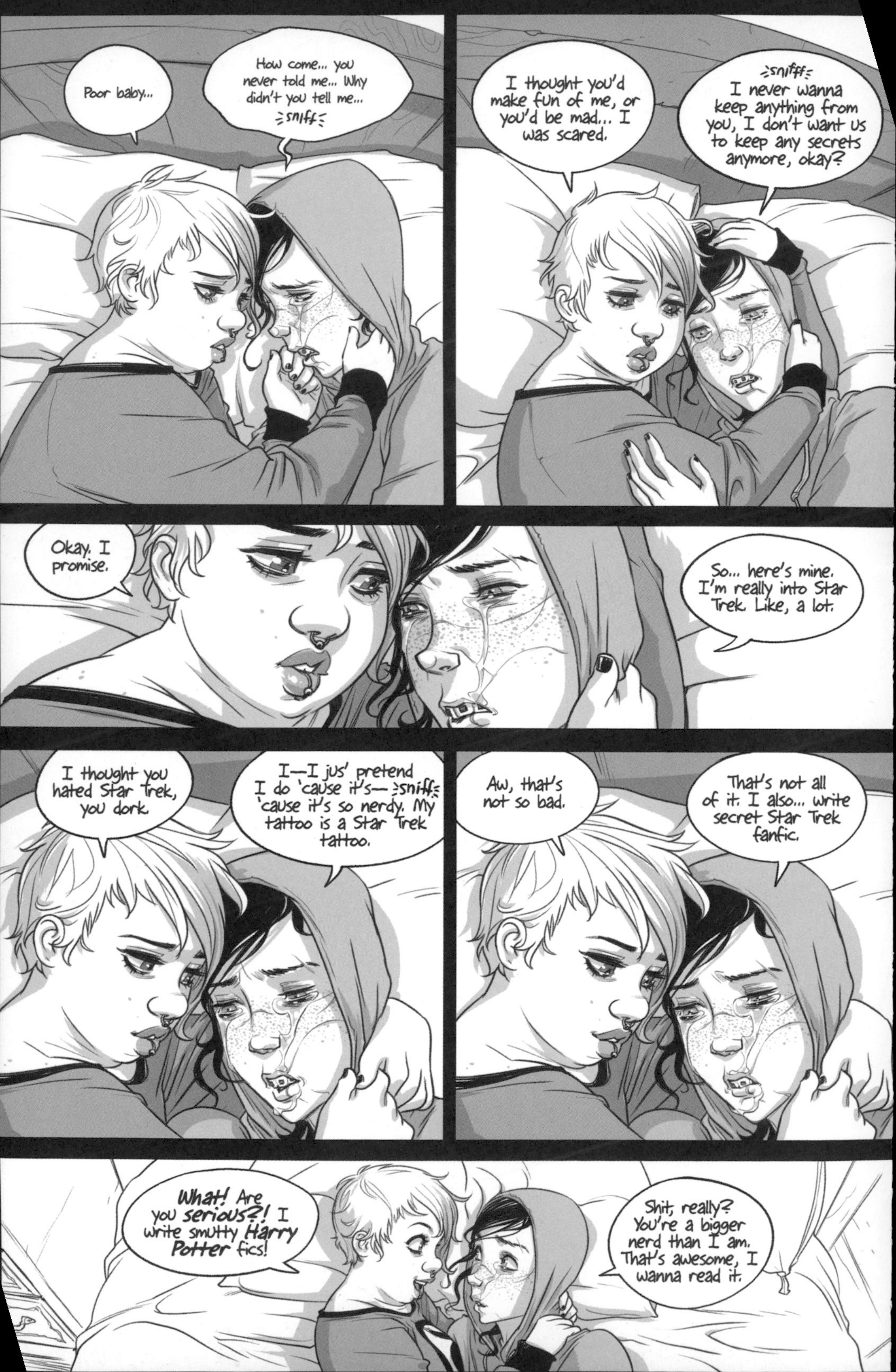
Poor baby...
How come... you never told me... Why didn't you tell me... ≈sniff≈
I thought you'd make fun of me, or you'd be mad... I was scared.
≈sniff≈ I never wanna keep anything from you, I don't want us to keep any secrets anymore, okay?
Okay. I promise.
So... here's mine. I'm really into Star Trek. Like, a lot.
I thought you hated Star Trek, you dork.
I—I jus' pretend I do 'cause it's— ≈sniff≈ 'cause it's so nerdy. My tattoo is a Star Trek tattoo.
Aw, that's not so bad.
That's not all of it. I also... write secret Star Trek fanfic.
What! Are you serious?! I write smutty Harry Potter fics!
Shit, really? You're a bigger nerd than I am. That's awesome, I wanna read it.

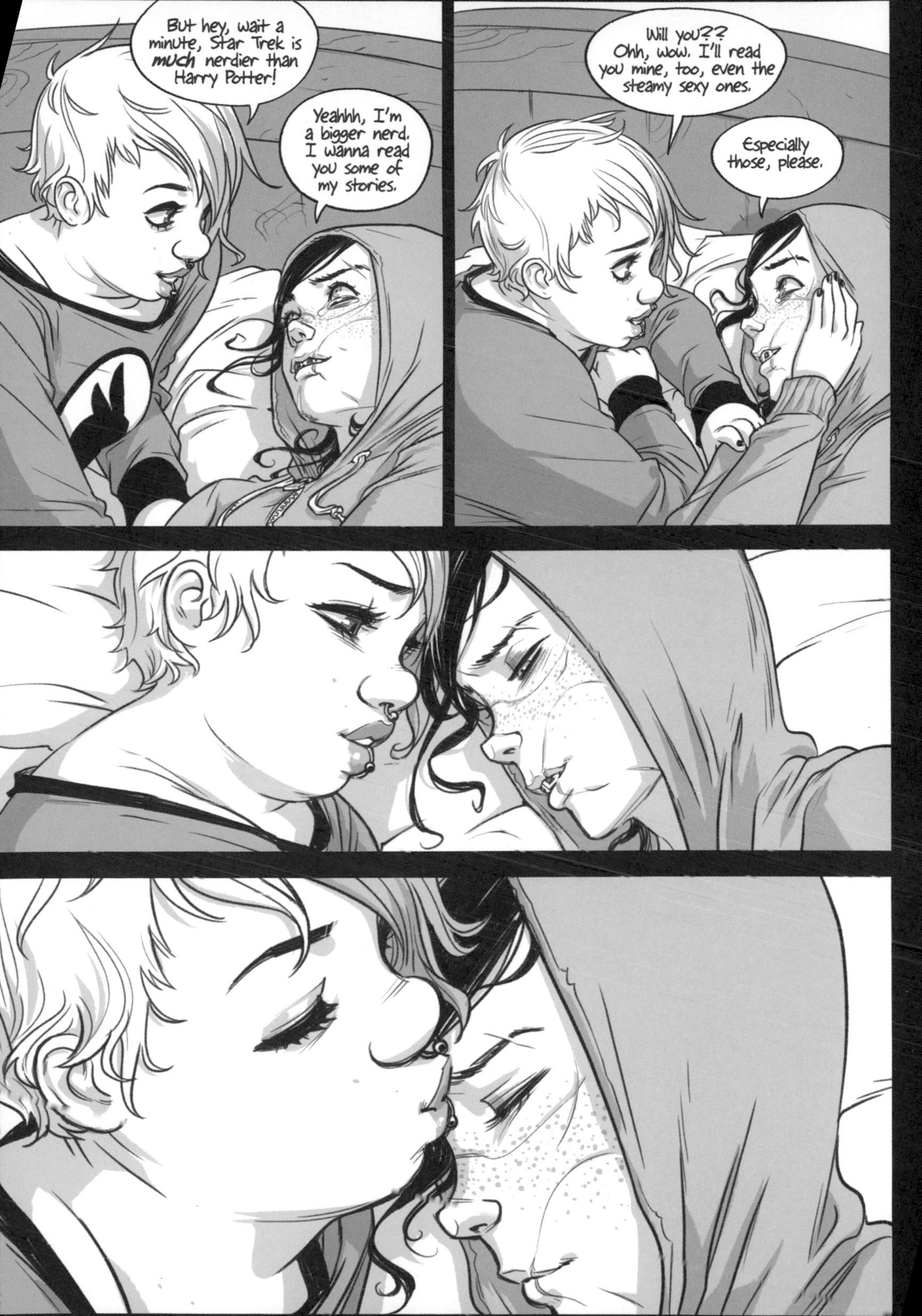
But hey, wait a minute, Star Trek is *much* nerdier than Harry Potter!
Yeahhh, I'm a bigger nerd. I wanna read you some of my stories.
Will you?? Ohh, wow. I'll read you mine, too, even the steamy sexy ones.
Especially those, please.

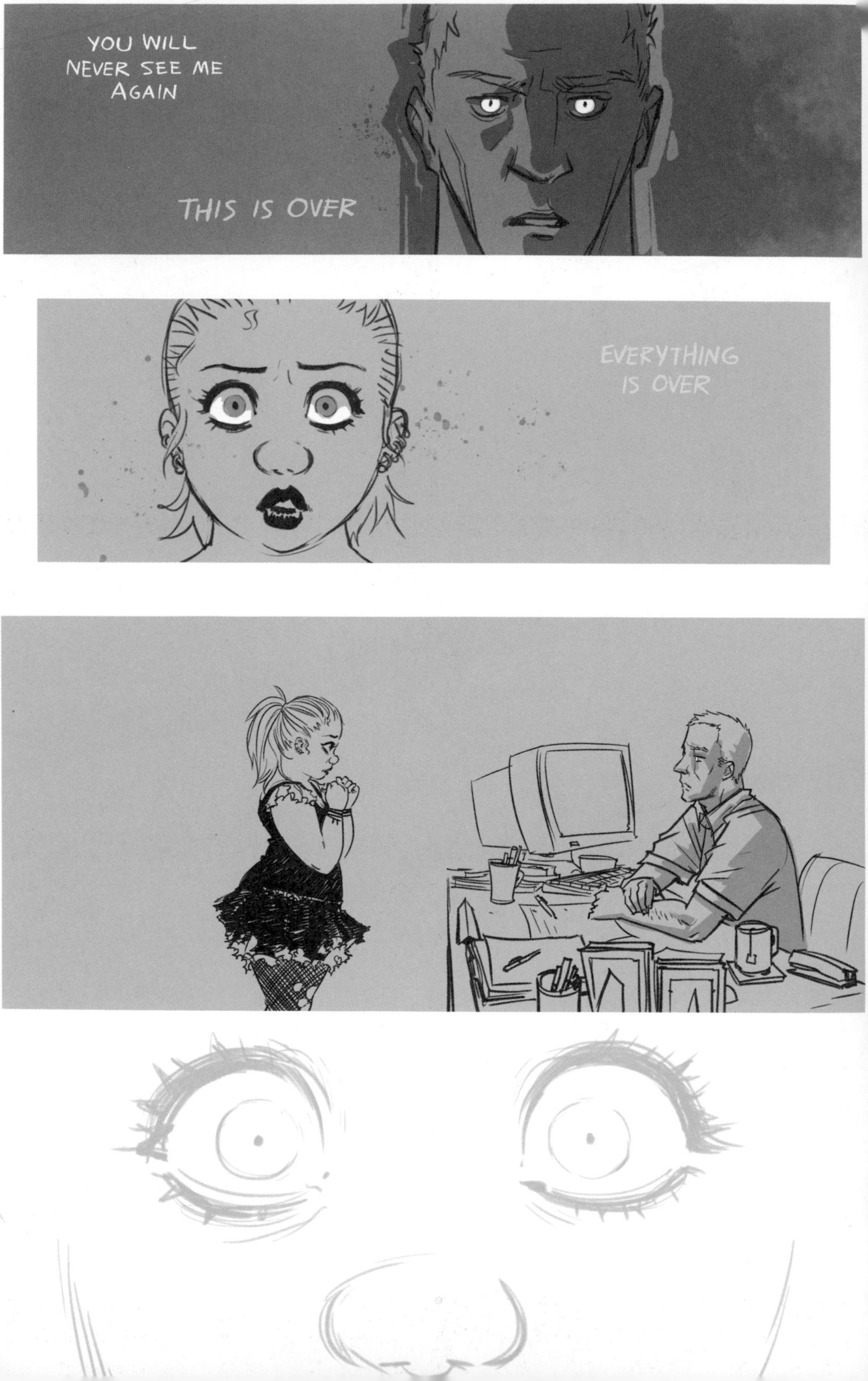
YOU WILL NEVER SEE ME AGAIN
THIS IS OVER
EVERYTHING IS OVER

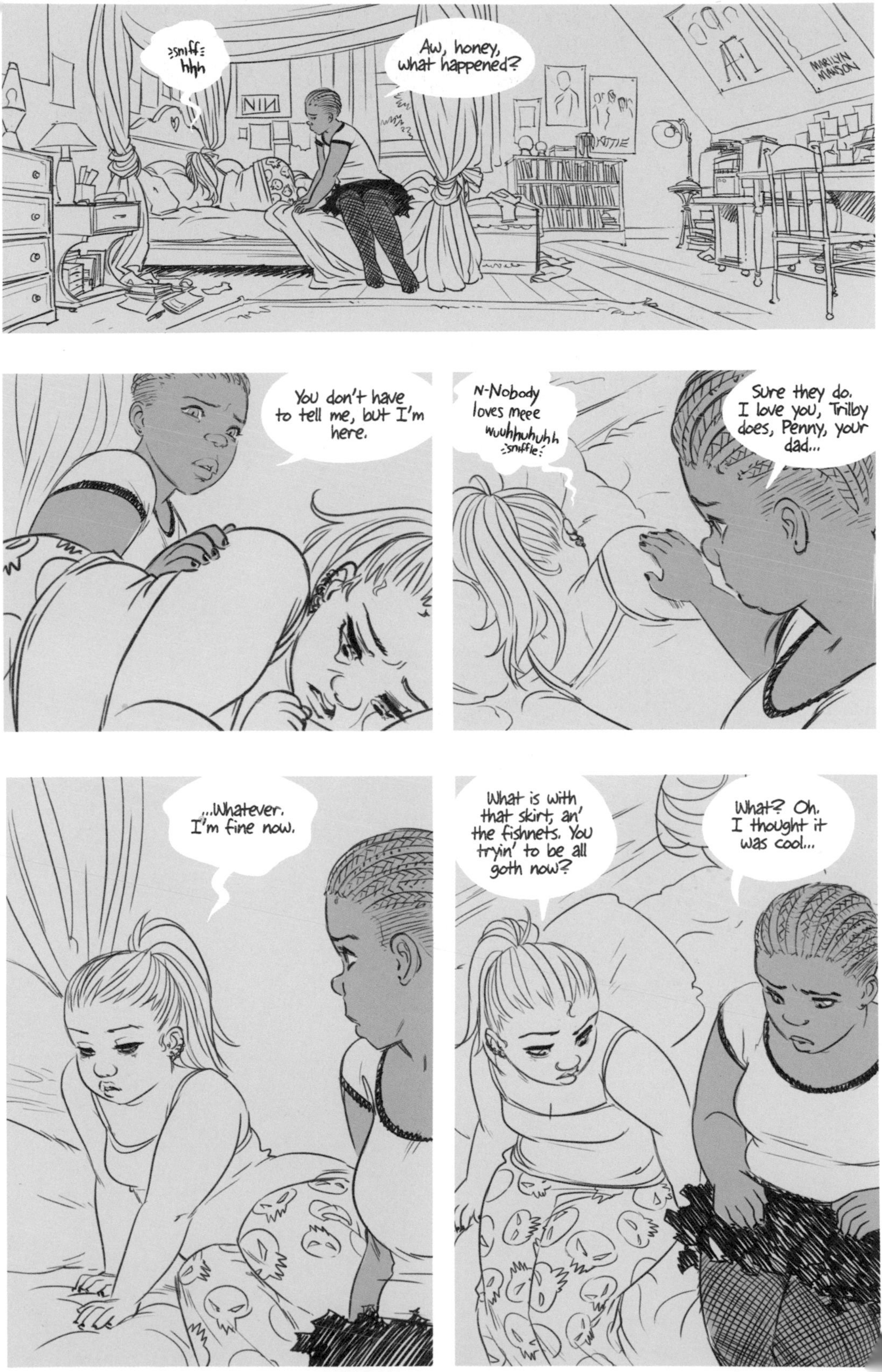
sniff
hhh
Aw, honey, what happened?
NIN
AFI
MARILYN MANSON
KITTIE
You don't have to tell me, but I'm here.
N-Nobody loves meee
wuuhhuhuhh
sniffle
Sure they do. I love you, Trilby does, Penny, your dad...
...Whatever. I'm fine now.
What is with that skirt, an' the fishnets. You tryin' to be all goth now?
What? Oh. I thought it was cool...

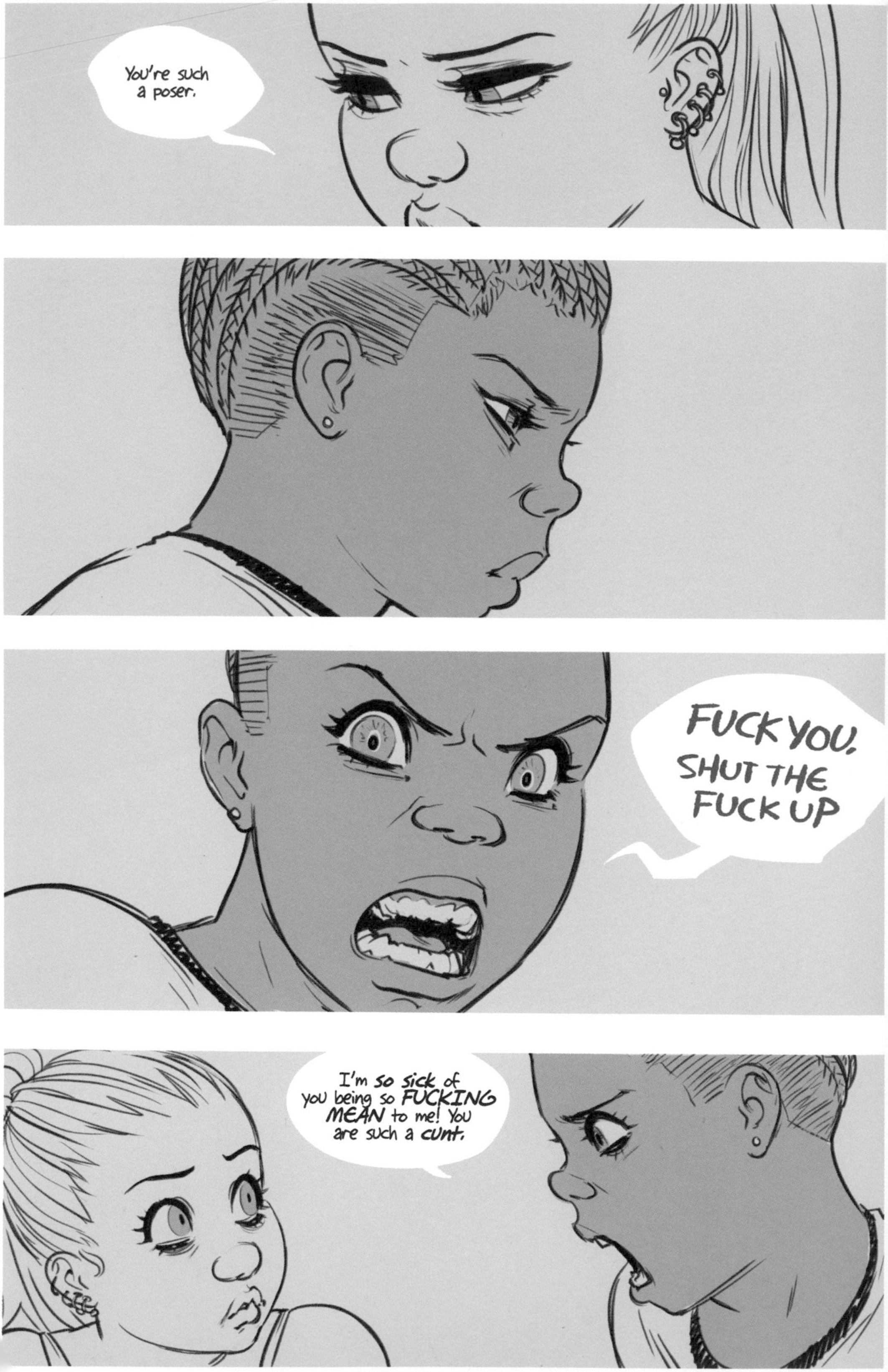
You're such a poser.
FUCK YOU. SHUT THE FUCK UP
I'm so sick of you being so FUCKING MEAN to me! You are such a cunt.

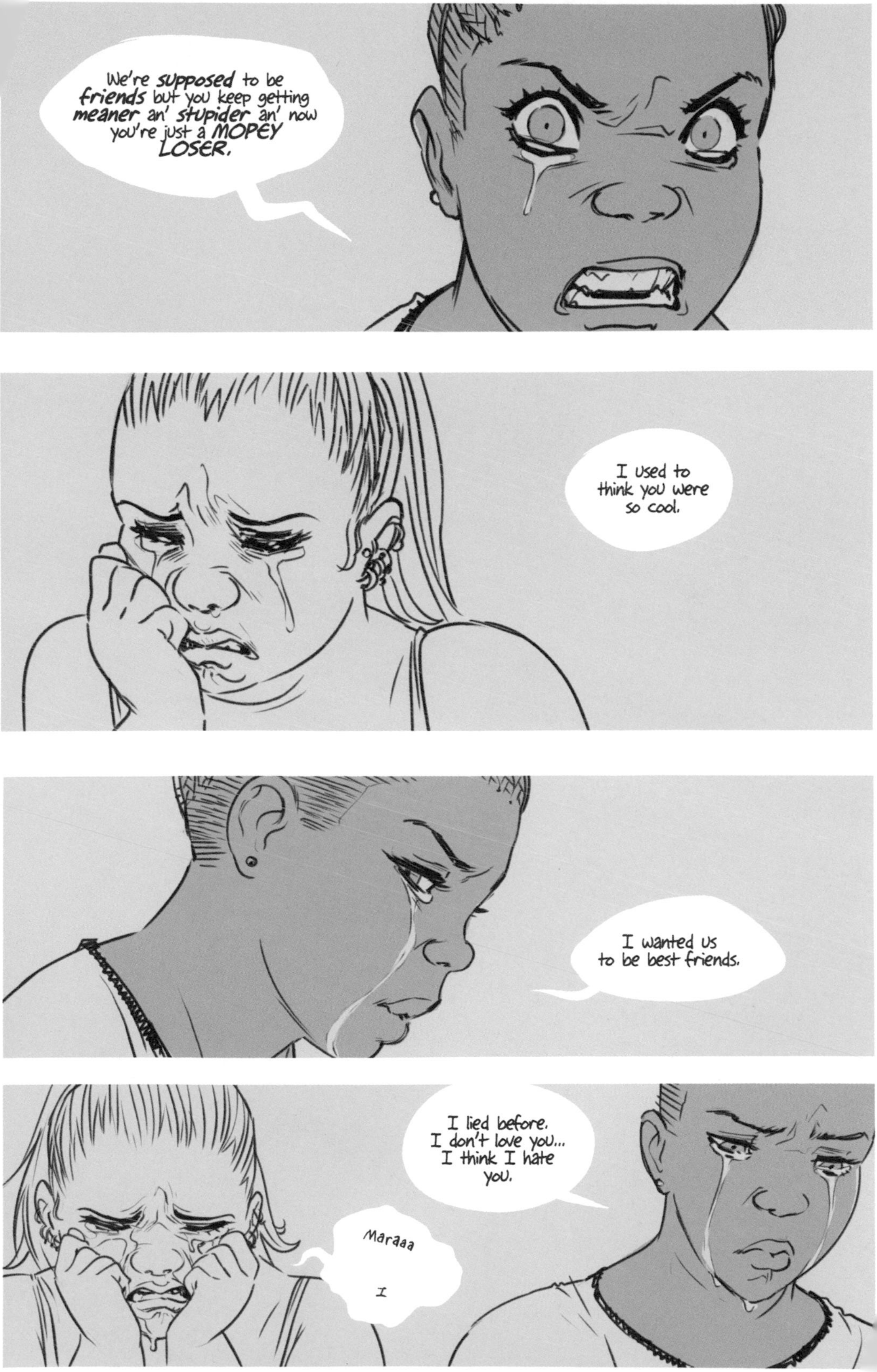
We're **supposed** to be **friends** but you keep getting **meaner** an' **stupider** an' now you're just a **MOPEY LOSER.**
I used to think you were so cool.
I wanted us to be best friends.
I lied before. I don't love you... I think I hate you.
Maraaa
I

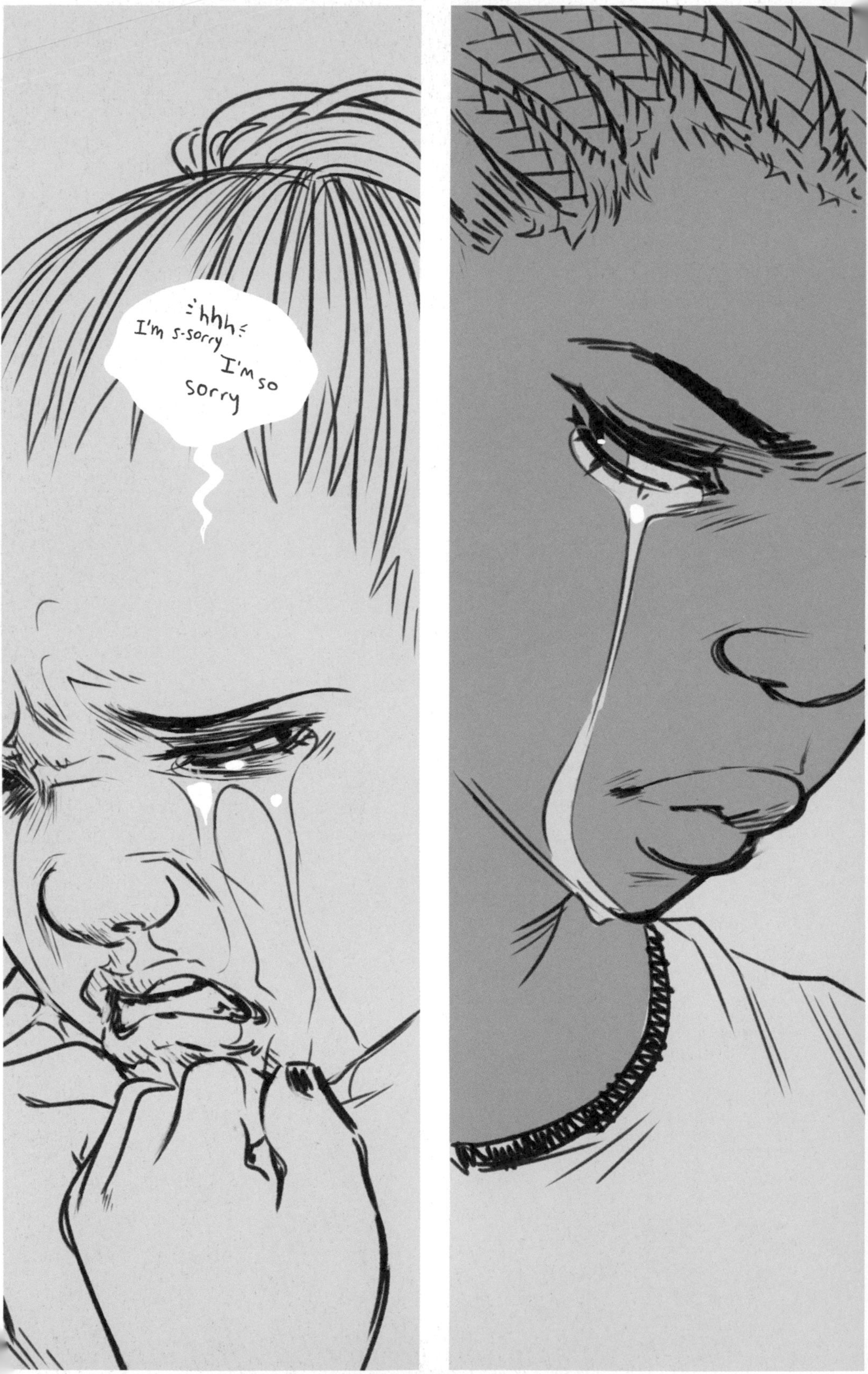
hhh
I'm s-sorry
I'm so sorry

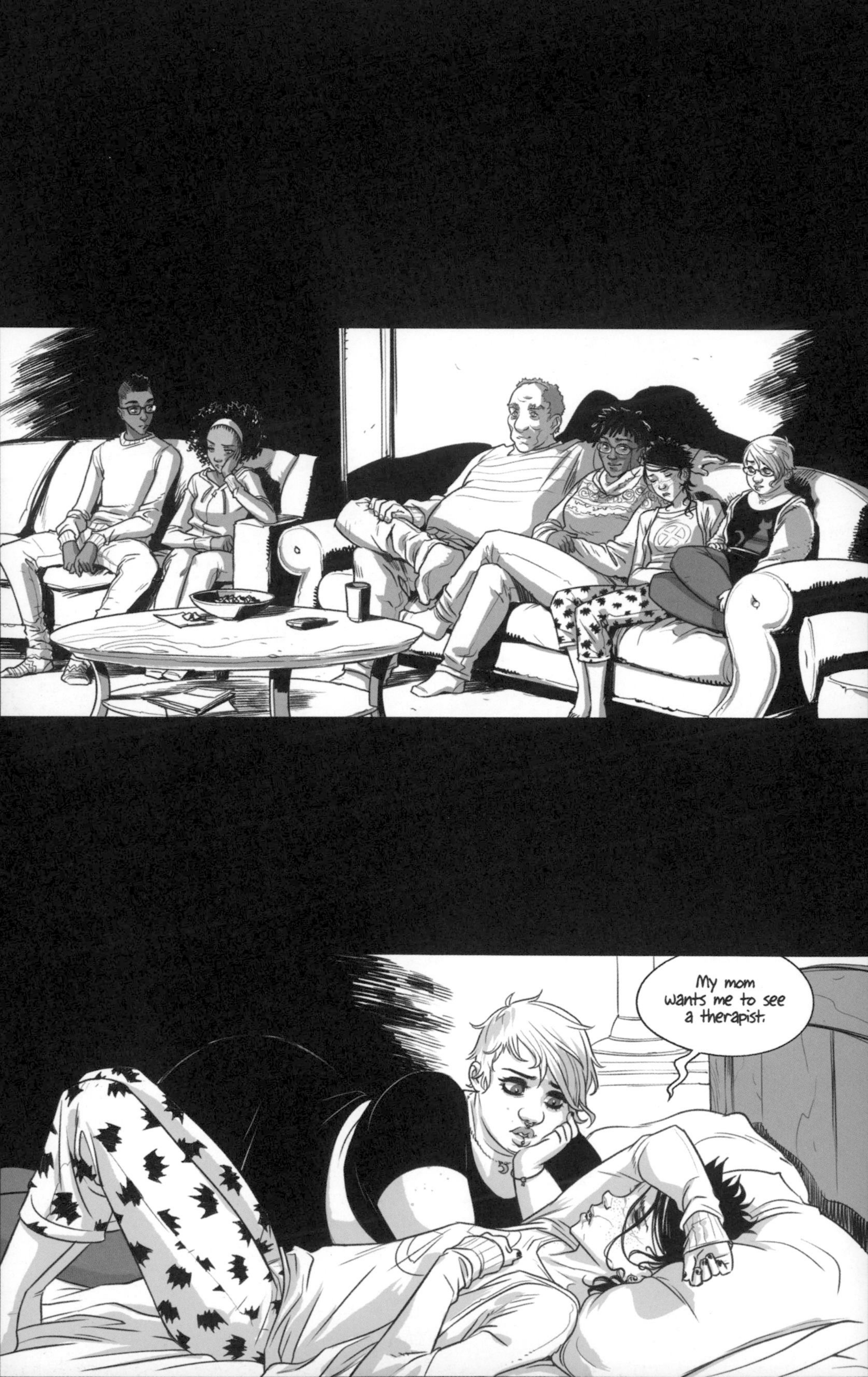
My mom wants me to see a therapist.

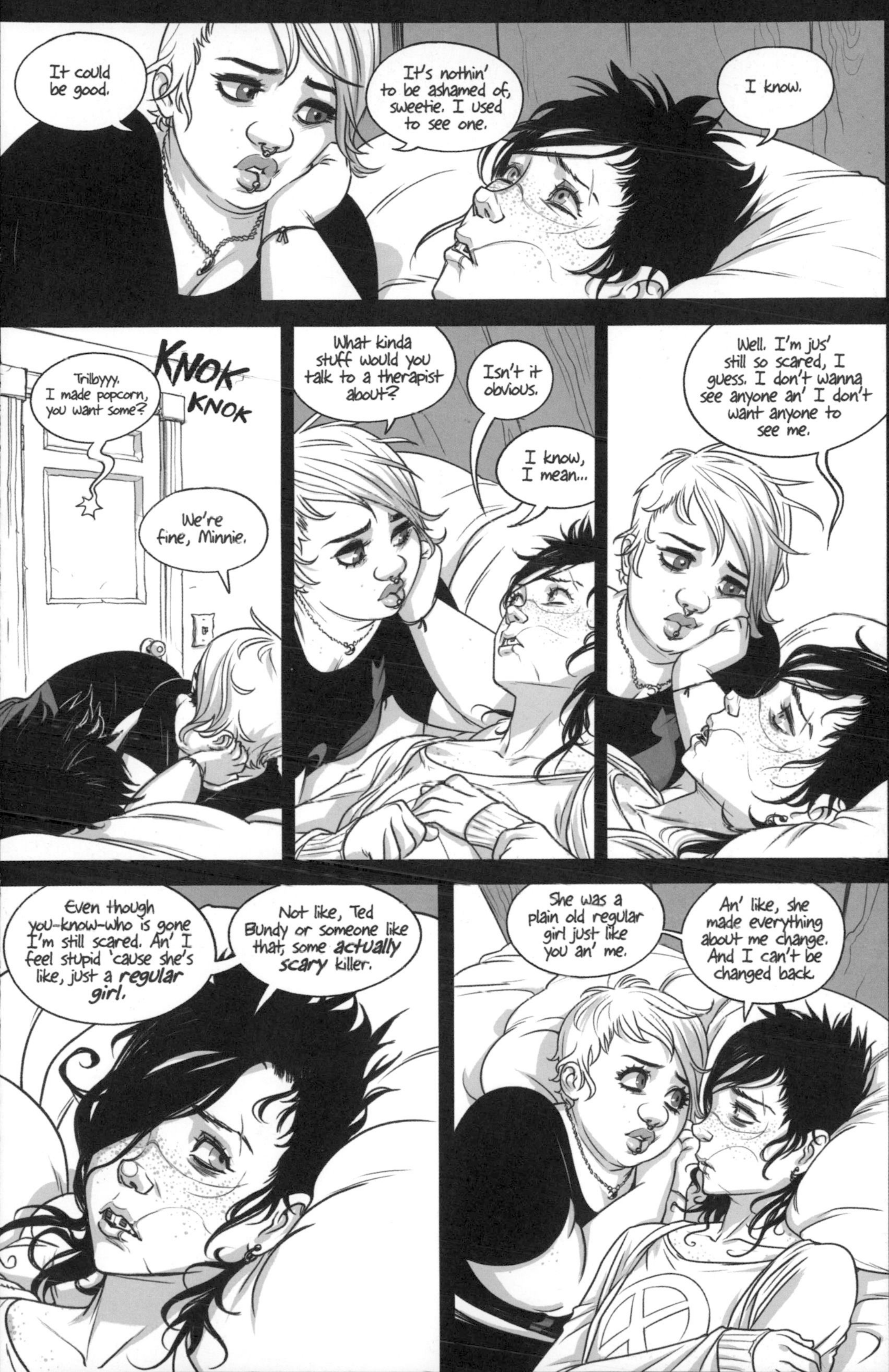
It could be good.
It's nothin' to be ashamed of, sweetie. I used to see one.
I know.
KNOK KNOK
Trilbyyy. I made popcorn, you want some?
We're fine, Minnie.
What kinda stuff would you talk to a therapist about?
Isn't it obvious.
I know, I mean...
Well. I'm jus' still so scared, I guess. I don't wanna see anyone an' I don't want anyone to see me.
Even though you-know-who is gone I'm still scared. An' I feel stupid 'cause she's like, just a **regular girl.**
Not like, Ted Bundy or someone like that, some **actually scary** killer.
She was a plain old regular girl just like you an' me.
An' like, she made everything about me change. And I can't be changed back.

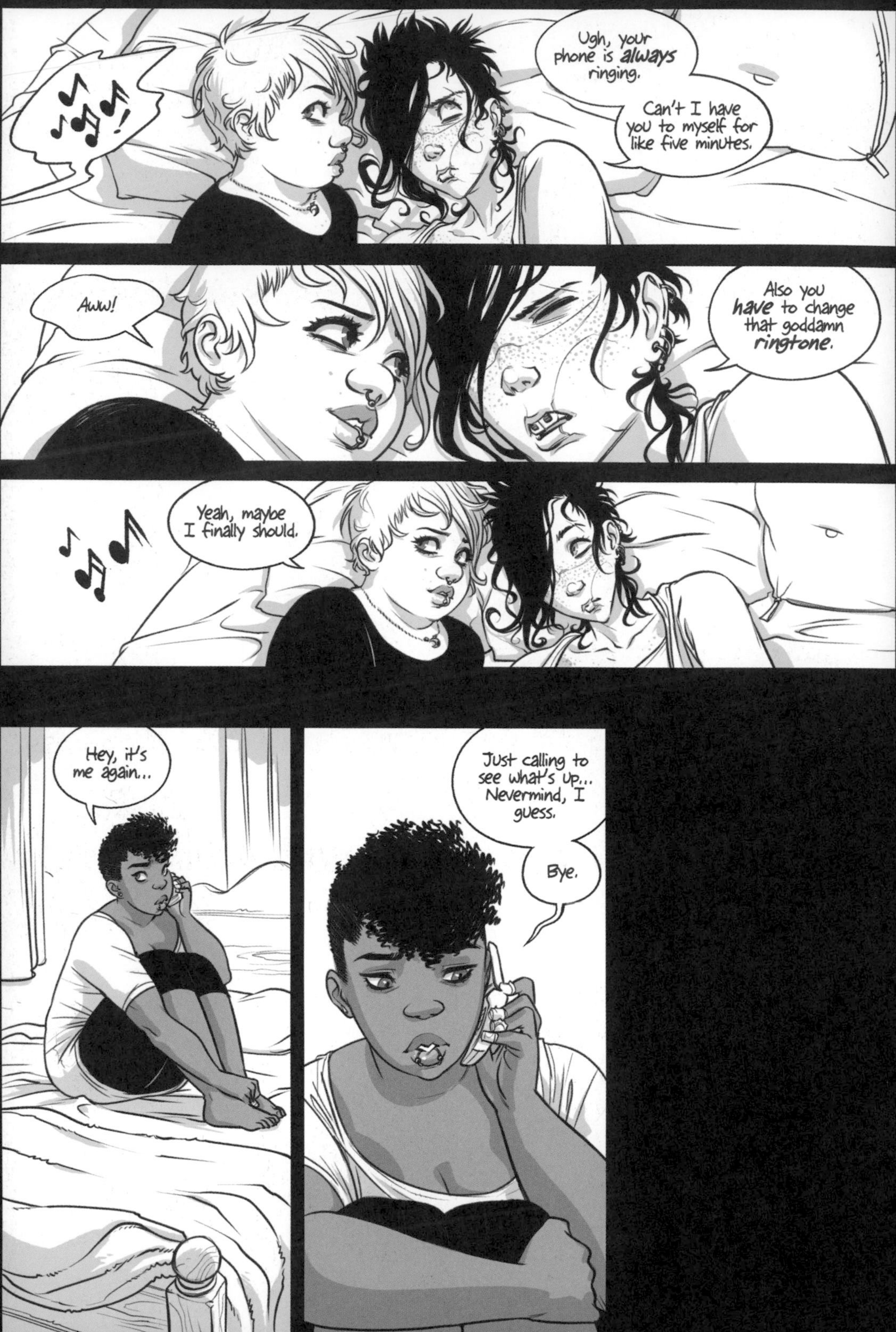
Ugh, your phone is always ringing.
Can't I have you to myself for like five minutes.
Aww!
Also you have to change that goddamn ringtone.
Yeah, maybe I finally should.
Hey, it's me again...
Just calling to see what's up... Nevermind, I guess.
Bye.

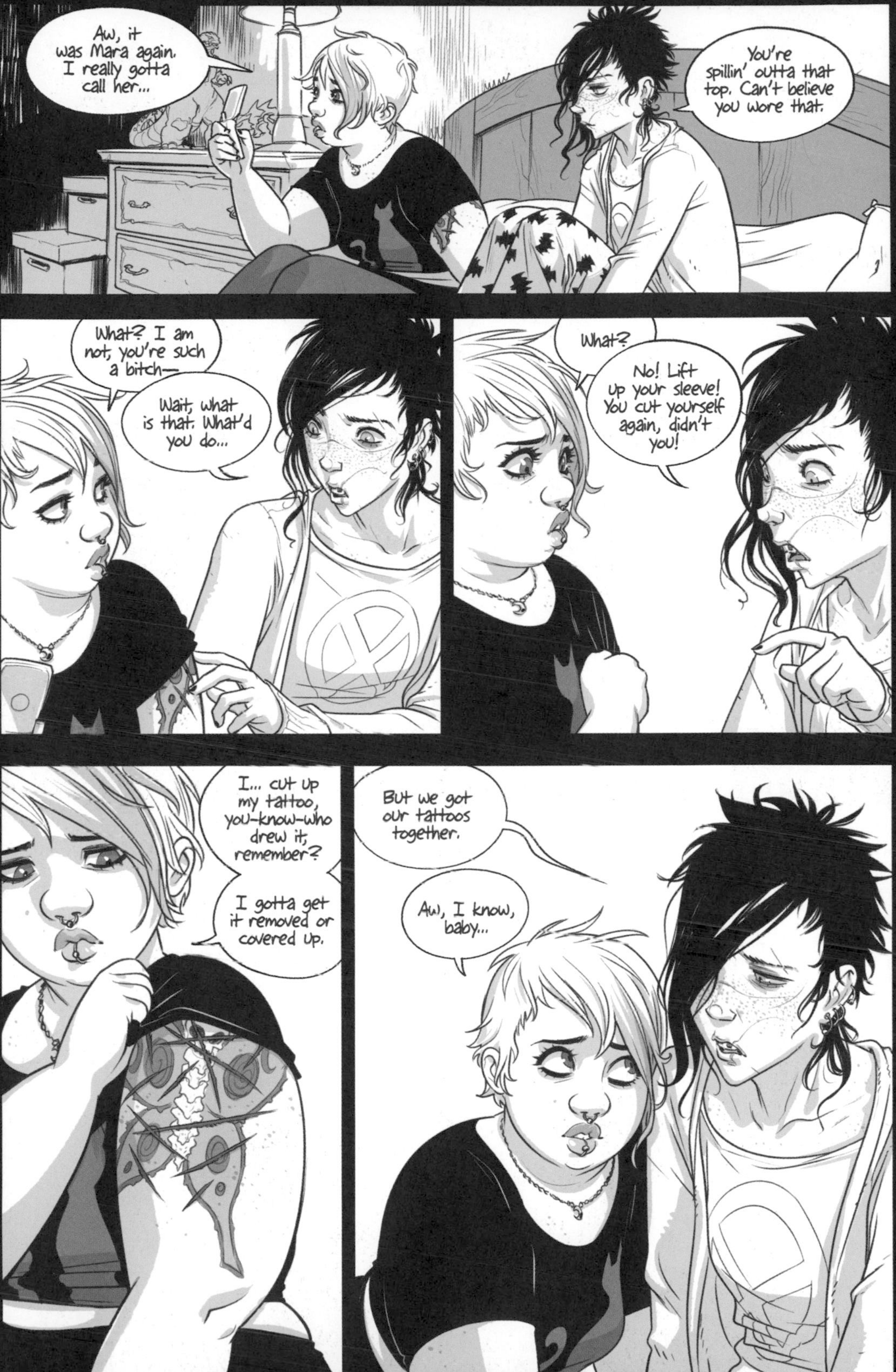
Aw, it was Mara again. I really gotta call her...
You're spillin' outta that top. Can't believe you wore that.
What? I am not, you're such a bitch—
Wait, what is that. What'd you do...
What?
No! Lift up your sleeve! You cut yourself again, didn't you!
I... cut up my tattoo, you-know-who drew it, remember?
I gotta get it removed or covered up.
But we got our tattoos together.
Aw, I know, baby...

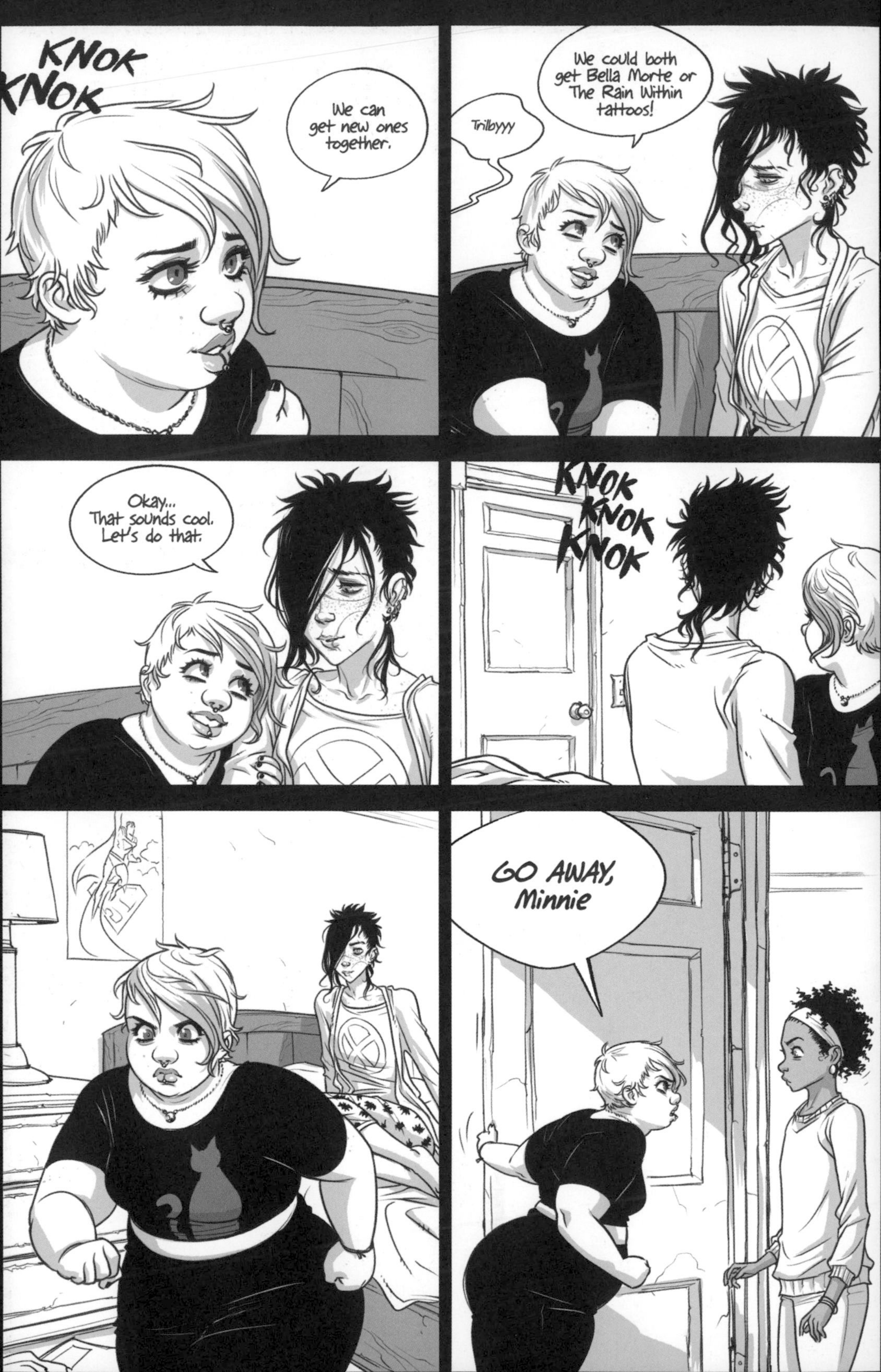
KNOK KNOK
We can get new ones together.
Trilbyyy
We could both get Bella Morte or The Rain Within tattoos!
Okay... That sounds cool. Let's do that.
KNOK KNOK KNOK
GO AWAY, Minnie

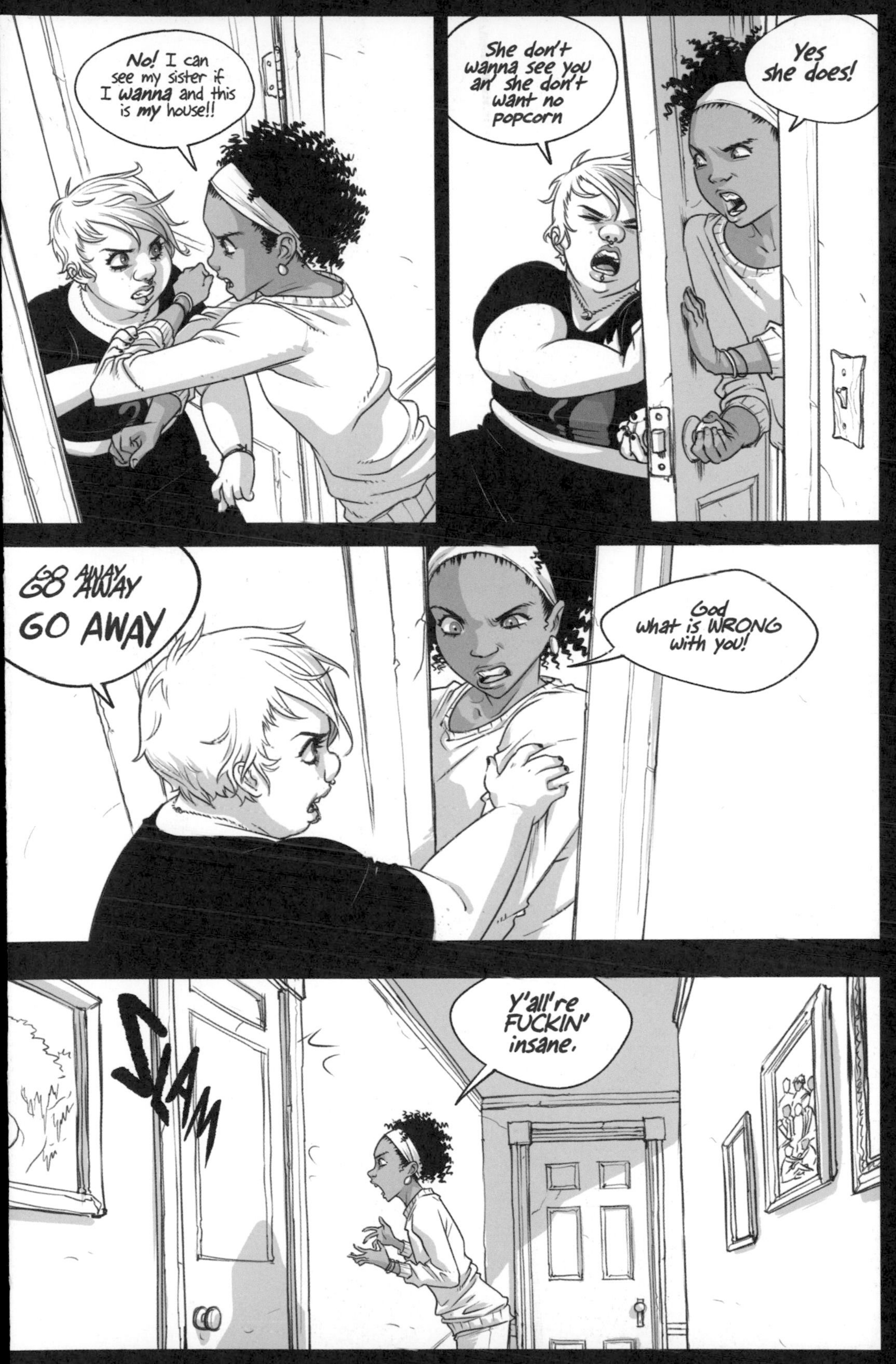
No! I can see my sister if I wanna and this is my house!!
She don't wanna see you an' she don't want no popcorn
Yes she does!
GO AWAY AWAY GO AWAY
God what is WRONG with you!
SLAM
Y'all're FUCKIN' insane.

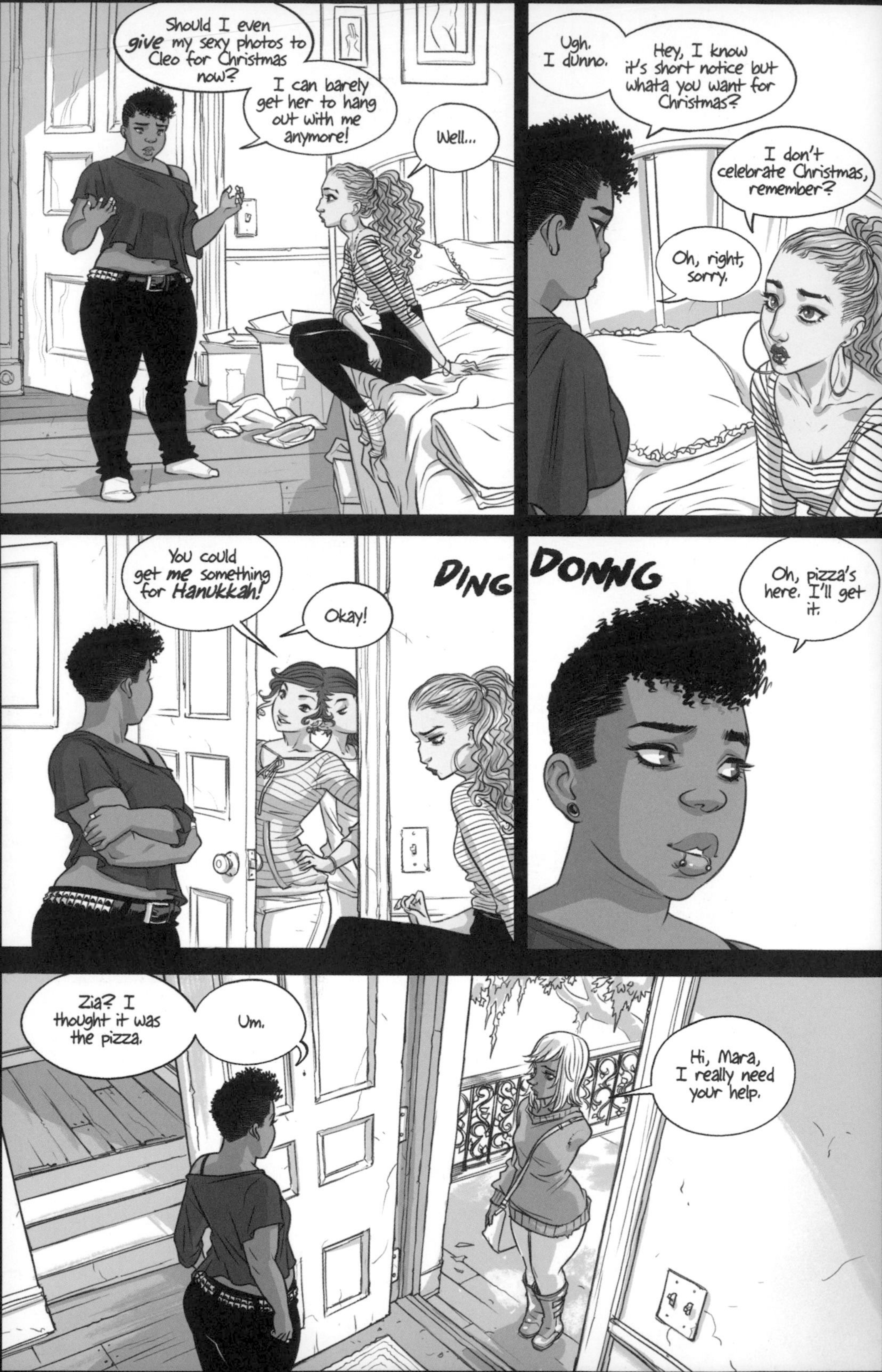
Should I even give my sexy photos to Cleo for Christmas now?
I can barely get her to hang out with me anymore!
Well...
Ugh. I dunno.
Hey, I know it's short notice but whata you want for Christmas?
I don't celebrate Christmas, remember?
Oh, right, sorry.
You could get me something for Hanukkah!
Okay!
DING
DONNG
Oh, pizza's here. I'll get it.
Zia? I thought it was the pizza.
Um.
Hi, Mara, I really need your help.

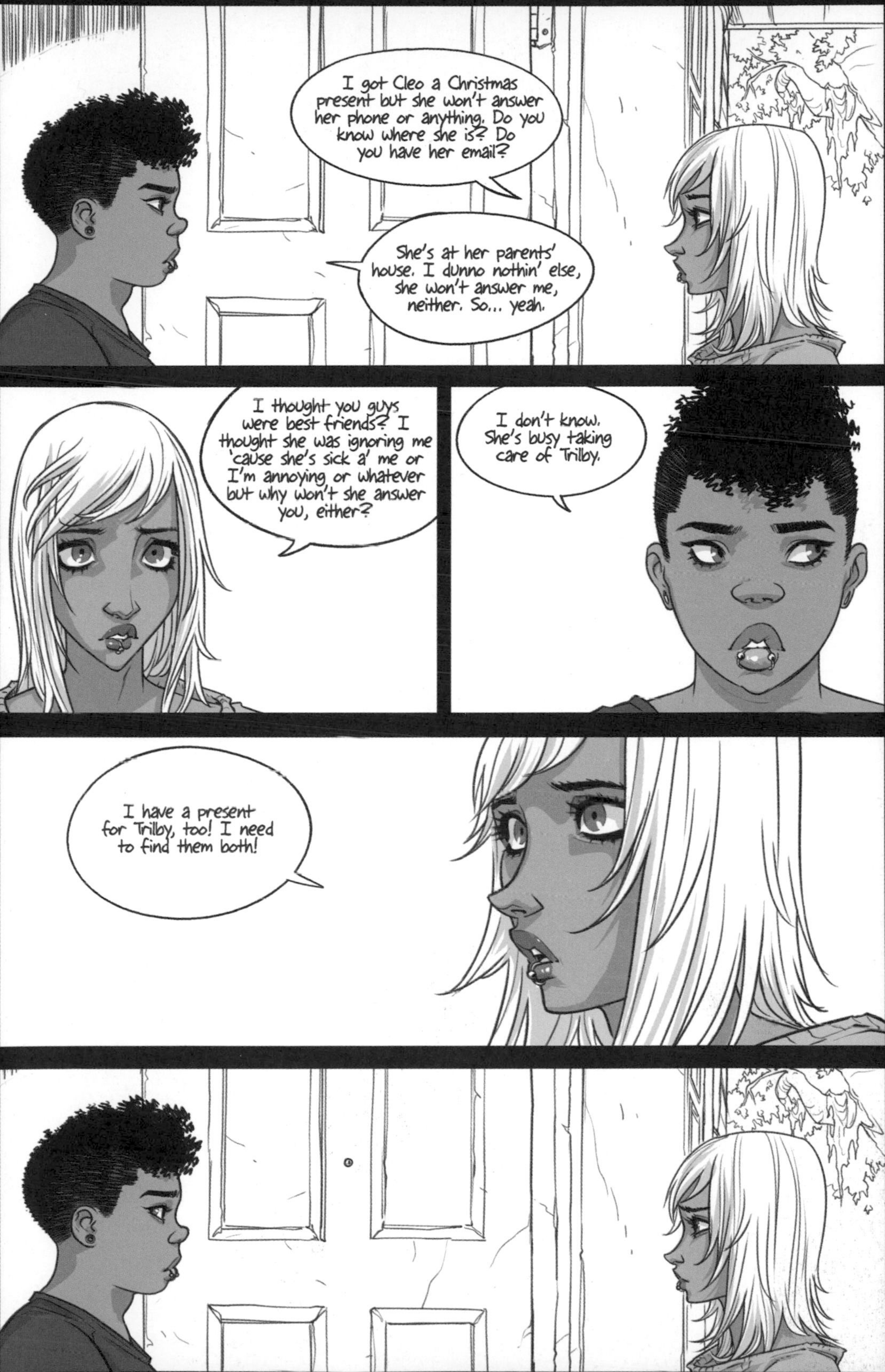
I got Cleo a Christmas present but she won't answer her phone or anything. Do you know where she is? Do you have her email?
She's at her parents' house. I dunno nothin' else, she won't answer me, neither. So... yeah.
I thought you guys were best friends? I thought she was ignoring me 'cause she's sick a' me or I'm annoying or whatever but why won't she answer you, either?
I don't know. She's busy taking care of Trilby.
I have a present for Trilby, too! I need to find them both!

34

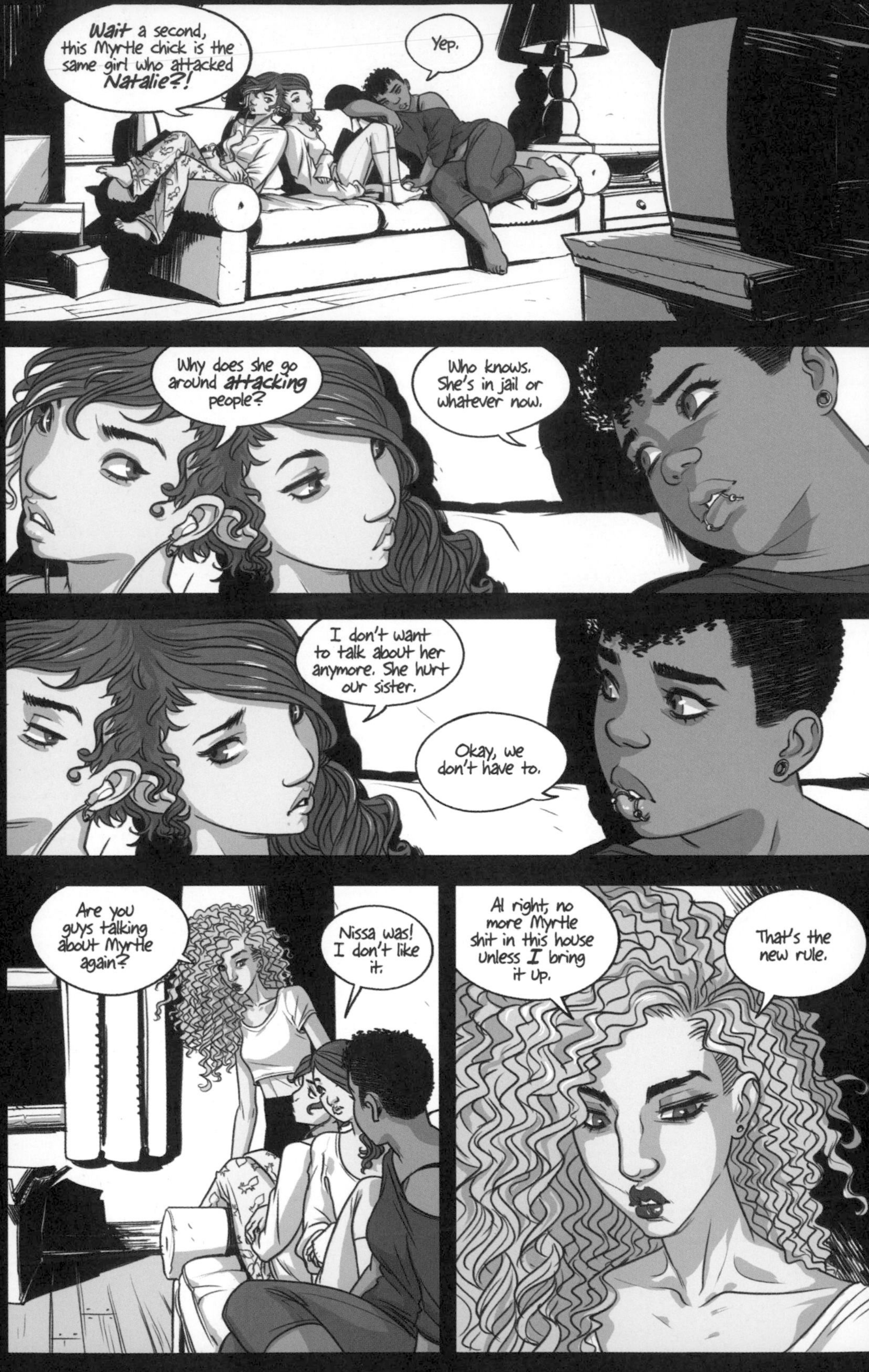

Wait a second, this Myrtle chick is the same girl who attacked Natalie?!
Yep.
Why does she go around attacking people?
Who knows. She's in jail or whatever now.
I don't want to talk about her anymore. She hurt our sister.
Okay, we don't have to.
Are you guys talking about Myrtle again?
Nissa was! I don't like it.
Al right, no more Myrtle shit in this house unless I bring it up.
That's the new rule.

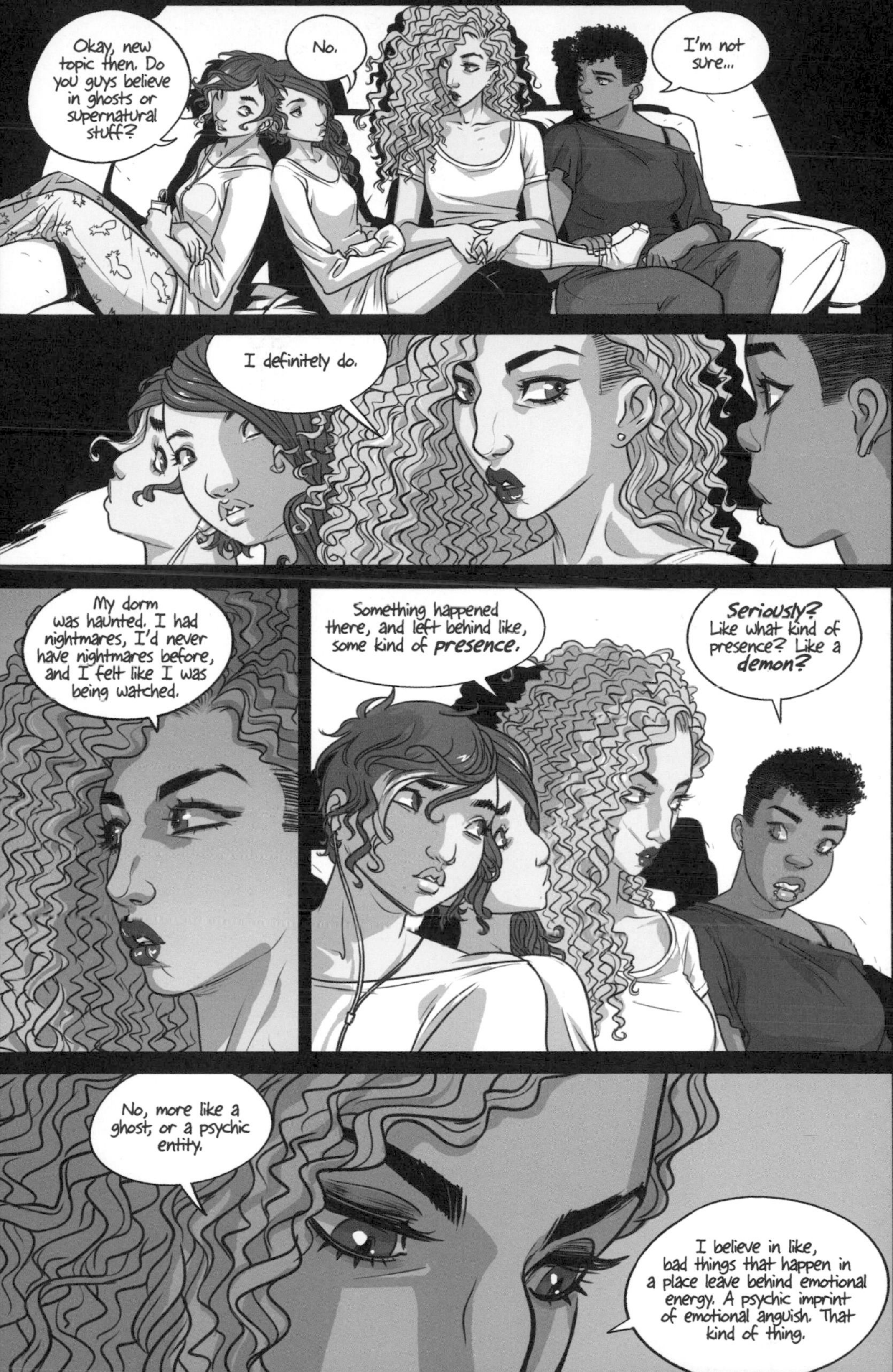
Okay, new topic then. Do you guys believe in ghosts or supernatural stuff?
No.
I'm not sure...
I definitely do.
My dorm was haunted. I had nightmares, I'd never have nightmares before, and I felt like I was being watched.
Something happened there, and left behind like, some kind of presence.
Seriously? Like what kind of presence? Like a demon?
No, more like a ghost, or a psychic entity.
I believe in like, bad things that happen in a place leave behind emotional energy. A psychic imprint of emotional anguish. That kind of thing.

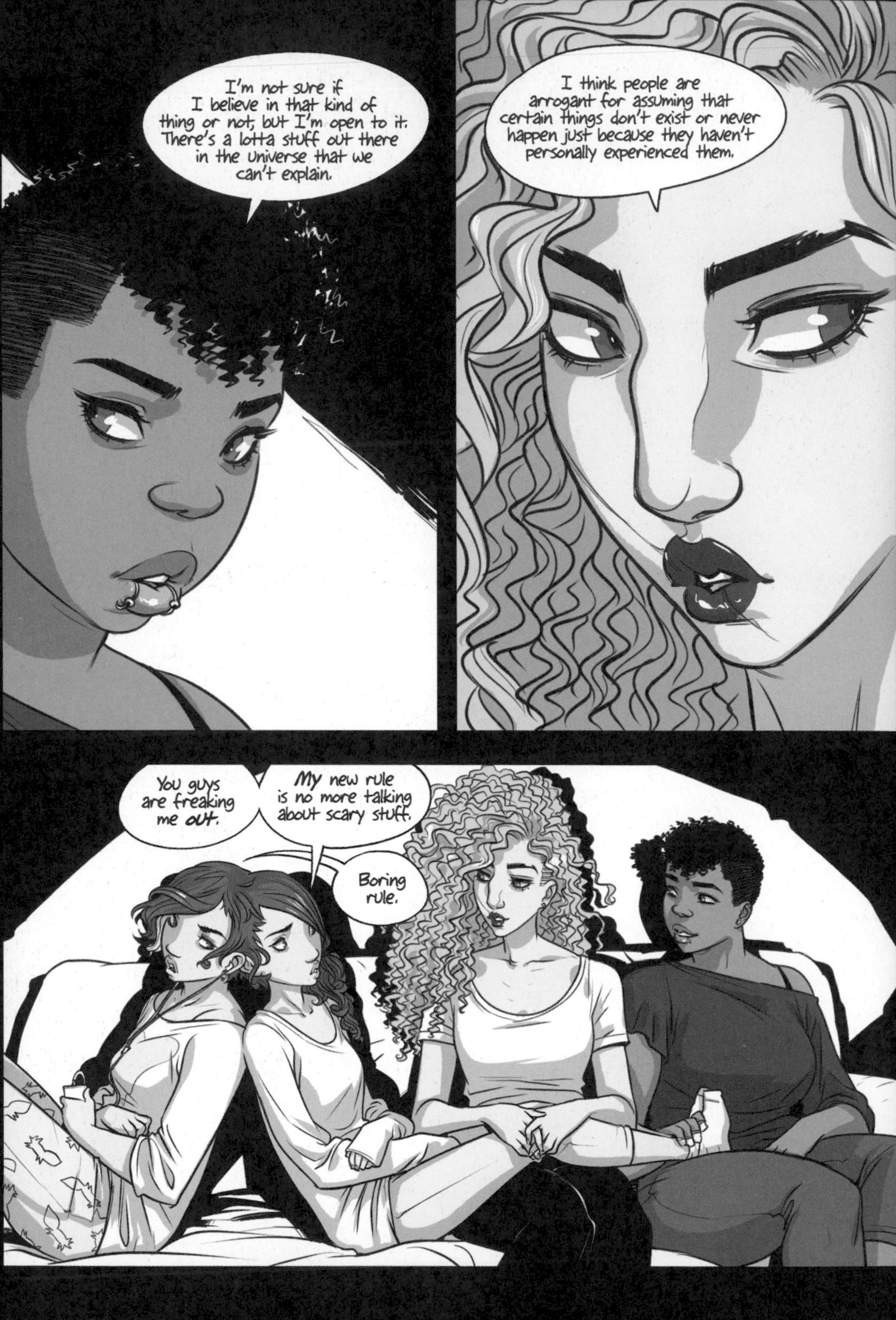
I'm not sure if I believe in that kind of thing or not, but I'm open to it. There's a lotta stuff out there in the universe that we can't explain.
I think people are arrogant for assuming that certain things don't exist or never happen just because they haven't personally experienced them.
You guys are freaking me *out*.
My new rule is no more talking about scary stuff.
Boring rule.

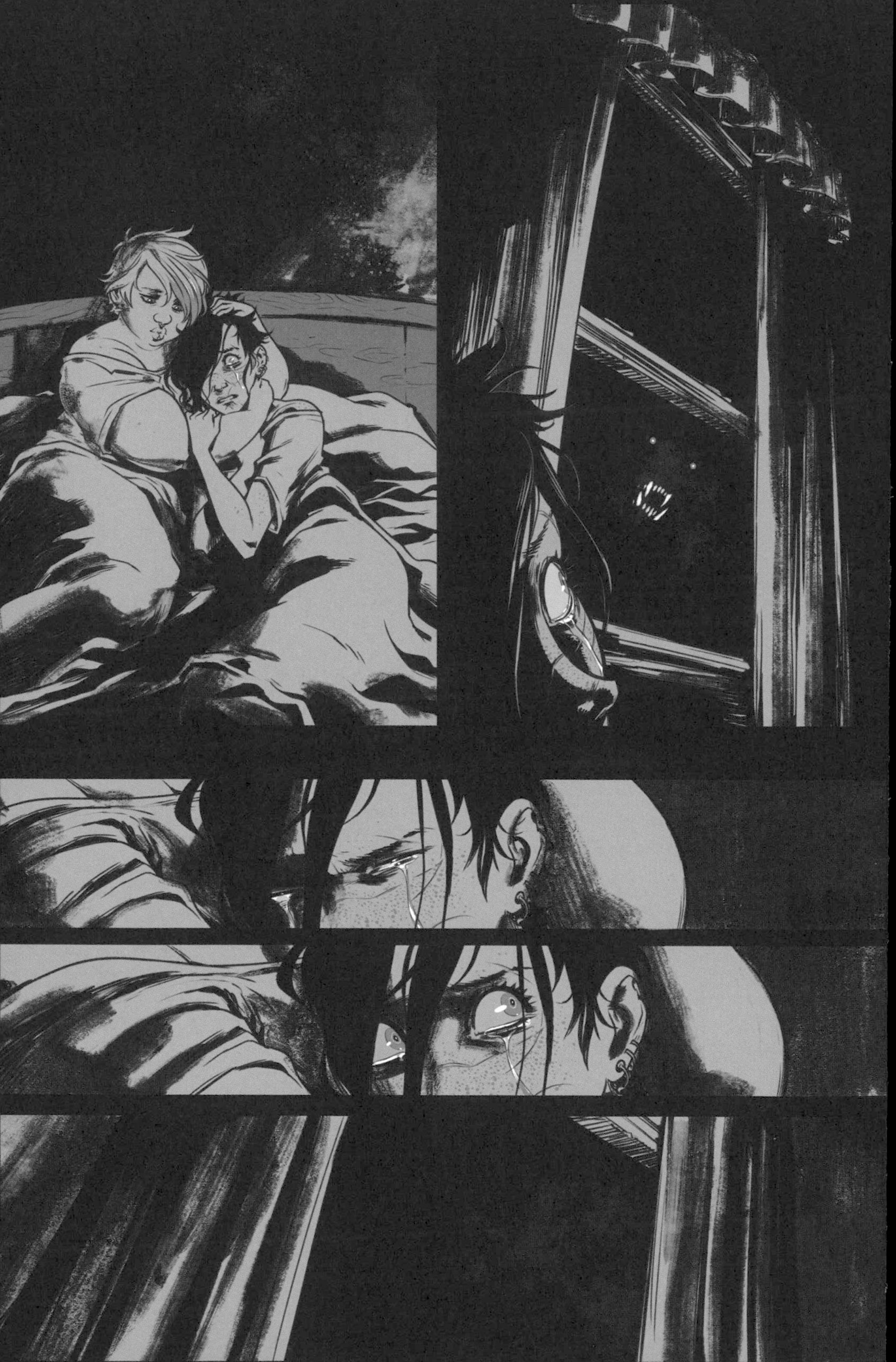

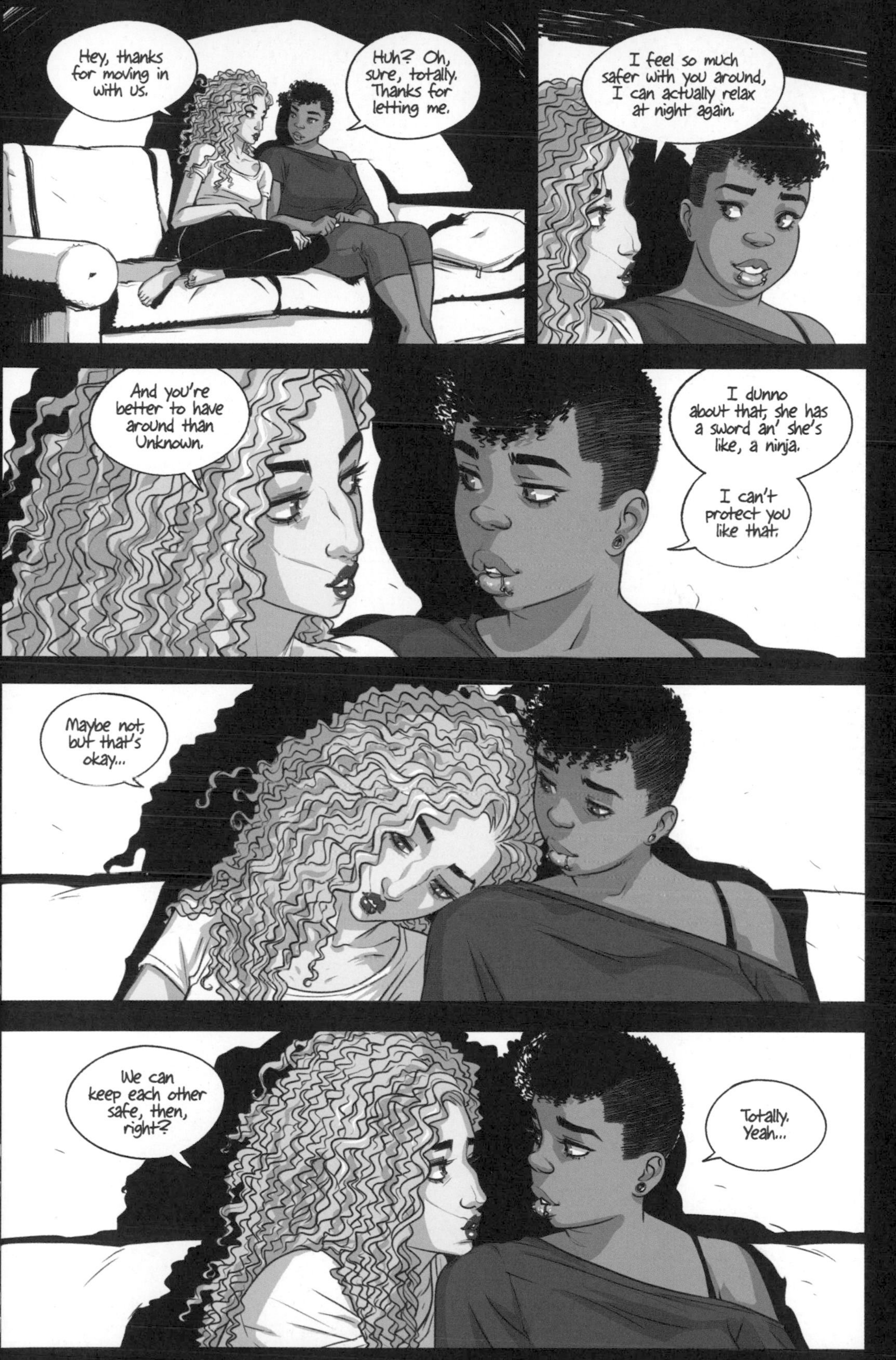
Hey, thanks for moving in with us.
Huh? Oh, sure, totally. Thanks for letting me.
I feel so much safer with you around, I can actually relax at night again.
And you're better to have around than Unknown.
I dunno about that, she has a sword an' she's like, a ninja.
I can't protect you like that.
Maybe not, but that's okay...
We can keep each other safe, then, right?
Totally. Yeah...

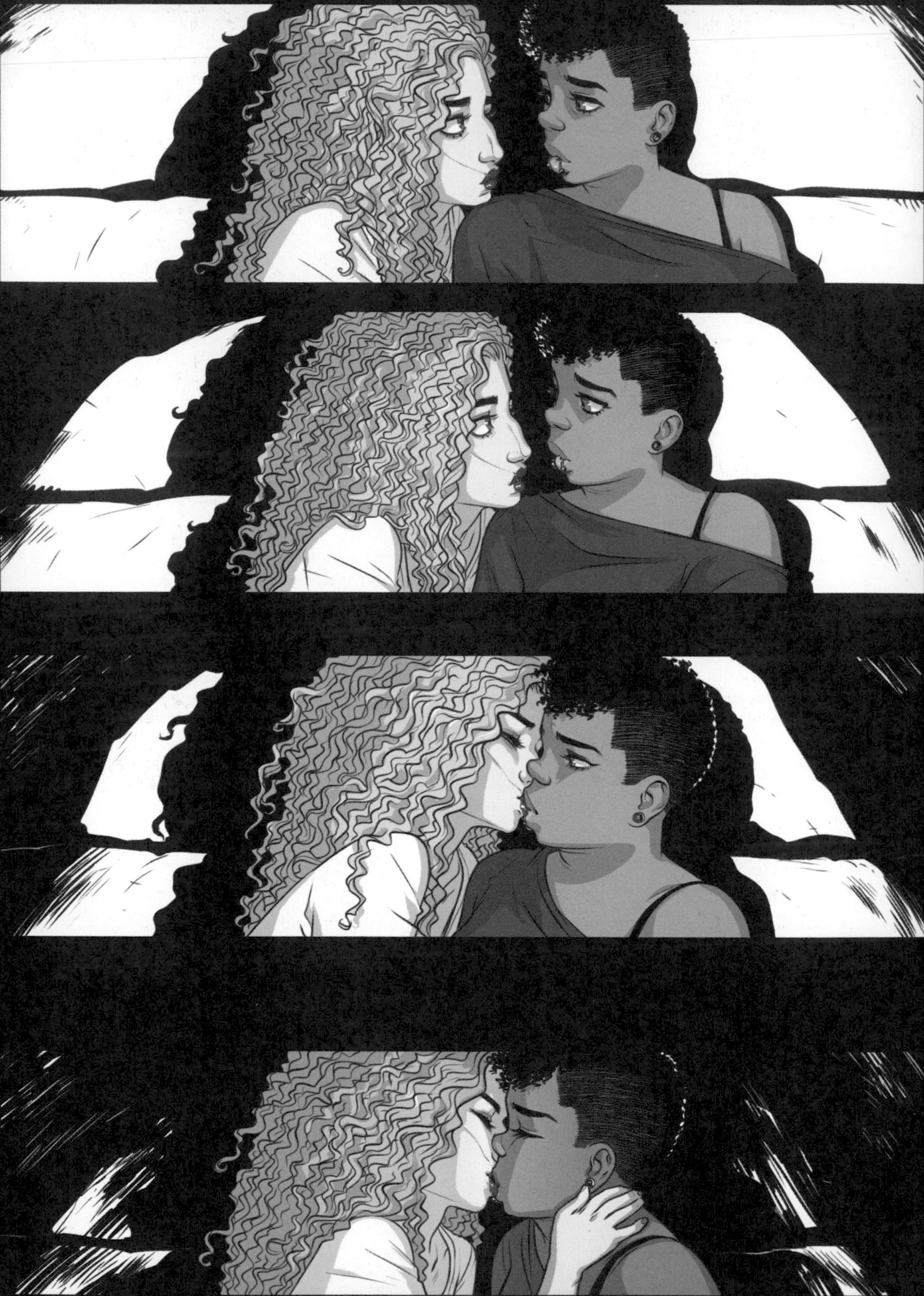

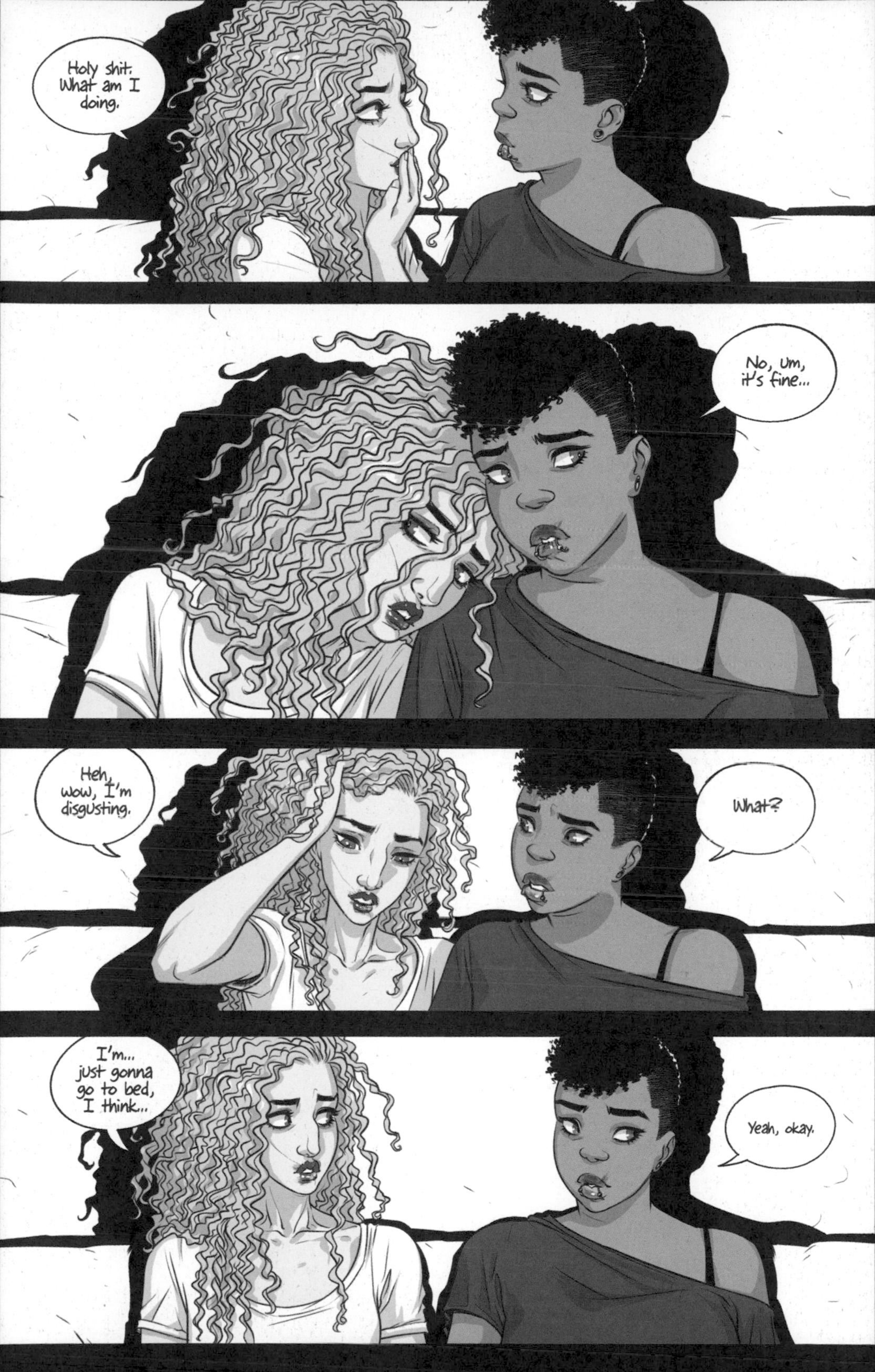
Holy shit. What am I doing.
No, um, it's fine...
Heh, wow, I'm disgusting.
What?
I'm... just gonna go to bed, I think...
Yeah, okay.

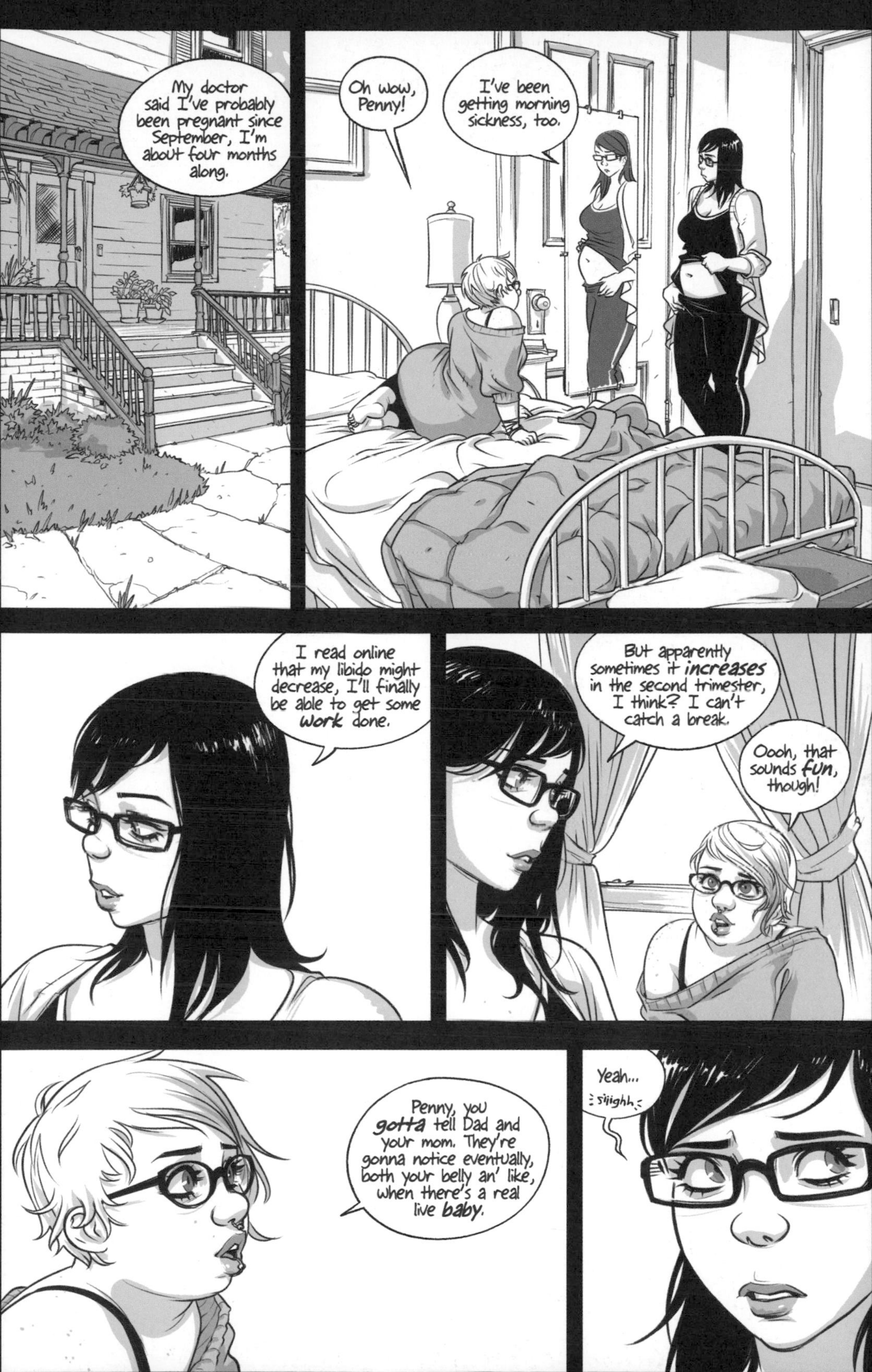
My doctor said I've probably been pregnant since September, I'm about four months along.
Oh wow, Penny!
I've been getting morning sickness, too.
I read online that my libido might decrease, I'll finally be able to get some work done.
But apparently sometimes it increases in the second trimester, I think? I can't catch a break.
Oooh, that sounds fun, though!
Penny, you gotta tell Dad and your mom. They're gonna notice eventually, both your belly an' like, when there's a real live baby.
Yeah...
siiighh

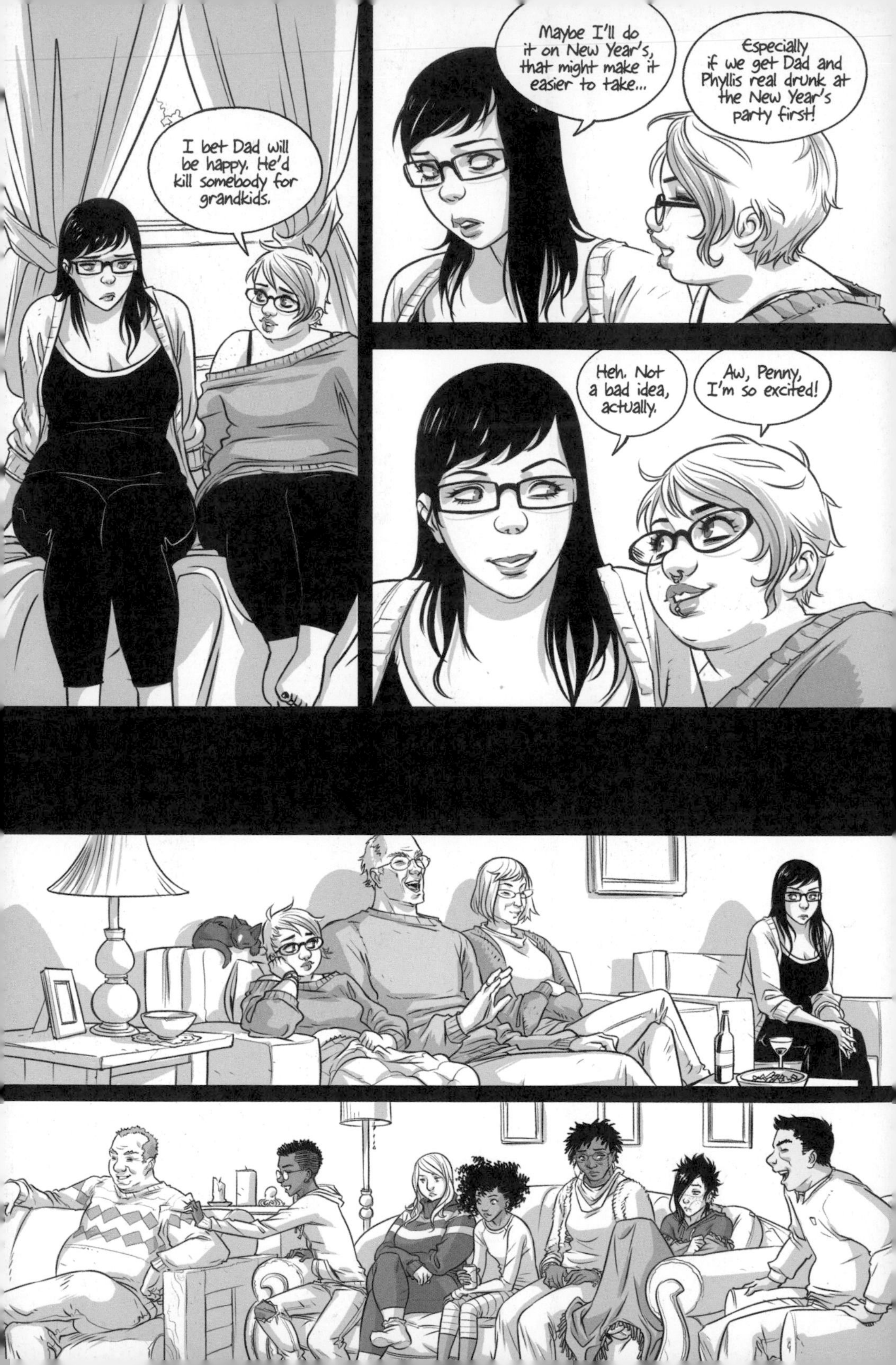
I bet Dad will be happy. He'd kill somebody for grandkids.
Maybe I'll do it on New Year's, that might make it easier to take...
Especially if we get Dad and Phyllis real drunk at the New Year's party first!
Heh. Not a bad idea, actually.
Aw, Penny, I'm so excited!

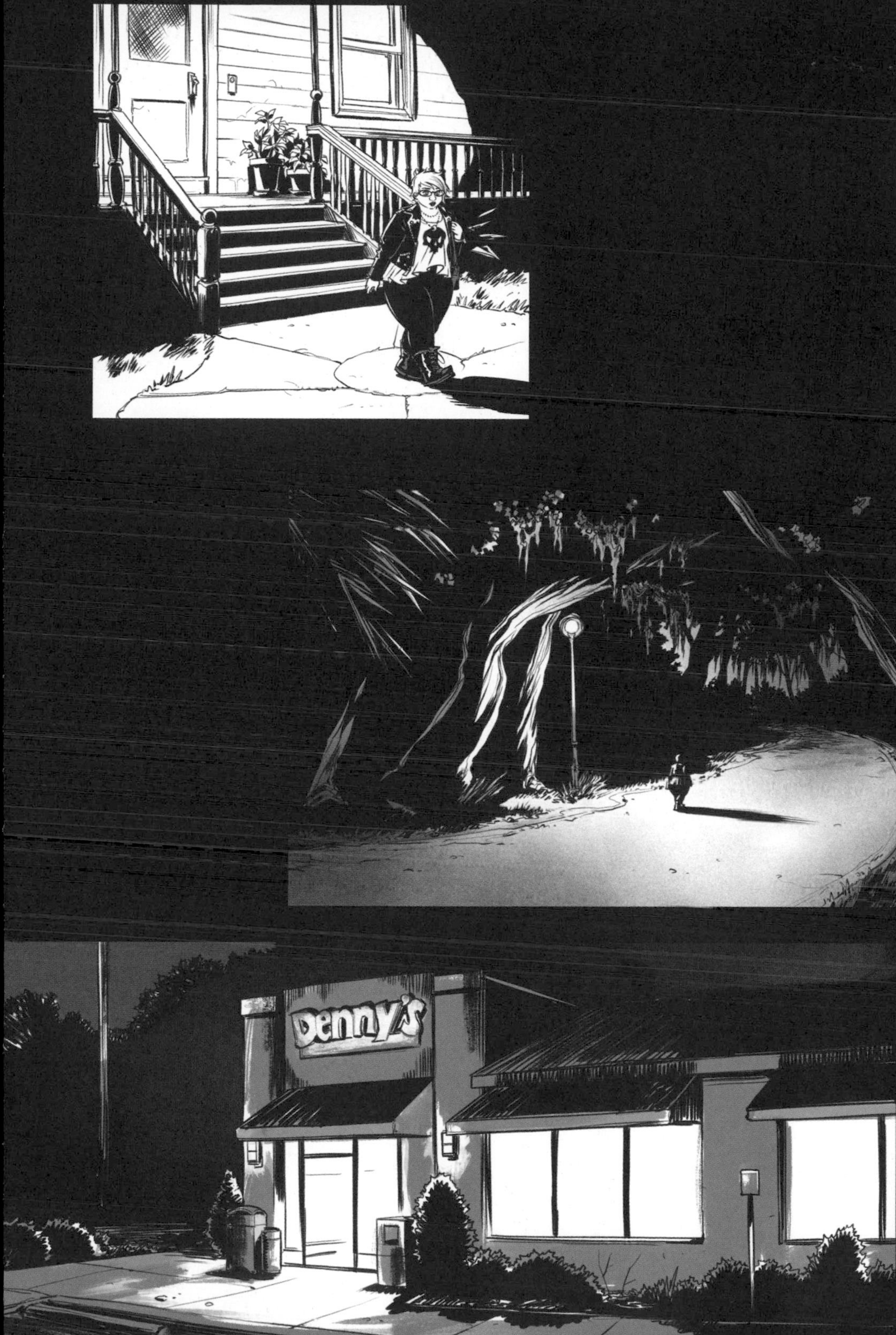
Denny's

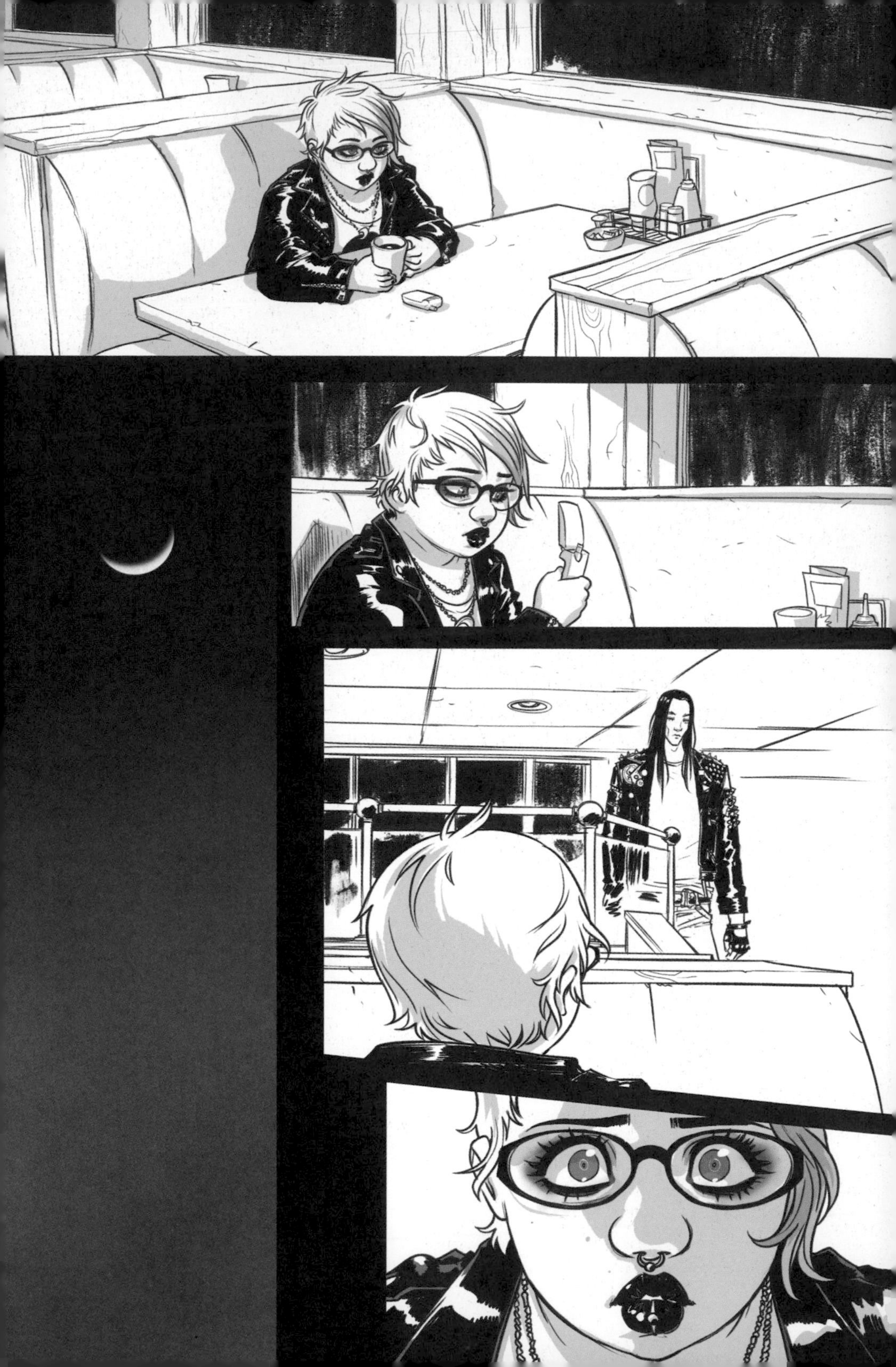

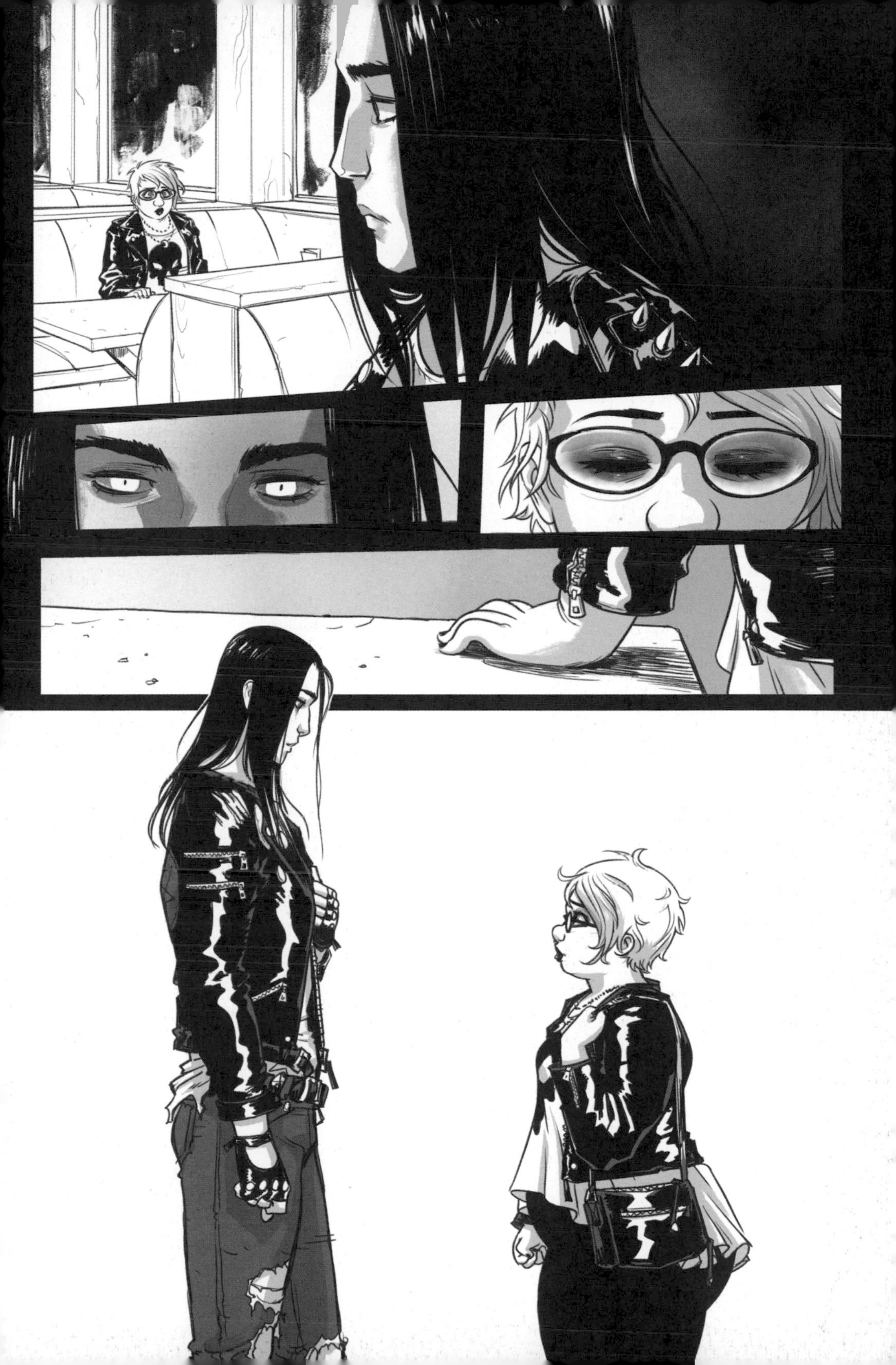

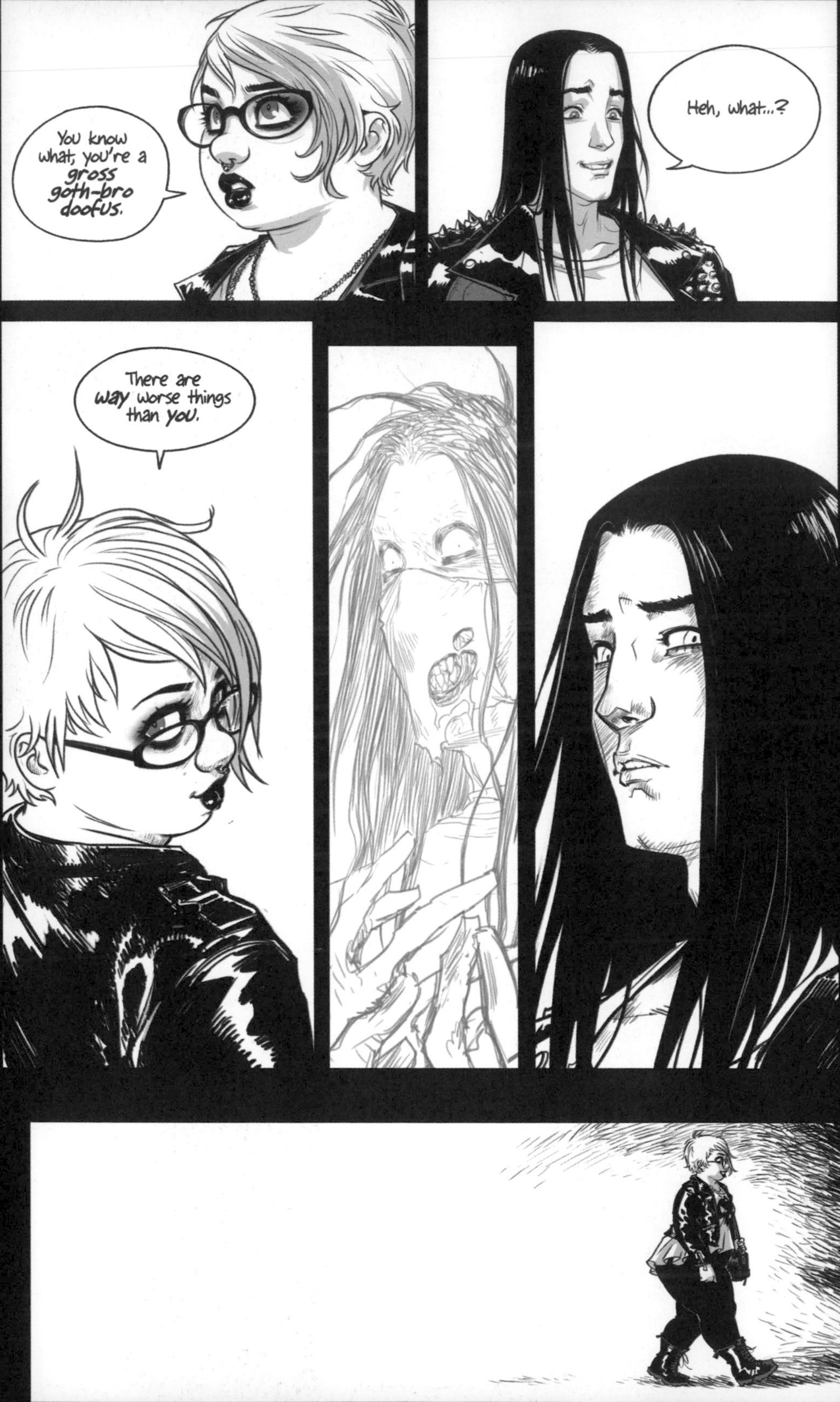
You know what, you're a gross goth-bro doofus.
Heh, what...?
There are way worse things than you.

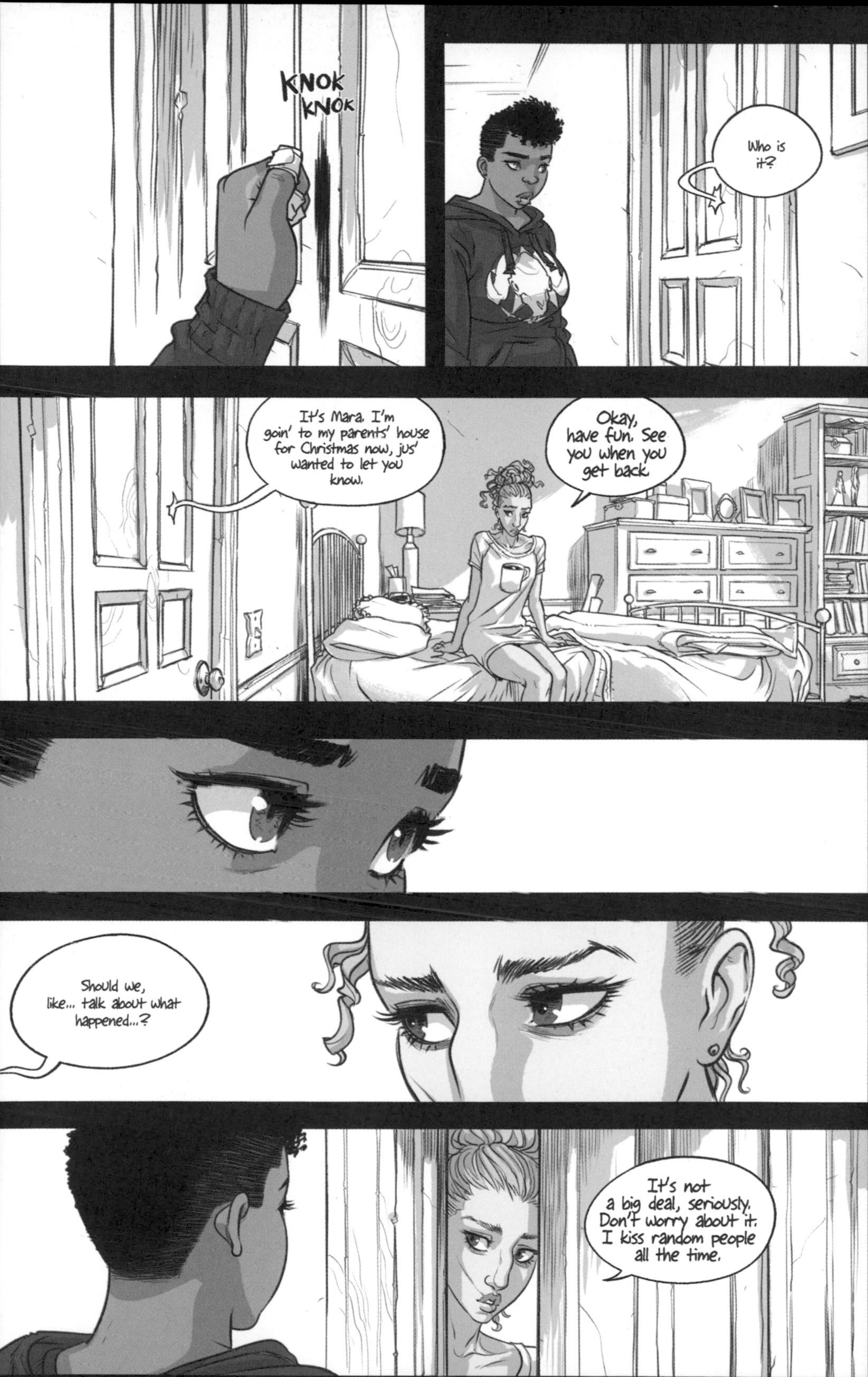
KNOK KNOK
Who is it?
It's Mara. I'm goin' to my parents' house for Christmas now, jus' wanted to let you know.
Okay, have fun. See you when you get back.
Should we, like... talk about what happened...?
It's not a big deal, seriously. Don't worry about it. I kiss random people all the time.

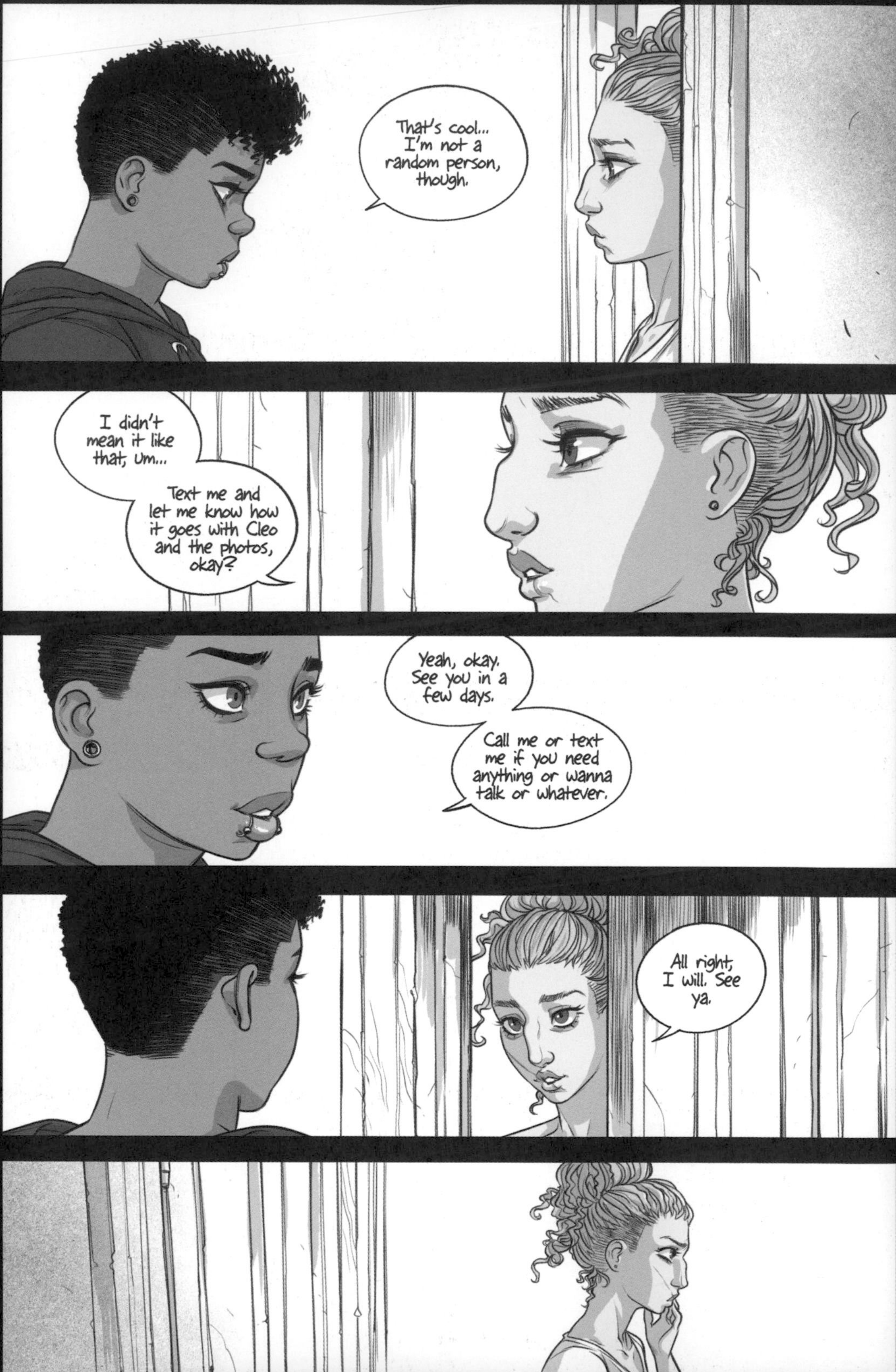
That's cool... I'm not a random person, though.
I didn't mean it like that, um...
Text me and let me know how it goes with Cleo and the photos, okay?
Yeah, okay. See you in a few days.
Call me or text me if you need anything or wanna talk or whatever.
All right, I will. See ya.

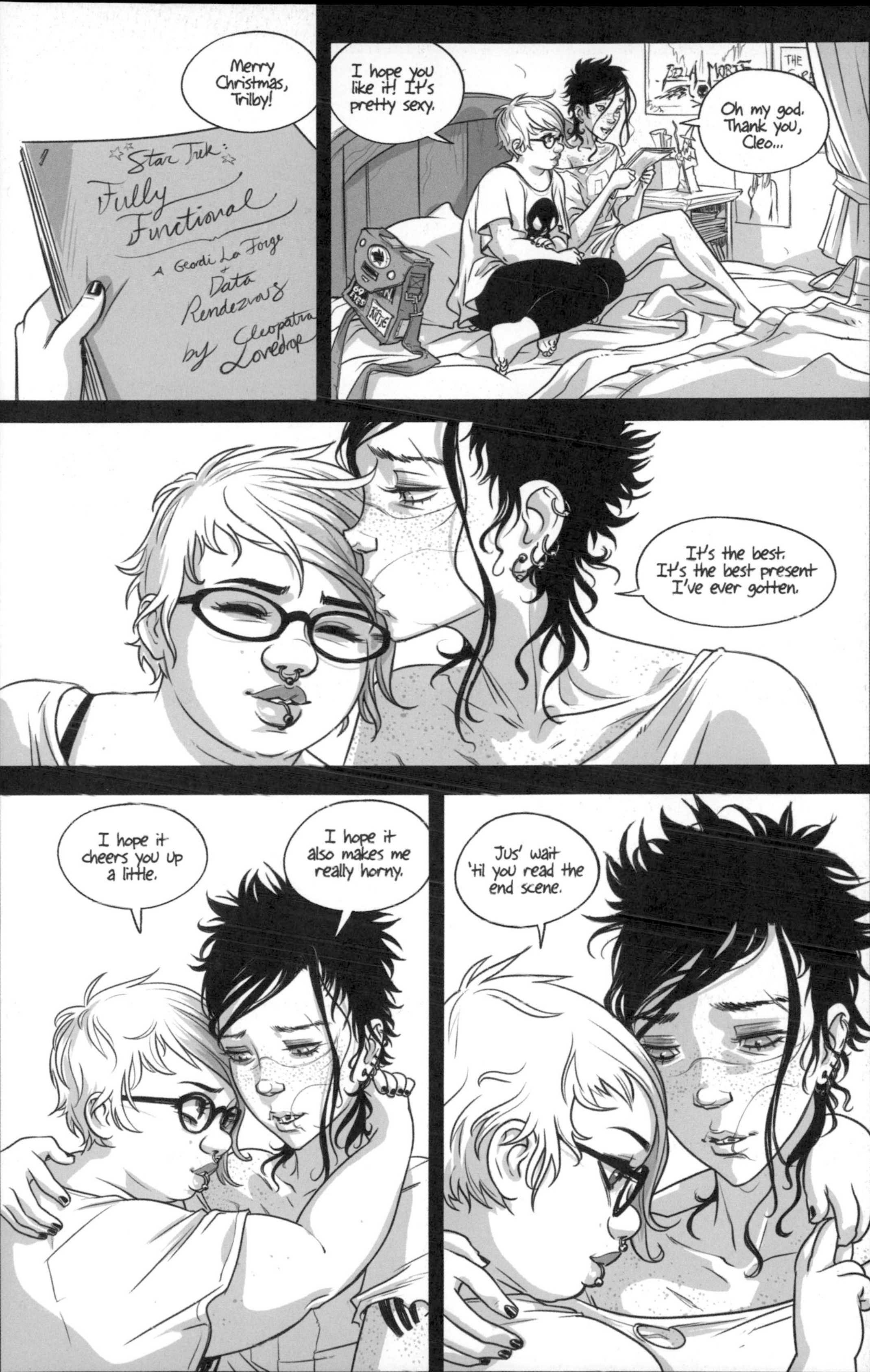
Merry Christmas, Trilby!
Star Trek: Fully Functional
A Geordi La Forge + Data Rendezvous
by Cleopatra Lovedrop
I hope you like it! It's pretty sexy.
Oh my god. Thank you, Cleo...
It's the best. It's the best present I've ever gotten.
I hope it cheers you up a little.
I hope it also makes me really horny.
Jus' wait 'til you read the end scene.

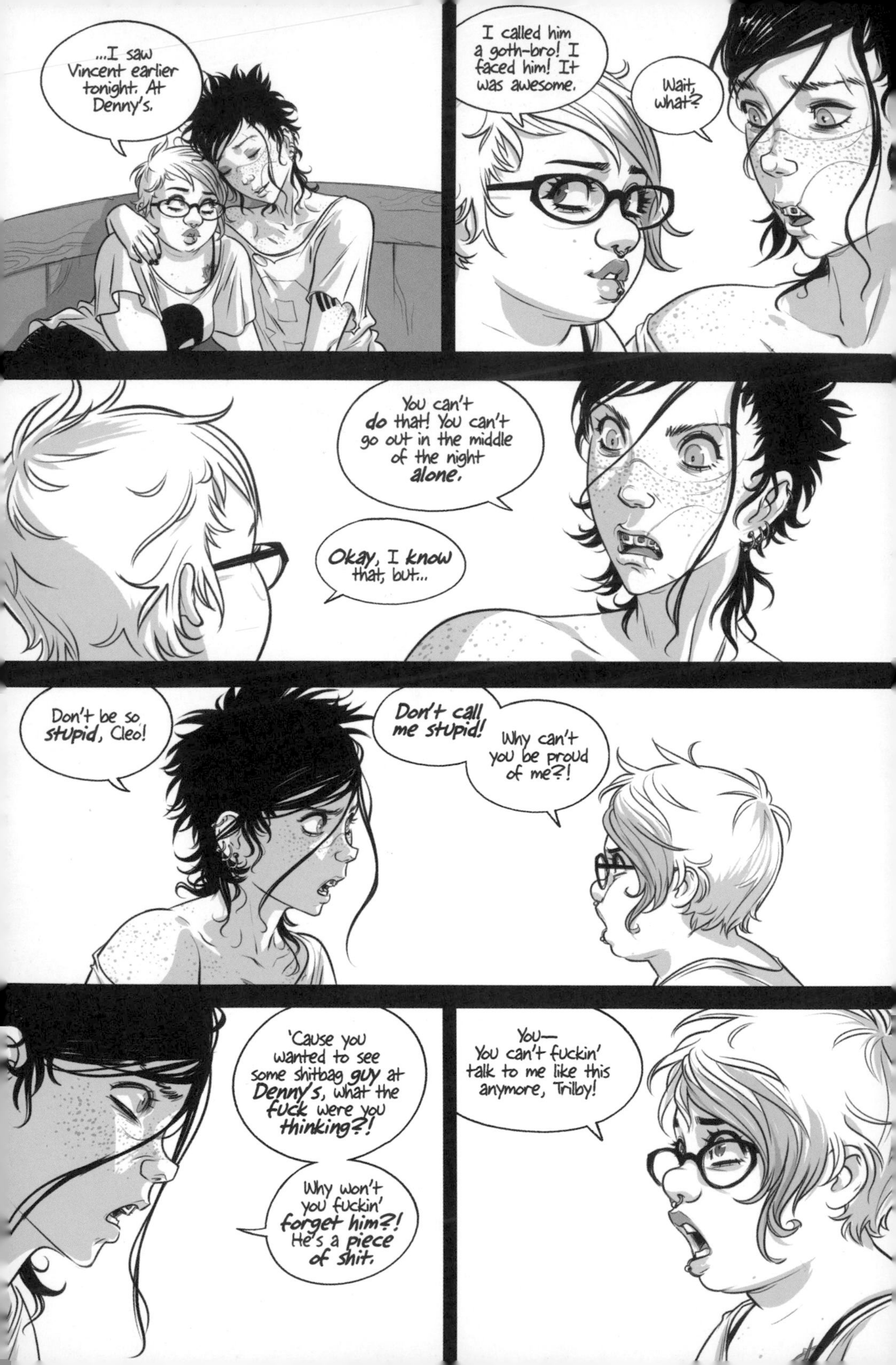
...I saw Vincent earlier tonight. At Denny's.
I called him a goth-bro! I faced him! It was awesome.
Wait, what?
You can't do that! You can't go out in the middle of the night alone.
Okay, I know that, but...
Don't be so stupid, Cleo!
Don't call me stupid!
Why can't you be proud of me?!
'Cause you wanted to see some shitbag guy at Denny's, what the fuck were you thinking?!
Why won't you fuckin' forget him?! He's a piece of shit.
You—
You can't fuckin' talk to me like this anymore, Trilby!

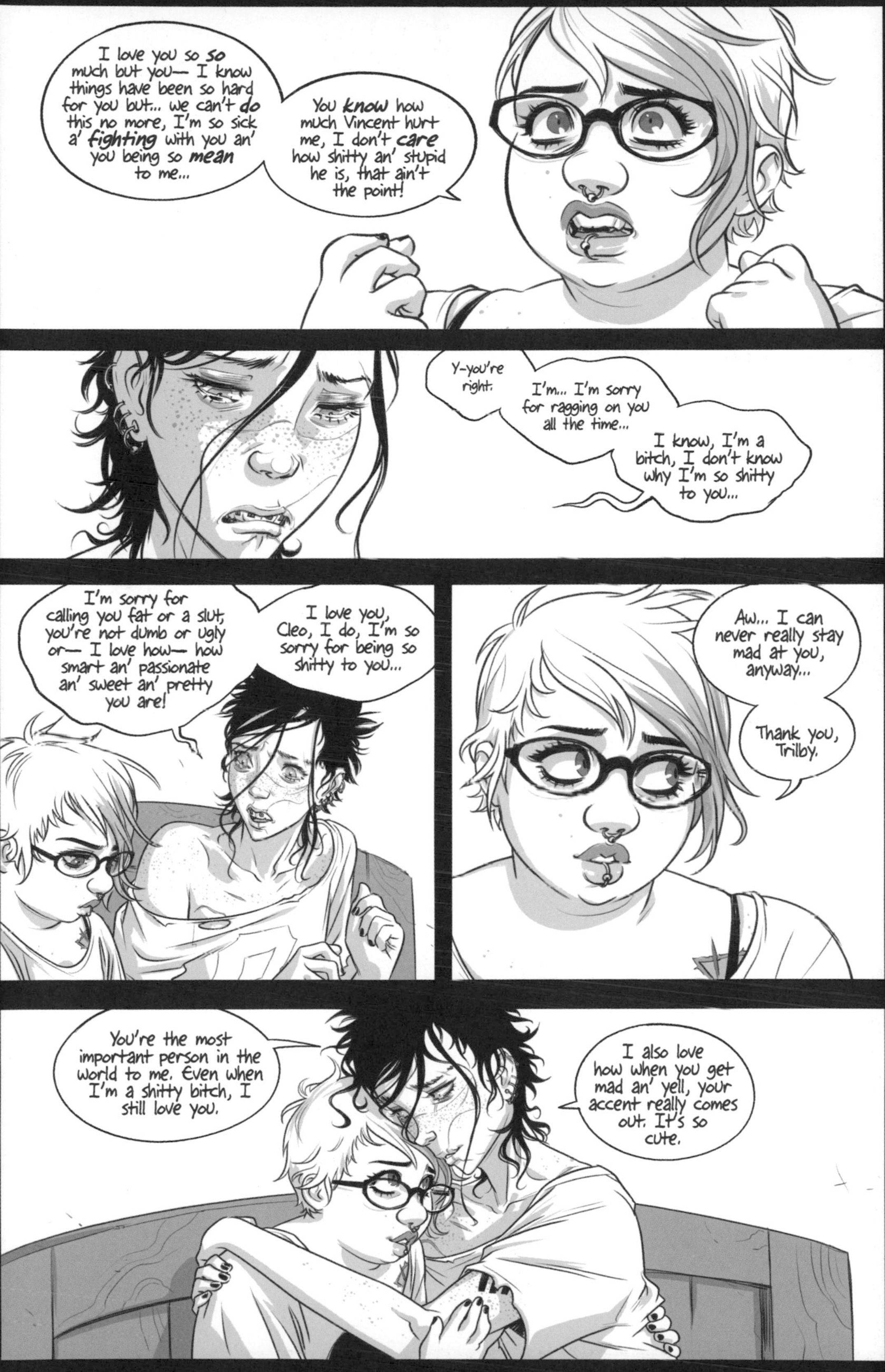
I love you so so much but you— I know things have been so hard for you but... we can't do this no more, I'm so sick a' fighting with you an' you being so mean to me...
You know how much Vincent hurt me, I don't care how shitty an' stupid he is, that ain't the point!
Y-you're right.
I'm... I'm sorry for ragging on you all the time...
I know, I'm a bitch, I don't know why I'm so shitty to you...
I'm sorry for calling you fat or a slut, you're not dumb or ugly or— I love how— how smart an' passionate an' sweet an' pretty you are!
I love you, Cleo, I do, I'm so sorry for being so shitty to you...
Aw... I can never really stay mad at you, anyway...
Thank you, Trilby.
You're the most important person in the world to me. Even when I'm a shitty bitch, I still love you.
I also love how when you get mad an' yell, your accent really comes out. It's so cute.

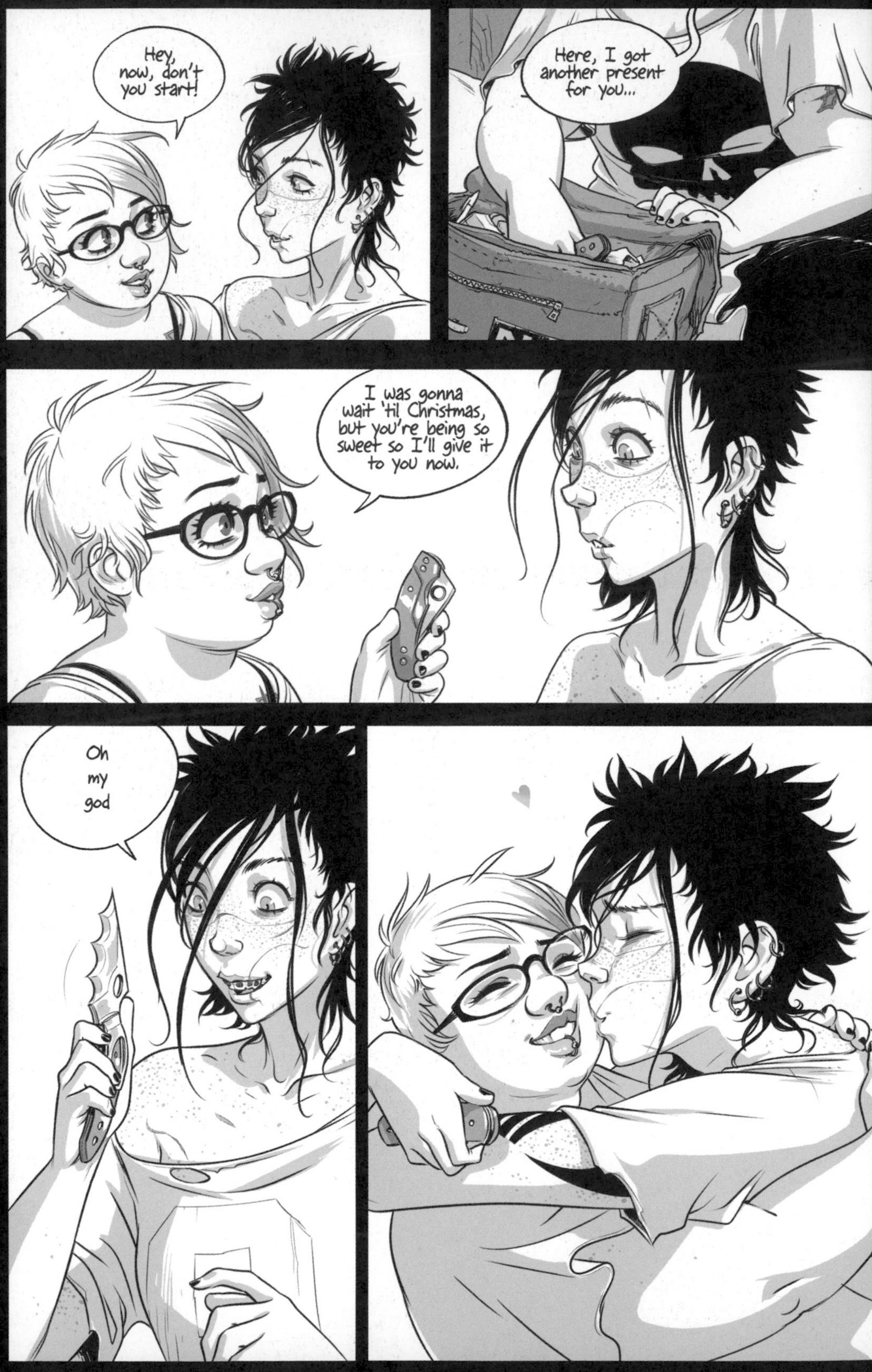
Hey, now, don't you start!
Here, I got another present for you...
I was gonna wait 'til Christmas, but you're being so sweet so I'll give it to you now.
Oh my god

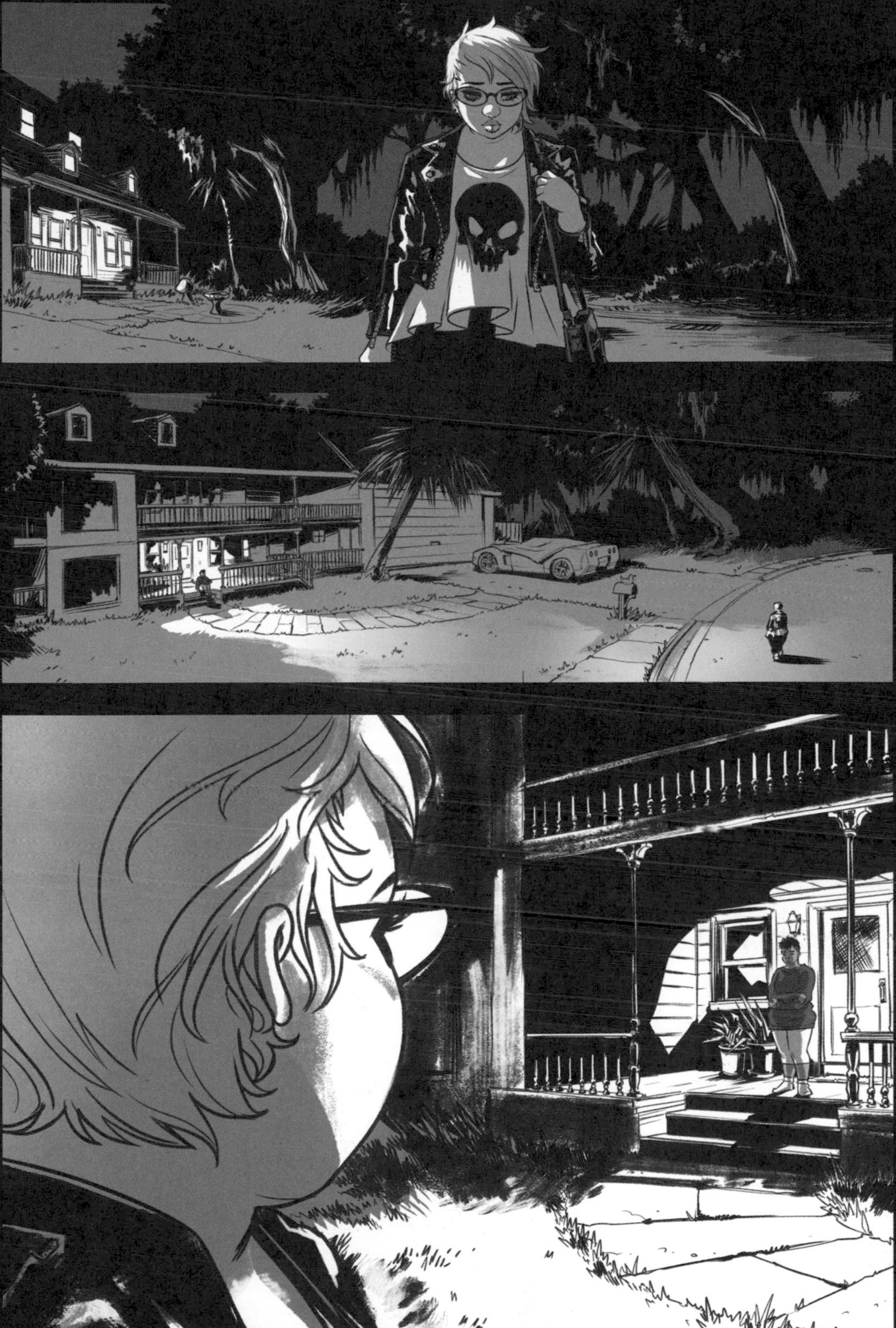

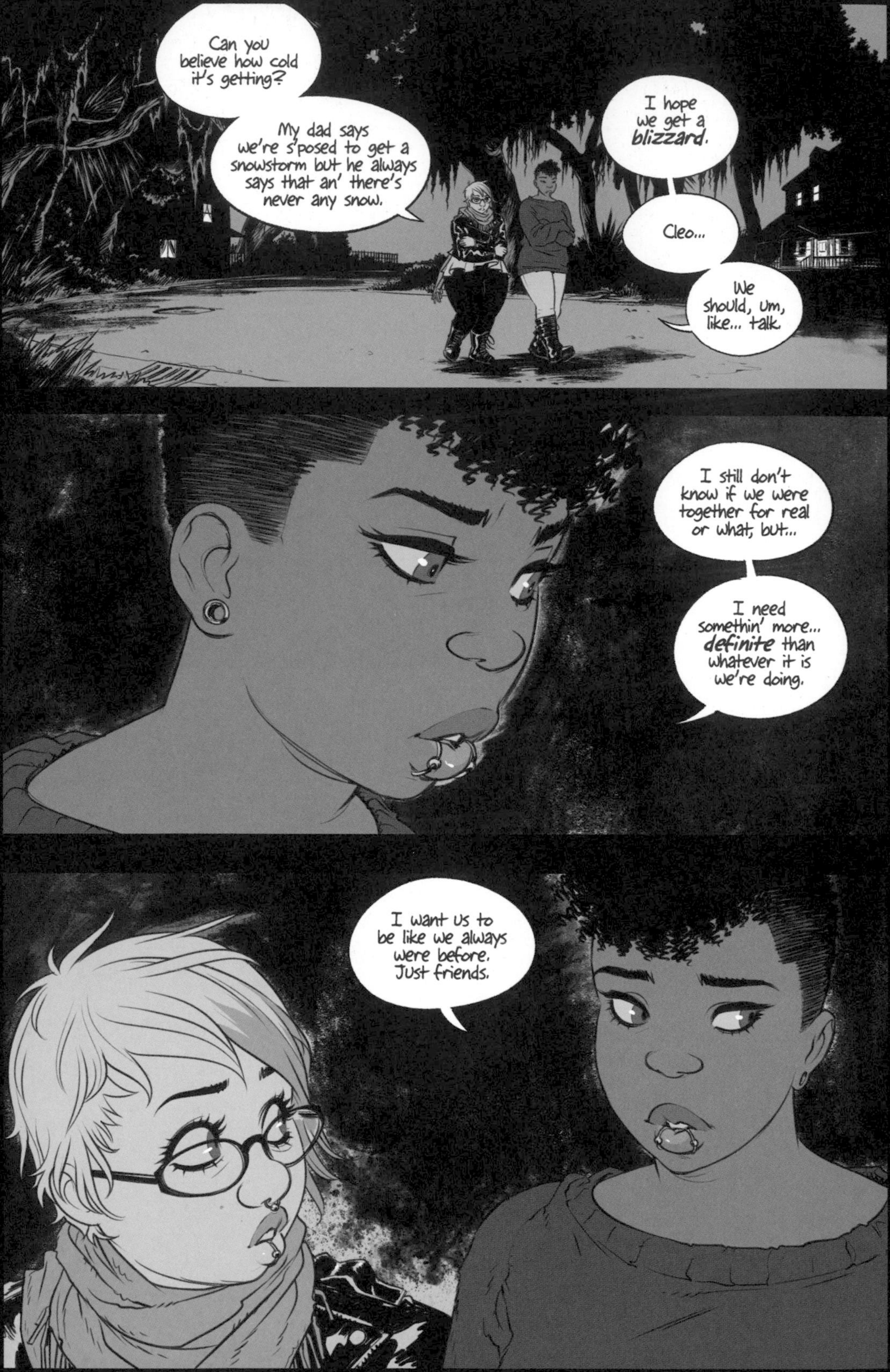
Can you believe how cold it's getting?
My dad says we're s'posed to get a snowstorm but he always says that an' there's never any snow.
I hope we get a *blizzard*.
Cleo...
We should, um, like... talk.
I still don't know if we were together for real or what, but...
I need somethin' more... *definite* than whatever it is we're doing.
I want us to be like we always were before. Just friends.

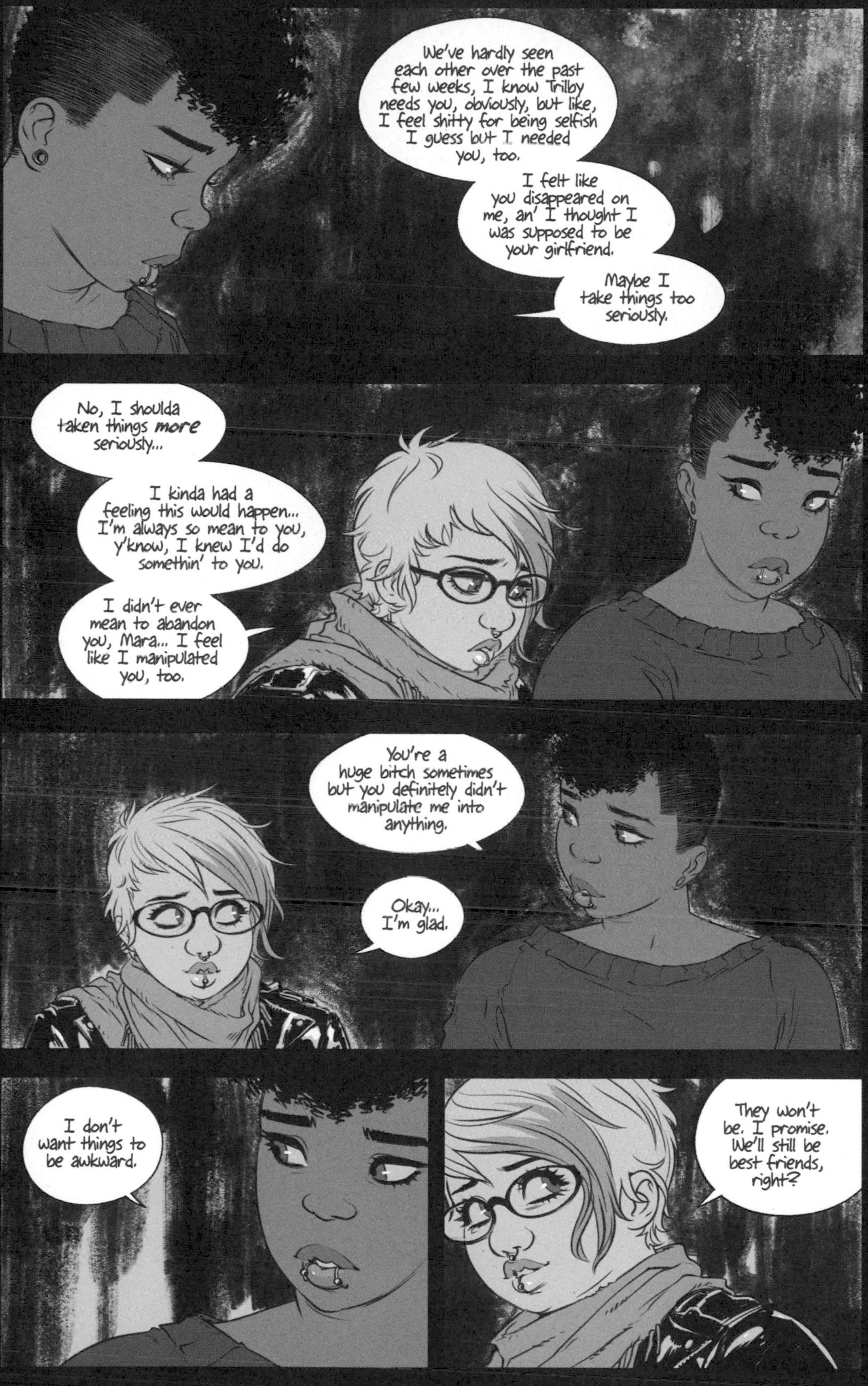
We've hardly seen each other over the past few weeks, I know Trilby needs you, obviously, but like, I feel shitty for being selfish I guess but I needed you, too.
I felt like you disappeared on me, an' I thought I was supposed to be your girlfriend.
Maybe I take things too seriously.
No, I shoulda taken things *more* seriously...
I kinda had a feeling this would happen... I'm always so mean to you, y'know, I knew I'd do somethin' to you.
I didn't ever mean to abandon you, Mara... I feel like I manipulated you, too.
You're a huge bitch sometimes but you definitely didn't manipulate me into anything.
Okay... I'm glad.
I don't want things to be awkward.
They won't be. I promise. We'll still be best friends, right?

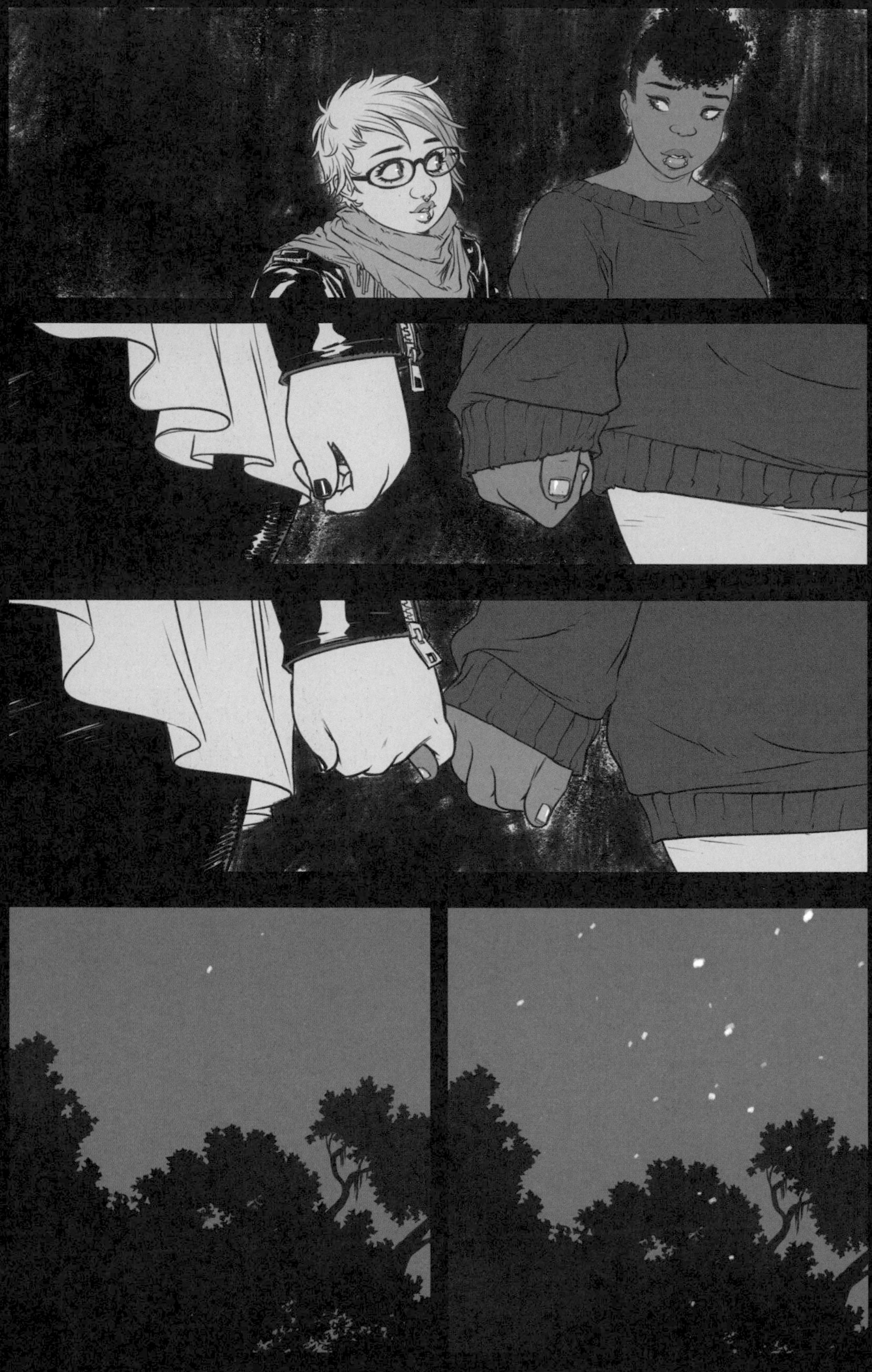

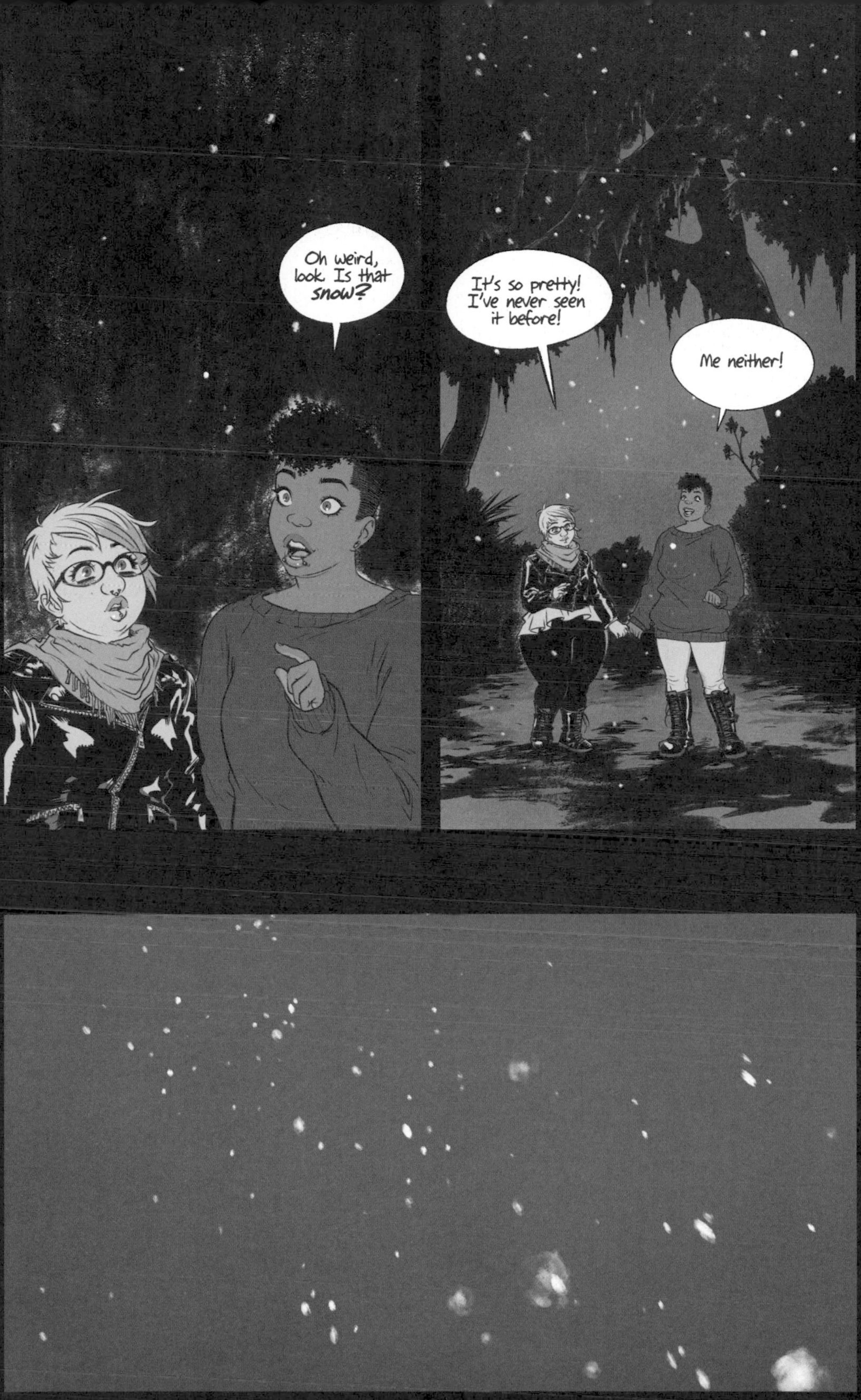
Oh weird, look. Is that snow?
It's so pretty! I've never seen it before!
Me neither!

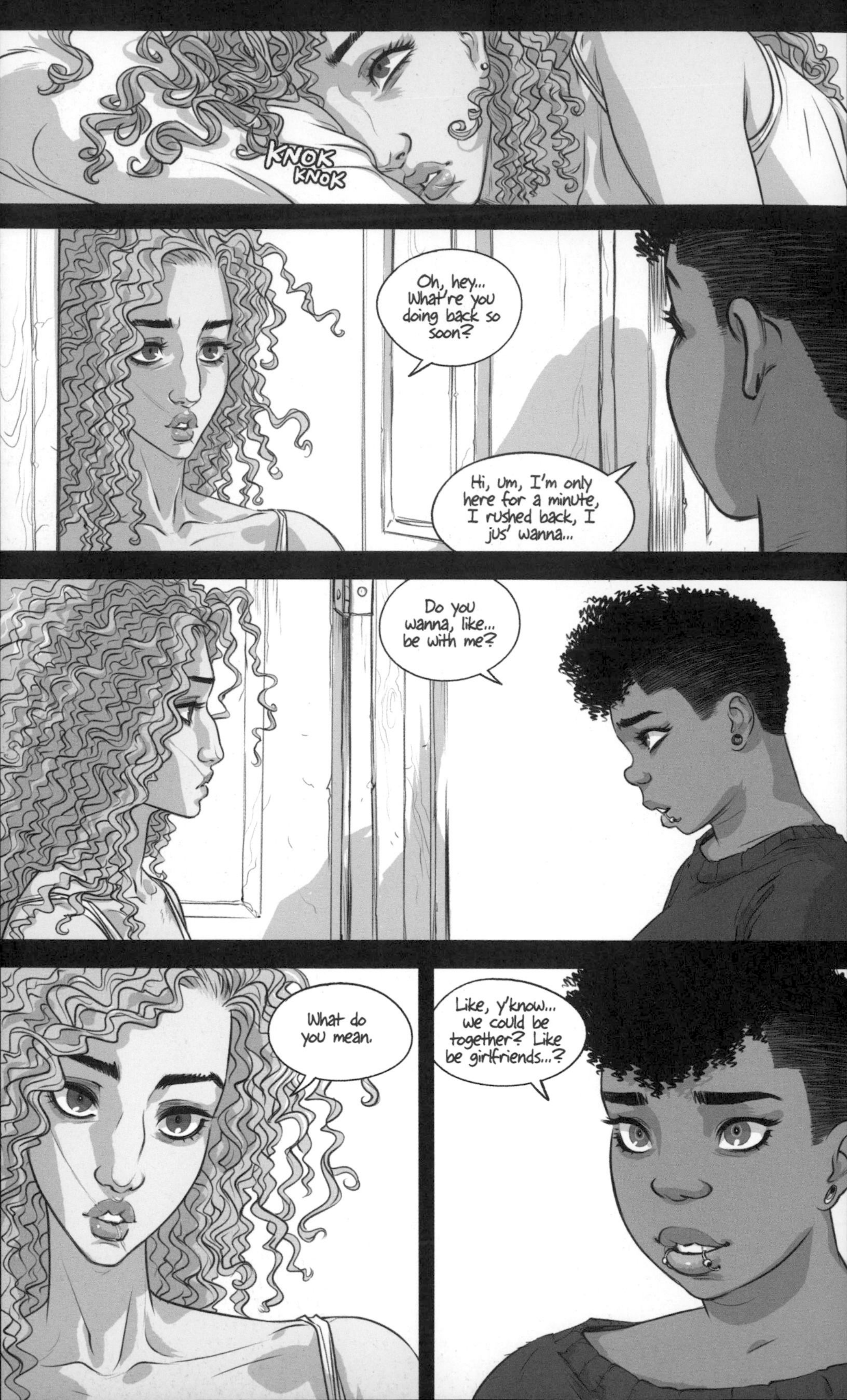
KNOK
KNOK
Oh, hey... What're you doing back so soon?
Hi, um, I'm only here for a minute, I rushed back, I jus' wanna...
Do you wanna, like... be with me?
What do you mean.
Like, y'know... we could be together? Like be girlfriends...?

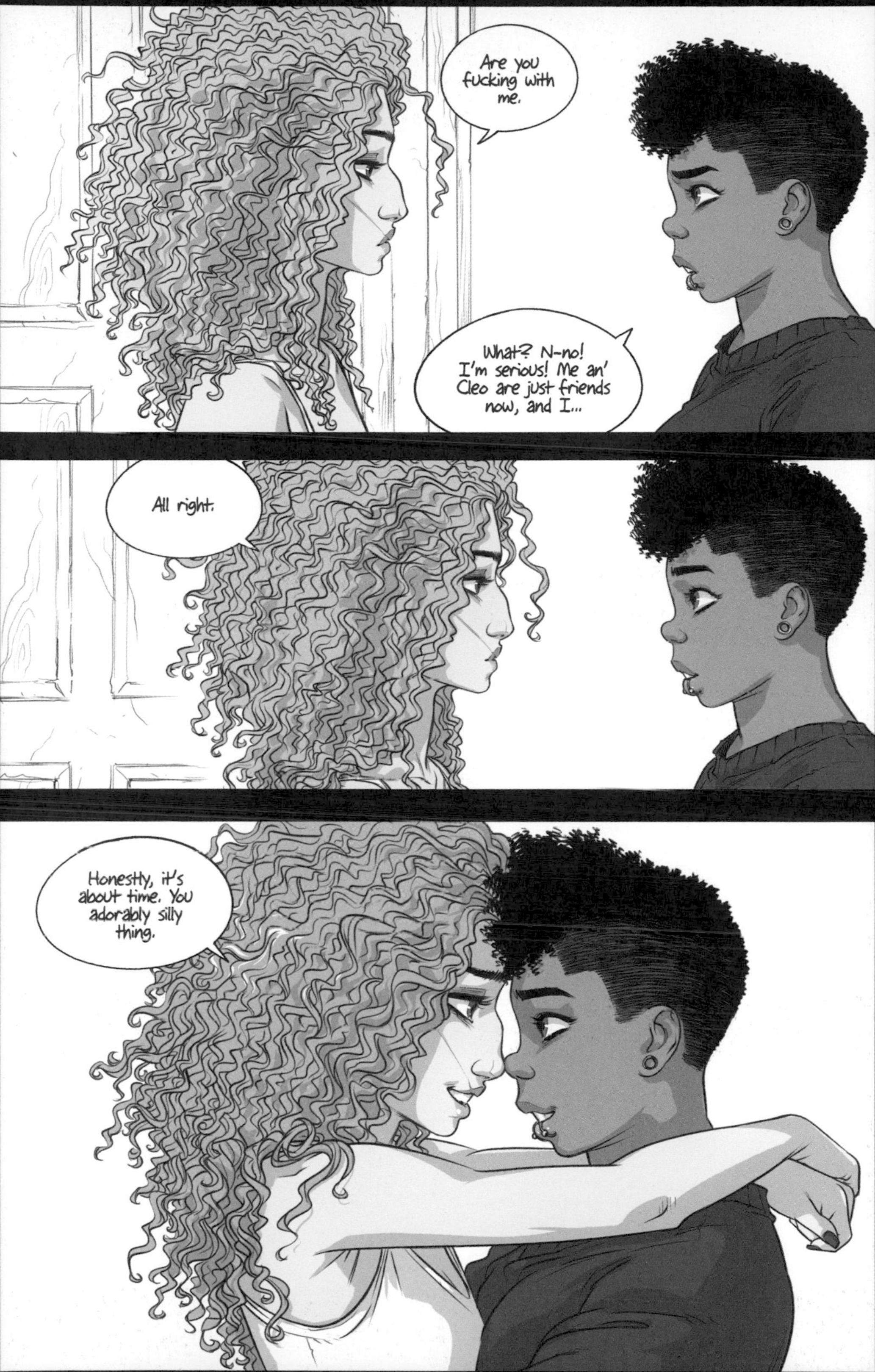
Are you fucking with me.
What? N-no! I'm serious! Me an' Cleo are just friends now, and I...
All right.
Honestly, it's about time. You adorably silly thing.

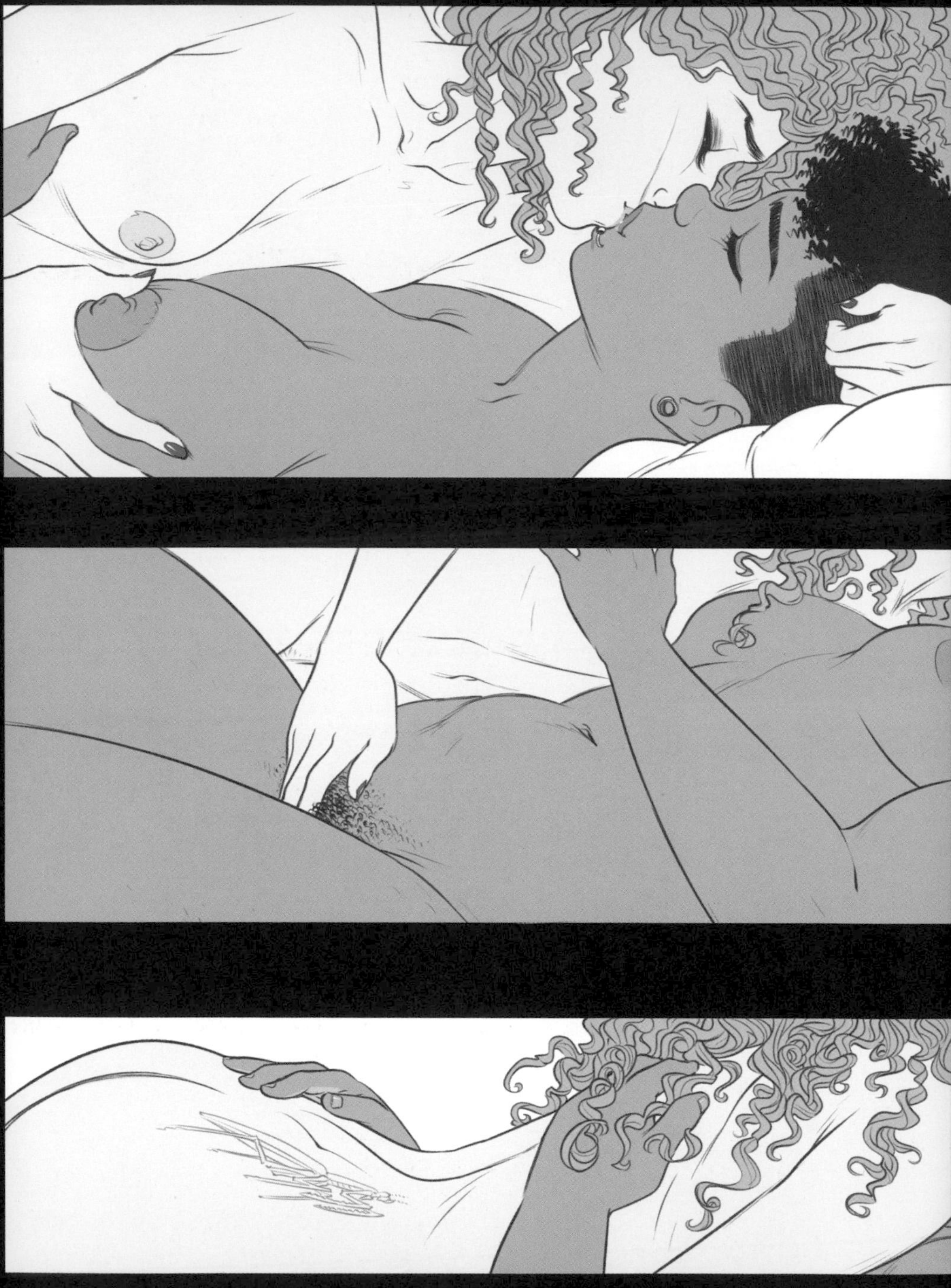

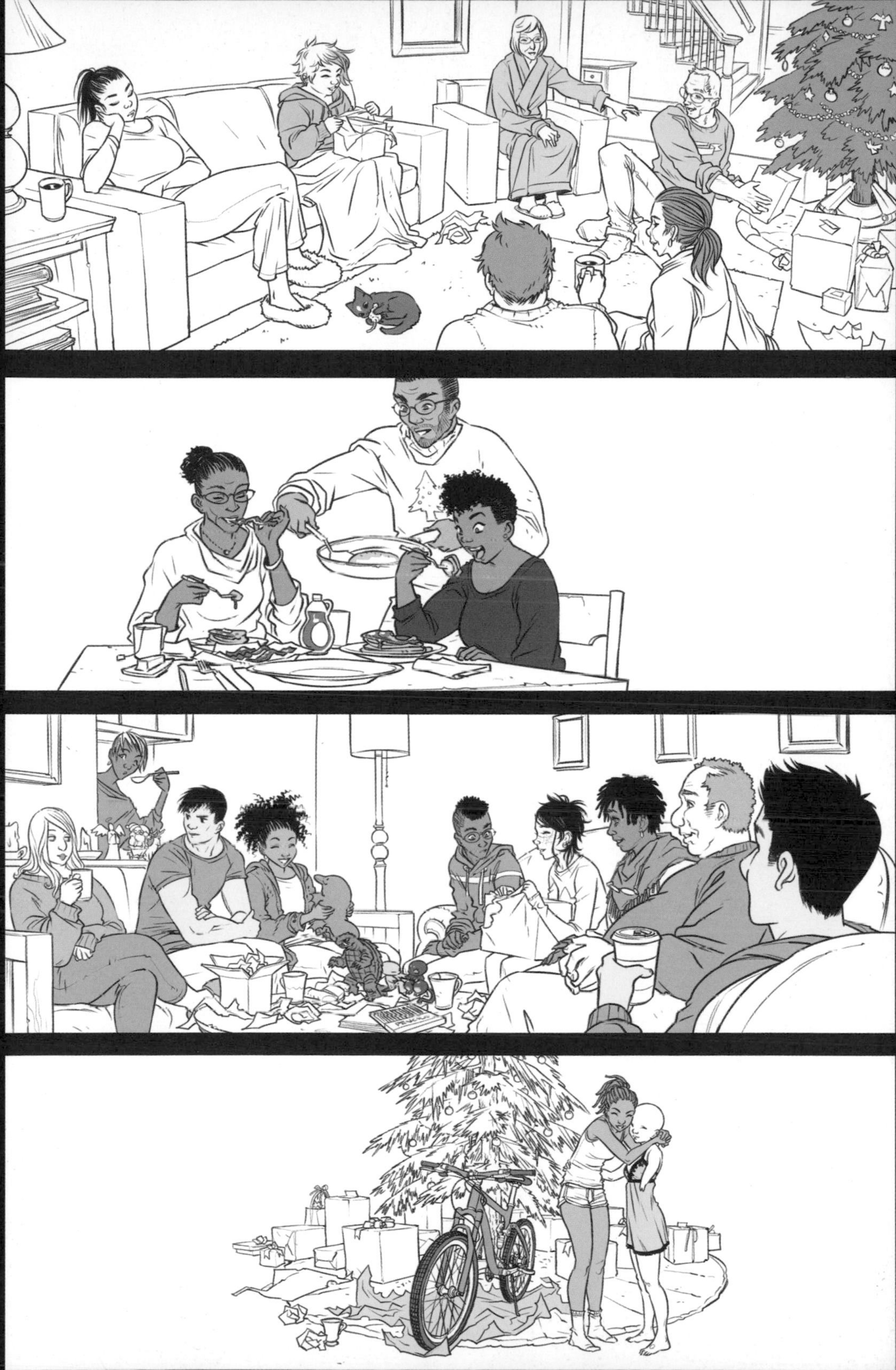

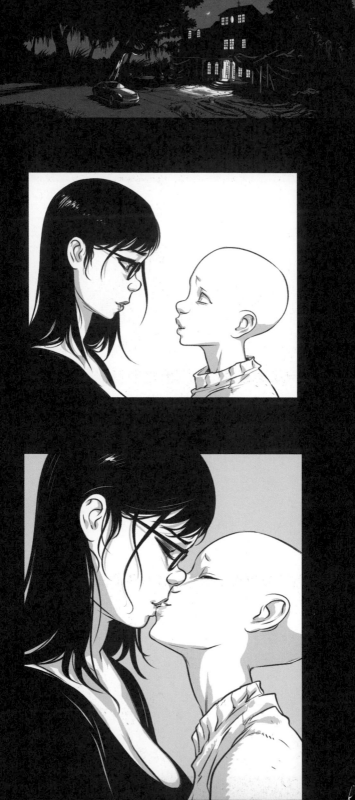

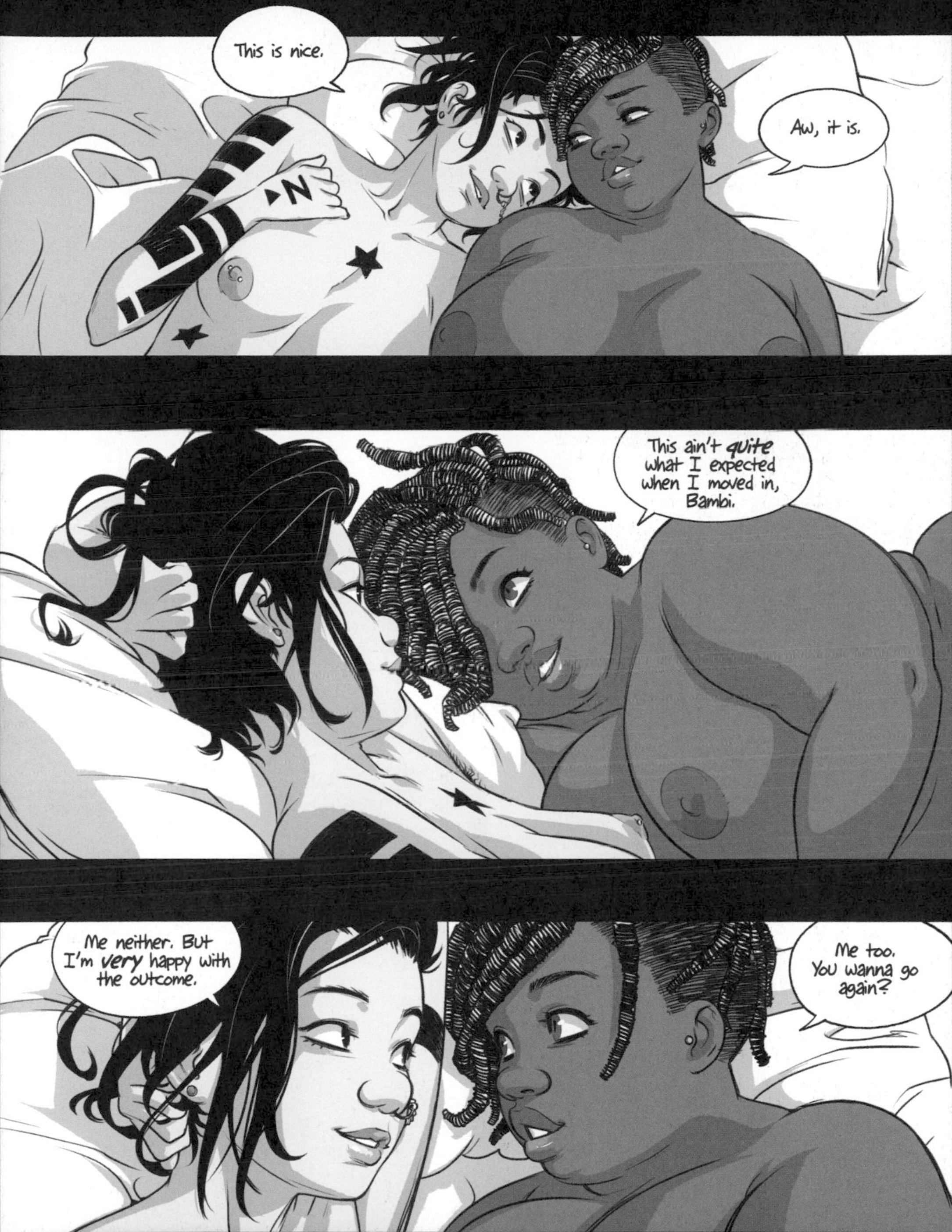
This is nice.
Aw, it is.
This ain't *quite* what I expected when I moved in, Bambi.
Me neither. But I'm *very* happy with the outcome.
Me too. You wanna go again?

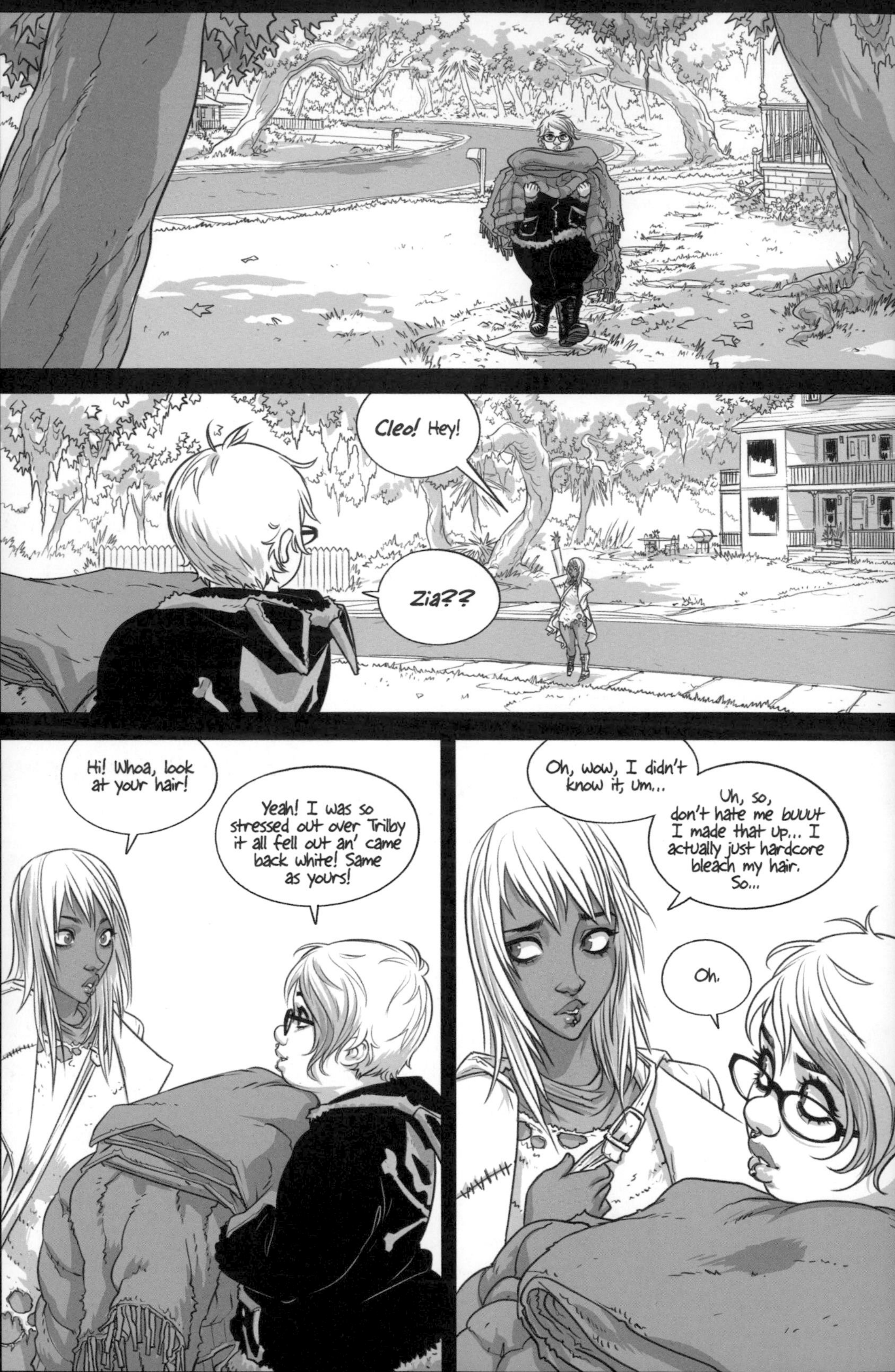
Cleo! Hey!
Zia??
Hi! Whoa, look at your hair!
Yeah! I was so stressed out over Trilby it all fell out an' came back white! Same as yours!
Oh, wow, I didn't know it, um...
Uh, so, don't hate me buuut I made that up... I actually just hardcore bleach my hair. So...
Oh.

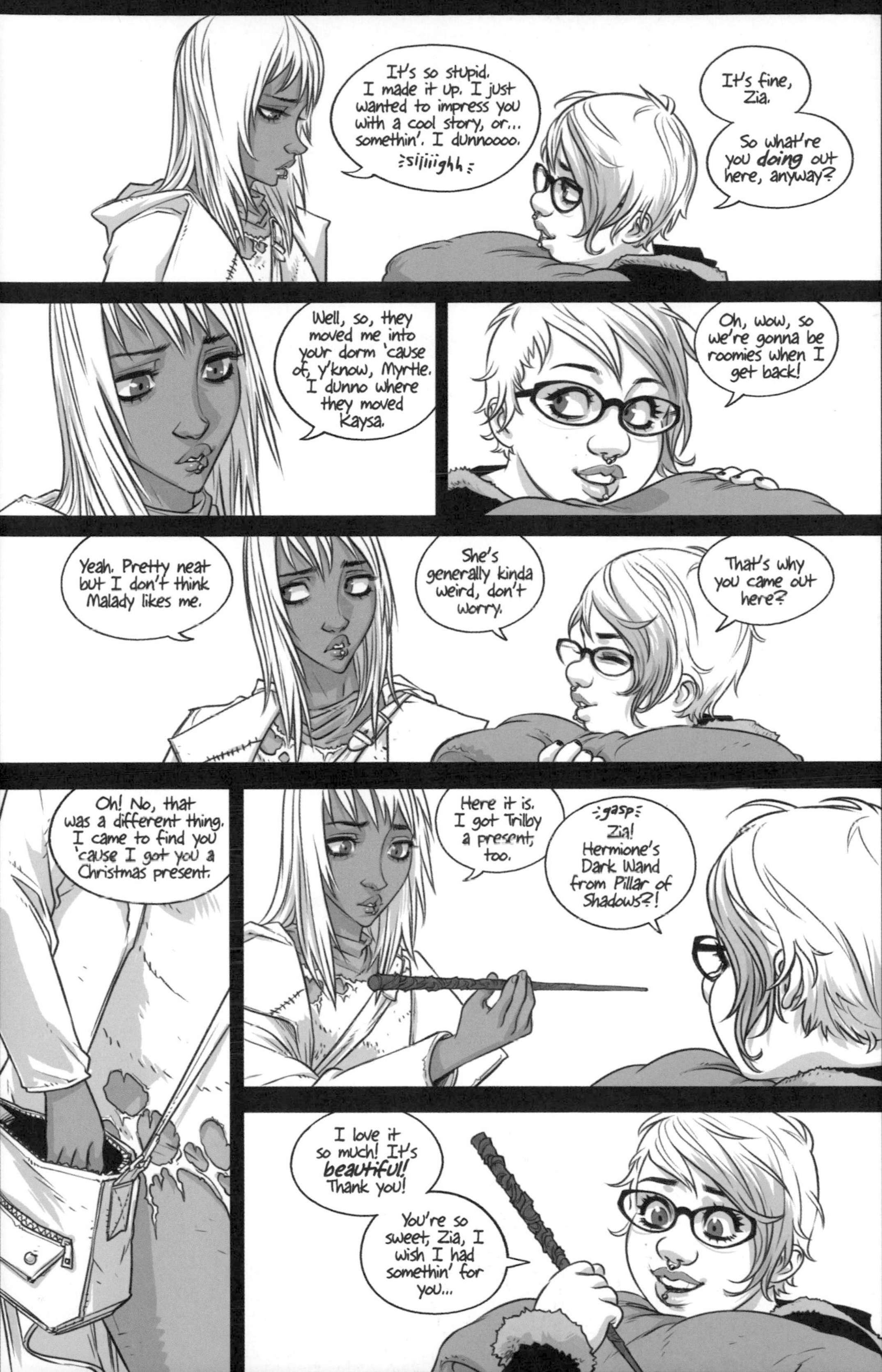

It's so stupid. I made it up. I just wanted to impress you with a cool story, or... somethin'. I dunnoooo.
siiiiighh
It's fine, Zia.
So what're you doing out here, anyway?
Well, so, they moved me into your dorm 'cause of, y'know, Myrtle. I dunno where they moved Kaysa.
Oh, wow, so we're gonna be roomies when I get back!
Yeah. Pretty neat but I don't think Malady likes me.
She's generally kinda weird, don't worry.
That's why you came out here?
Oh! No, that was a different thing. I came to find you 'cause I got you a Christmas present.
Here it is. I got Trilby a present, too.
gasp
Zia! Hermione's Dark Wand from Pillar of Shadows?!
I love it so much! It's beautiful! Thank you!
You're so sweet, Zia, I wish I had somethin' for you...

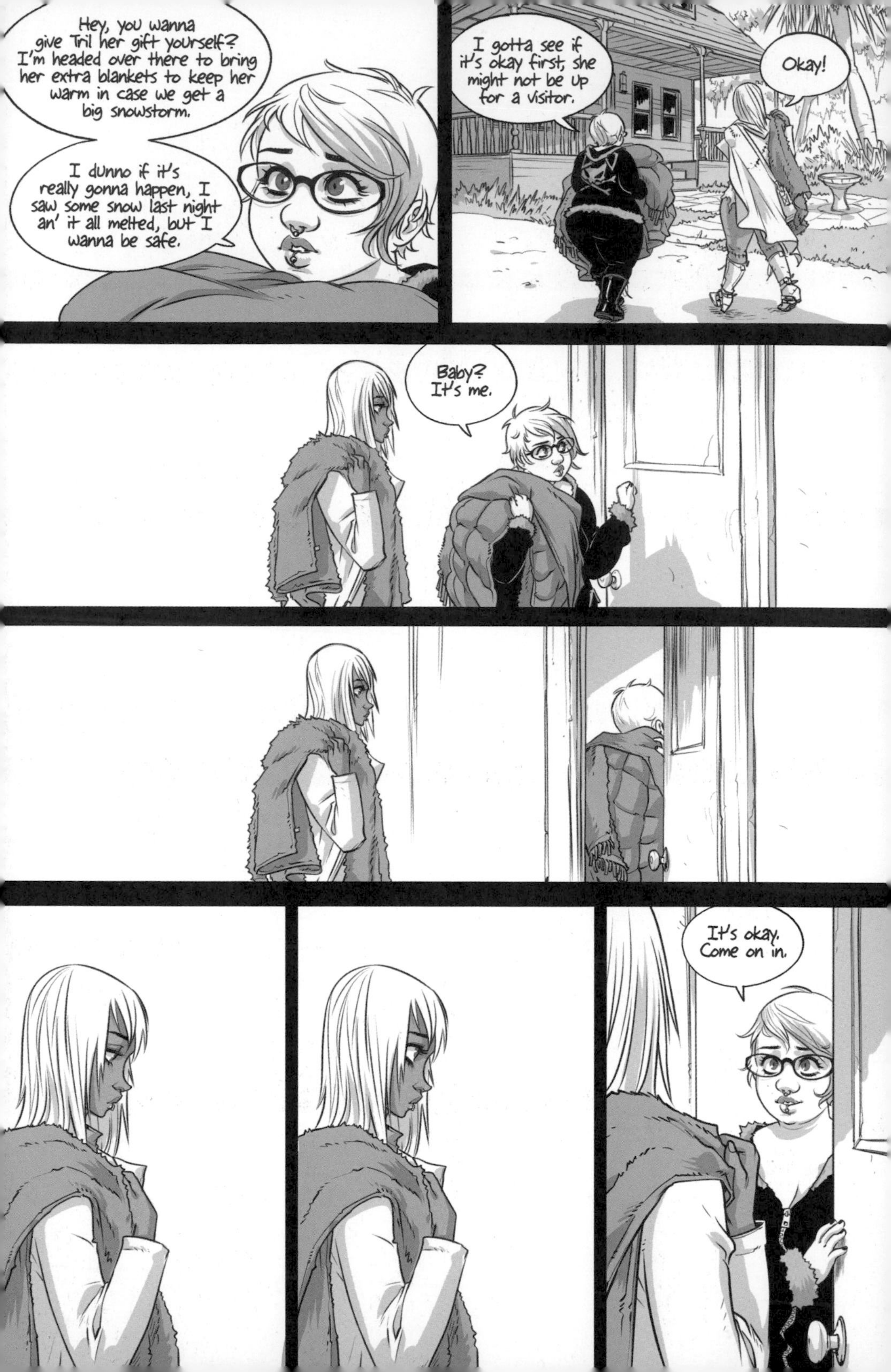
Hey, you wanna give Tril her gift yourself? I'm headed over there to bring her extra blankets to keep her warm in case we get a big snowstorm.
I dunno if it's really gonna happen, I saw some snow last night an' it all melted, but I wanna be safe.
I gotta see if it's okay first, she might not be up for a visitor.
Okay!
Baby? It's me.
It's okay. Come on in.

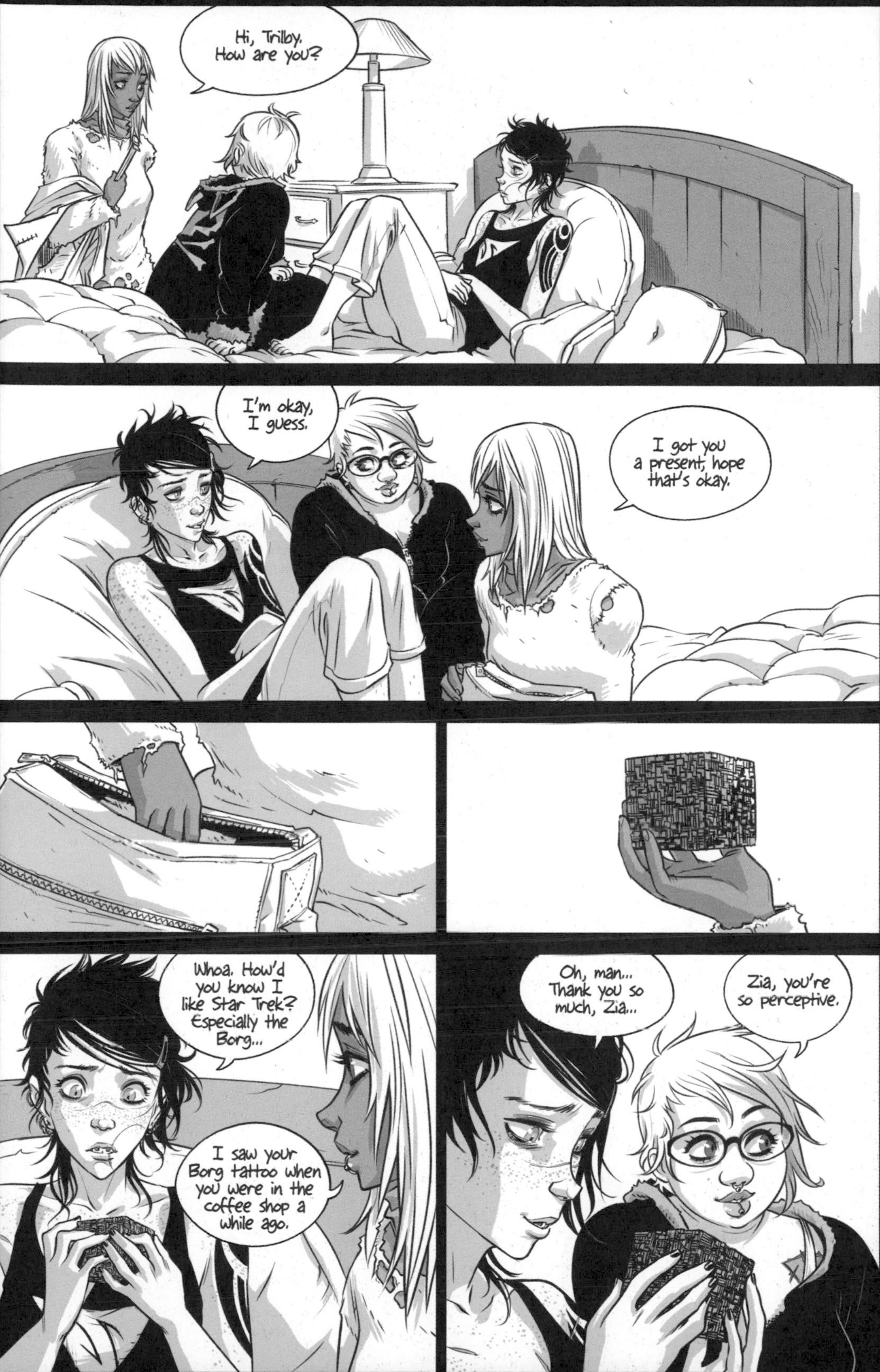
Hi, Trilby. How are you?
I'm okay, I guess.
I got you a present, hope that's okay.
Whoa. How'd you know I like Star Trek? Especially the Borg...
I saw your Borg tattoo when you were in the coffee shop a while ago.
Oh, man... Thank you so much, Zia...
Zia, you're so perceptive.

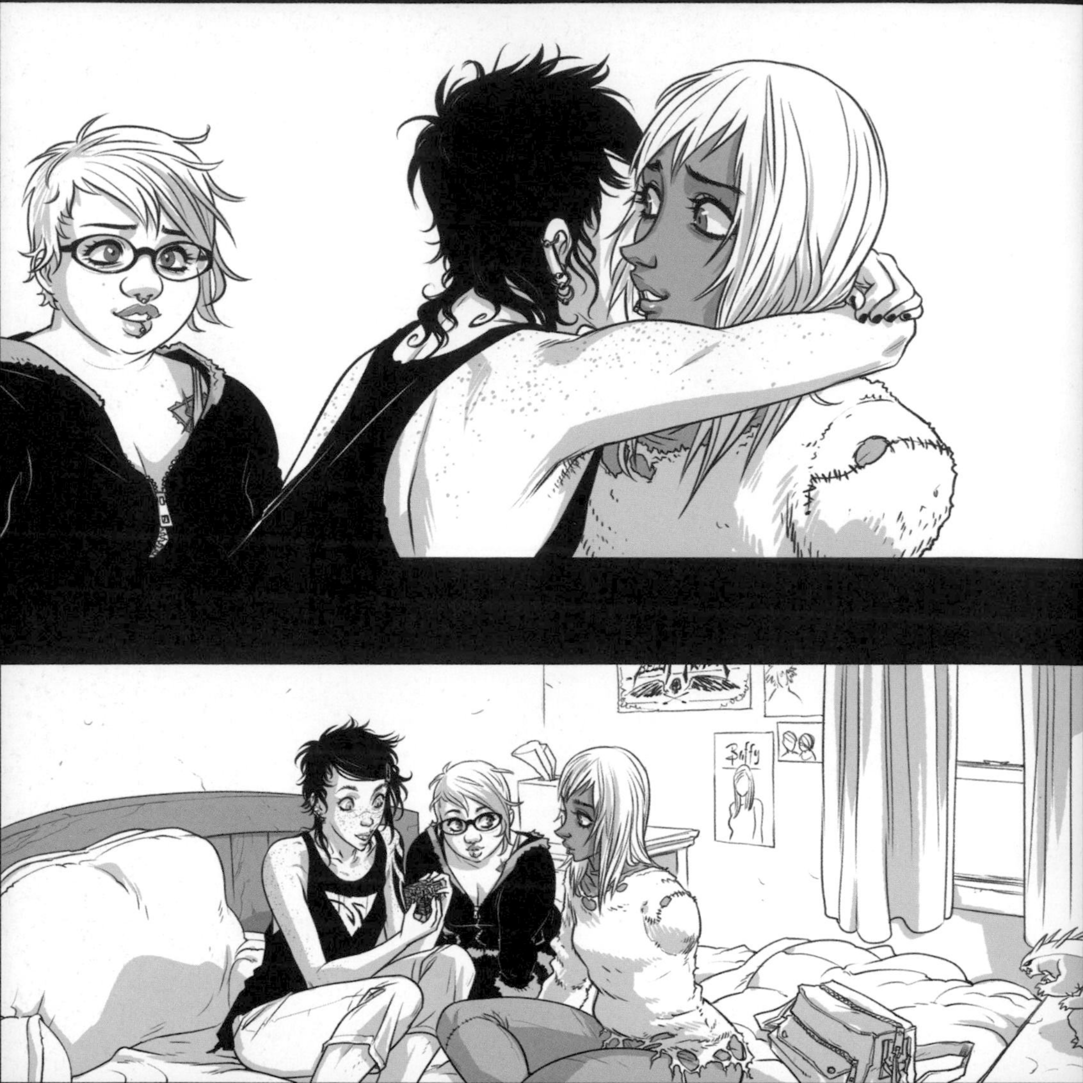
Buffy

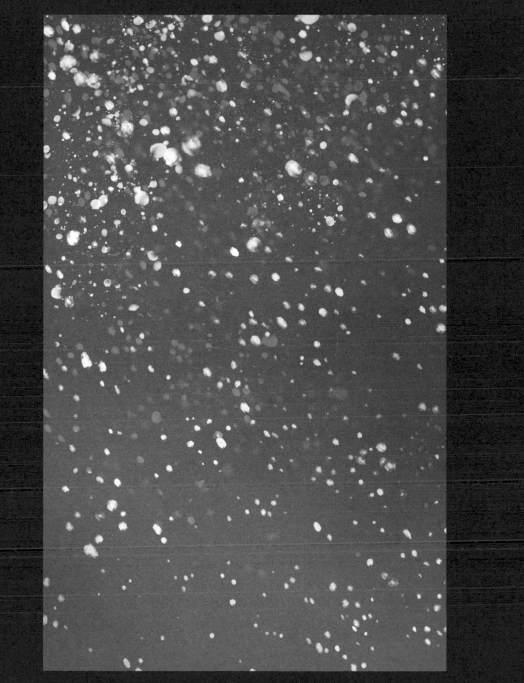

35

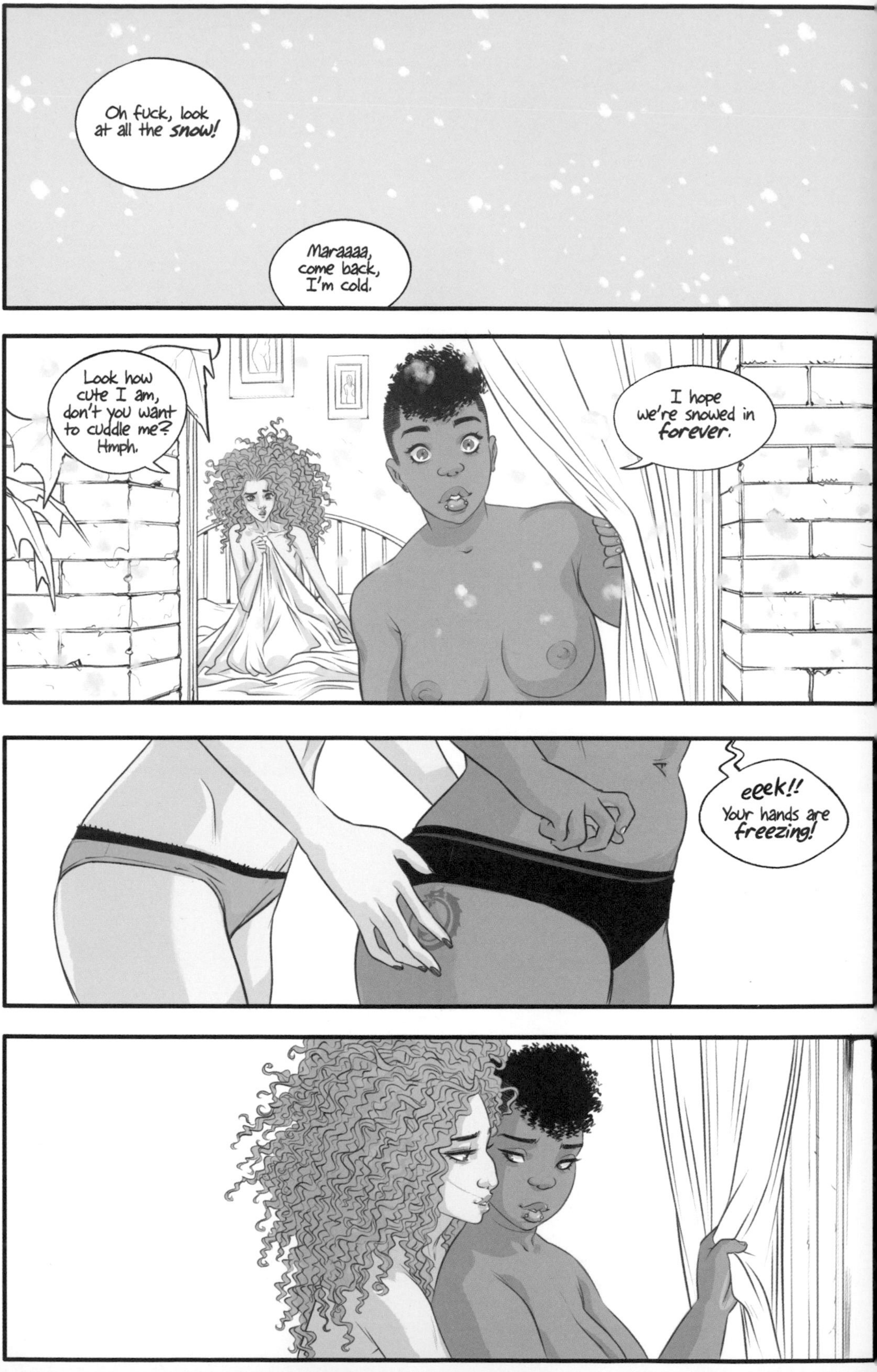
Oh fuck, look at all the snow!
Maraaaa, come back, I'm cold.
Look how cute I am, don't you want to cuddle me? Hmph.
I hope we're snowed in forever.
eeek!! Your hands are freezing!

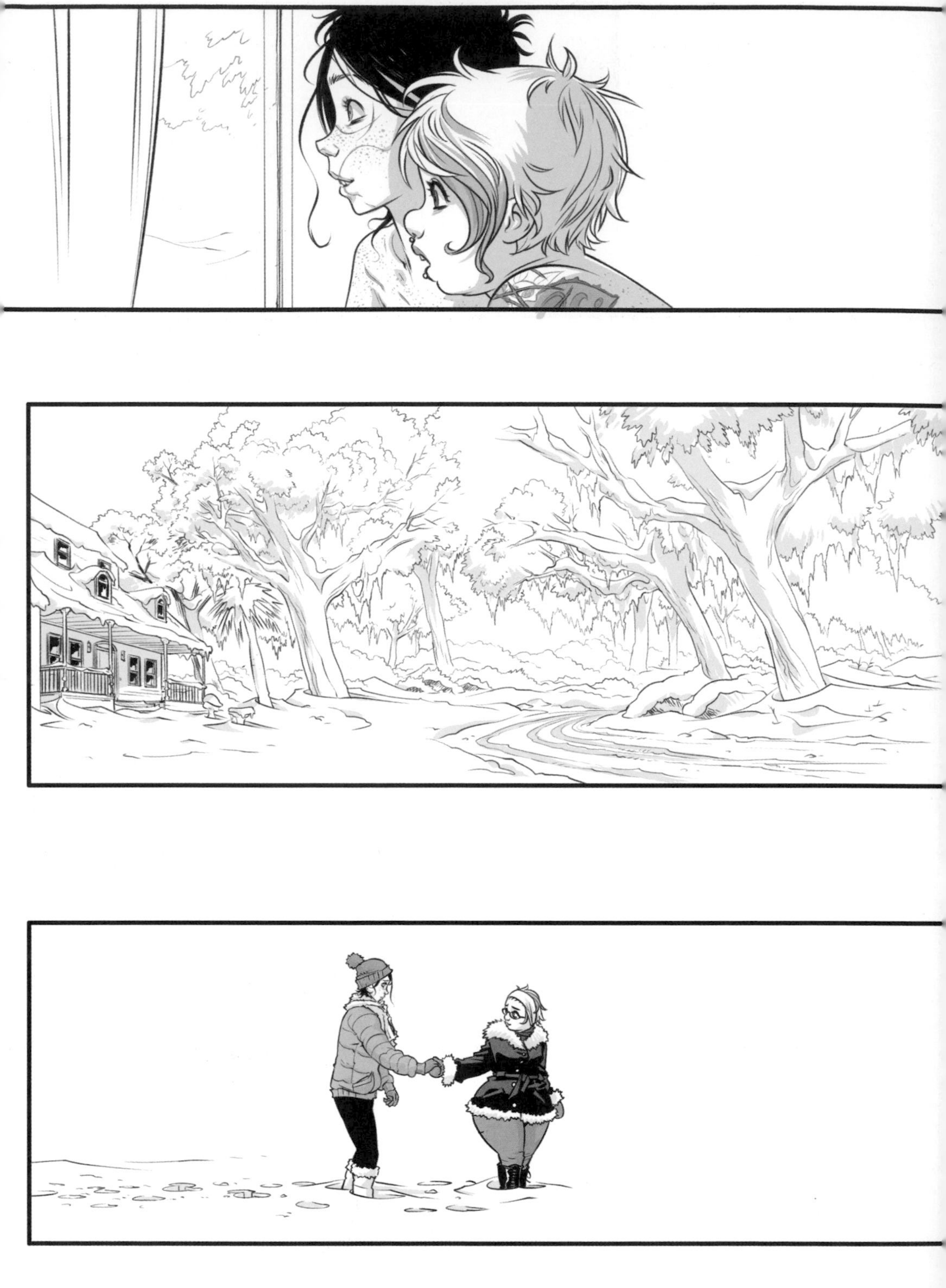

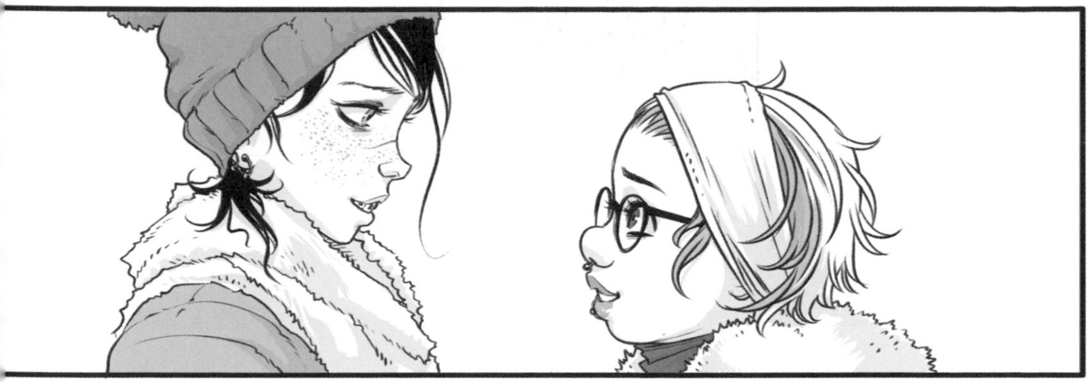

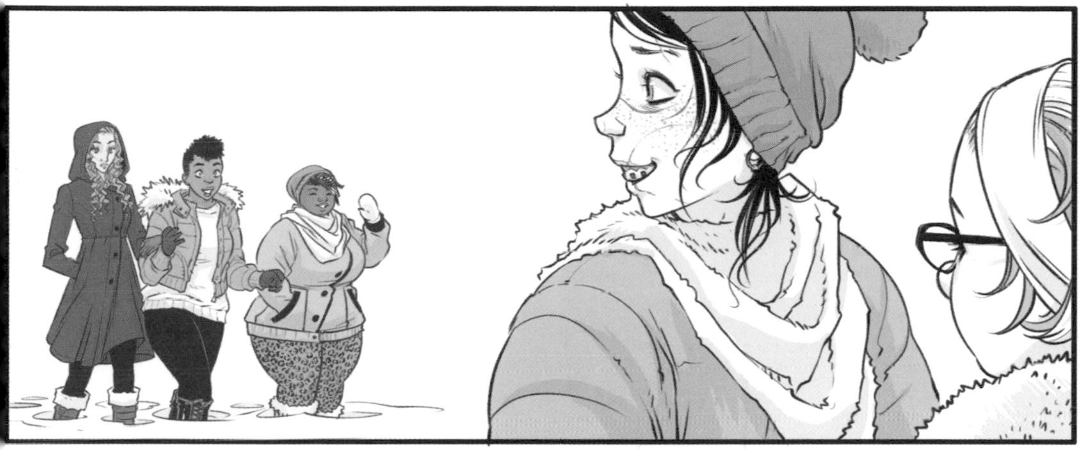

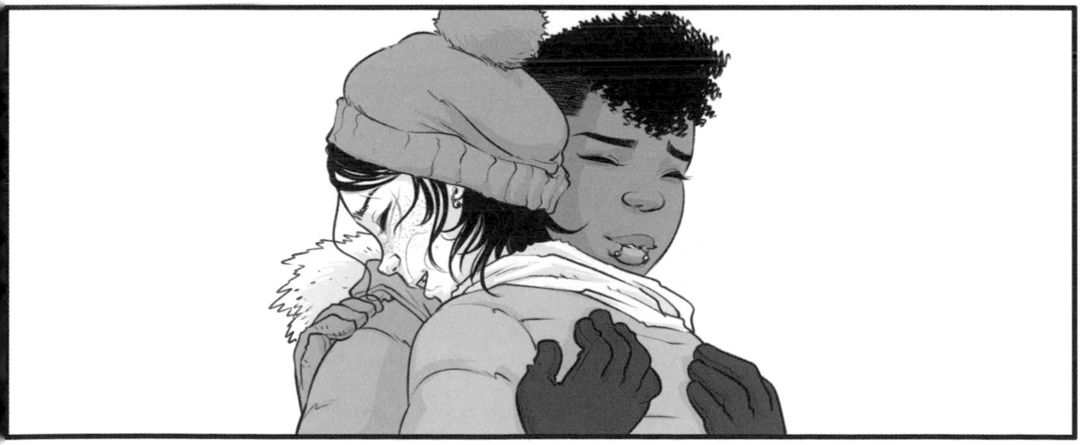

the
end

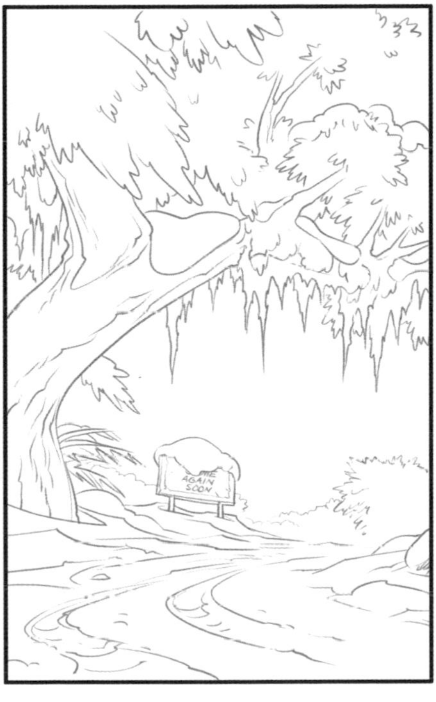
AGAIN SOON

AFTERWORD

BEFORE I SAY ANYTHING ELSE, I WANT TO SAY I'M SORRY for the word "g***y" being in volume 4, in the scene where Cleo is talking about her novel to Myrtle. It was something I'd meant to remove when it came time for a reprint, but I forgot, and only remembered it when I was flipping through volume 4 to look something up for reference while working on volume 7. I take full responsibility and I apologize.

I thought for weeks about what to say in this afterword. I thought about not doing one at all, not every book has one, most don't, but I liked the personal feeling of the new editions of the previous six volumes so I want to continue that. Having volume 7 end without any word from me seemed cold. As I'm writing this, I finished *Wet Moon* 7 about three weeks ago and I've been slobbing around since then and going through the crash that always happens to me after I finish a big project, it's like my body realizes the work is finally done and it's allowed to shut down and sleep.

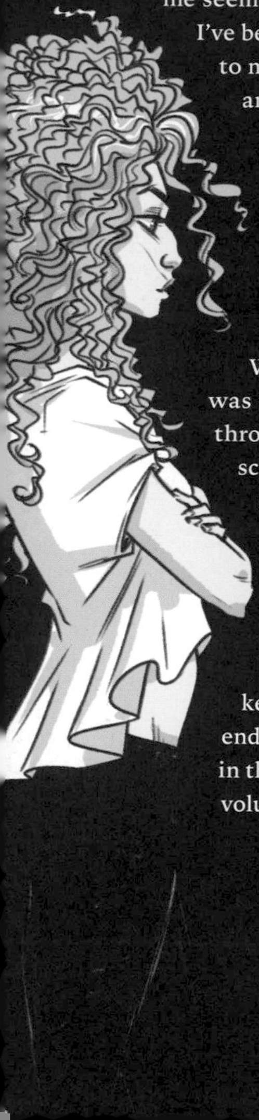

After I uploaded the final page of the book, I had a brief surge of emotion, it was finally done after so long, but besides that it still doesn't really seem real that it's done. I wish I could wait and hold the printed book in my hands, really process it and get some perspective on it, and THEN write the afterword and have it magically appear in the book.

Working on volume 7 on and off over the years taught me a lot. At times it was a struggle but it helped me have fun making comics again. This book went through so many changes and drafts, some of which I had fully thumbnailed before scrapping, and originally it was going to be over 300 pages before I decided to change one pivotal story point which required half of the book to be deleted and the rest completely rewritten. It was like when I was struggling with volume 6, originally I'd done a whole version of the book where Trilby had died but it just wasn't working, and when I changed it to have her survive, everything fell into place. It resulted in a shorter book that was smaller in scope, but that was what it needed and I couldn't see it until I made that one key change. The same thing happened with volume 7, originally it was a grander ending, at least grand as far as *Wet Moon* goes, and I do still like some of the stuff in that older version but once I made that one big change, it helped me realize that volume 7 didn't need to be "big" to be an ending.

When I started *Wet Moon* in 2004, I didn't have any expectations for what would happen with it. I loved the characters, of course, but it started as more of a goof-off sort of thing, like all the weird, silly, funny things I could think of thrown into one comic, me following my whims without much thought to what it would mean or how it would be received, or what it was actually about. I'm still not sure if *Wet Moon* is actually "about" anything, but I like to think that's part of its charm, so much of what the comic is and has become is what people, you guys, the readers and fans, bring to it. At the time leading up to volume 1 there was already a fanbase for the characters online, I'd been drawing Cleo and some of the other characters for a while and posting them on Deviantart before there was ever a comic, so I knew the characters resonated with some people, but I didn't understand what it meant until later. I understand it now, after years of working on this comic and interacting with fans both new and old (I still hear from fans who've been around since the Deviantart days, who have stuck with me and *Wet Moon* for almost 20 years!). You guys have helped shape *Wet Moon* into what it is now.

I think sometimes I would lose sight of what *Wet Moon* was, and sometimes I'd get discouraged (there have been a LOT of bad reviews over the years, haha), and I'd forget why I loved it in the first place. Sometimes I felt pressured to give *Wet Moon* more direction and structure, sometimes I felt lost with what it should be, sometimes I felt like I'd forgotten how to have fun with it and enjoy doing it (I mean I was also super depressed for a while so that didn't help either) but you all were always there to remind me. It seemed like every time I felt lost, out of the blue I'd get a wonderful message from a fan about how much *Wet Moon* meant to them or how they were excited about the next book and how they were willing to wait for it no matter how long it took me. I seriously must have some of the most patient, understanding fans out there, patiently waiting for years for me to finish. Thank you to everyone who ever reached out to me in any way, I can't say how much it means to me and how amazing and humbling it is to know that my work has had a positive effect on some people's lives. Everyone reading this afterword: you guys are the absolute best. I couldn't have done *Wet Moon* without you.

But... you know, I'm not sure if I feel like *Wet Moon* is really over. I had so much fun doing this book that I found myself thinking of new ideas of what to do with the characters, and found myself casually brainstorming for a book where the characters are in their 30s, like 15 years later. Penny's kid would be a bratty teenage asshole! Natalie and Mara would be married (and of course there'd be a flashback to their wedding so I can draw their dresses)! Maybe Cleo is famous after her novel is published and made into a movie. Maybe Trilby works with other people who have survived attacks like hers. Maybe Myrtle is released and trying to start a new life. Maybe Trilby and Cleo live together with a bunch of Meiko's kittens. I'm getting ahead of myself!

Anyway, if I keep writing I'll just get more mushy and corny, gushing about how all my readers are so incredible, wonderful, compassionate, encouraging, patient, and inspiring, you are all an integral part of my life and my work and have made me a better, kinder, more humble person. Thank you so much, truly.

—SOPHIE
May 2018

ACKNOWLEDGMENTS

Thank you most to Mom and Dad, Zach, Erin, Kelly, Robin, Angie, James, Joe, Jill, and everyone at Oni for being so patient and accommodating.

Thank you to Michelle for being so understanding when I disappeared for months trying to finish this book.

Thank you to Carrie, my therapist. I couldn't have done it without her.

Thank you so much to everyone who's supported and encouraged me throughout the years: Candace, Andrea, Jessi, Amy R., Allison, Nancy, Jenn, Robert, Amy C., Nnedi, Aimee, Mandy, Michelle N., Heather, Becky, Rynn, Yhasmine, Rian, and all my amazing, wonderful, very patient fans. Thank you from the bottom of my heart.

Special thank you to Ariel Cruz for writing the music and lyrics for the Slutty Angels and being such a big fan, and to Andy Deane, Tony Lechmanski, Gopal Metro, Micah Consylman, and Jordan Marchini for making me feel super special and for making music that has been such a big inspiration for my comics. Also, special thanks to my wonderful landlords, Margot and Mike.

And last but certainly not least, thank you to my horrible cat Rambo.

morning cold

— PLAYLIST —

THE RAIN WITHIN — **CLOSE YOUR EYES**

THE BIRTHDAY MASSACRE — **DIARIES**

BELLA MORTE — **REFLECTIONS**

LA SCALTRA — **LUCIAN**

KATE BOY — **HIGHER**

GEORGE WINSTON — **NIGHT, PART ONE: SNOW**

THE RAIN WITHIN — **WHILE I AM HERE**

FORGE THE PAST — **SNOWFALL MORNING**

DEMI LOVATO — **NIGHTINGALE**

TEGAN AND SARA — **FAINT OF HEART**

BELLA MORTE — **MY ONLY ONE**

CARLY RAE JEPSEN — **FAVOURITE COLOUR**

FORGE THE PAST — **SLEEP AWAY THE COLD**

KELLY CLARKSON — **NOSTALGIC**

THUMBNAILS

for pages that were eventually abandoned in the revision process. But oh, what could have been!

I debated with myself a lot over whether to include this page of Myrtle in her cell. Originally it was going to go at the very end of the book after the acknowledgements and everything, like a stinger after the credits in a movie, and it is nice to see what became of Myrtle and it's nice to see her face when she's finally at peace while looking out at the full moon, but it didn't feel right to include it. I had so many different little scenes like this that would've been another button on the end of the book, but I tried to trust my gut and go with what felt right regardless of how much I liked it. Sometimes I know if story beats or pacing or whatever are right or wrong just by feeling it out even if I can't fully explain why.

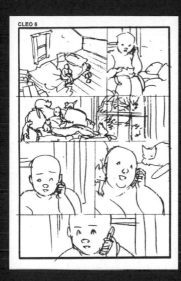

This is a page where Cleo talks to her mom, Kate, who lives up north with a bunch of cats. I still really like this scene and it would be cool to finally see Cleo's mom, but it felt out of place so I cut it.

Trilby, Cleo, and Zia smoke weed! This would've been super fun to draw, not just the characters getting stoned but Zia being more part of the group and her making real friends for the first time. Even though Zia isn't in the final scene of the book, in my head she becomes an integral part of the circle of friends. I ALMOST put her in that final scene, originally she was going to sleep over with Trilby and Cleo and be there with them when they see the snow outside, but I decided that Cleo and Trilby needed the moment for just the two of them. But ugh, now I want to go back and draw Zia showing up out of nowhere at the last minute but my editor Robin would kill me, haha.*

*ROBIN'S NOTE: It's true, I would kill her.

SOPHIE CAMPBELL likes cats, Gamera, tea, *Final Fantasy 7*, and ice cream. She hates frogs, snakes, dogs, and traveling. She currently resides in Rochester, New York.

FOLLOW SOPHIE AT:

—twitter.com/mooncalfe1—mooncalfe.tumblr.com—
—mooncalfe-art.tumblr.com—shadoweyescomic.tumblr.com—
—cantlookbackcomic.tumblr.com—

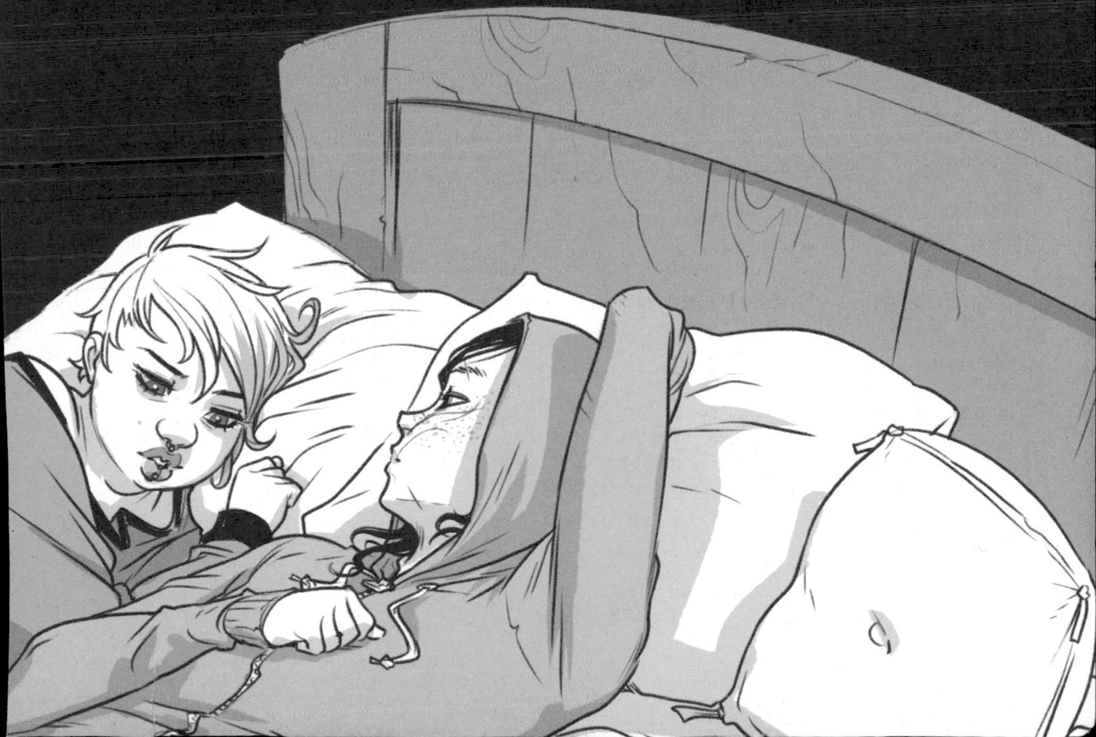

MORE WET MOON

1
Sophie Campbell
WET MOON
FEEBLE WANDERINGS

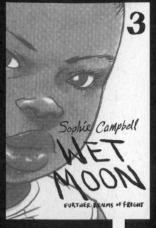

Wet Moon, Book 1:
Feeble Wanderings

ISBN 978-1-62010-304-3

2
WET MOON
UNSEEN FEET
Sophie Campbell

Wet Moon, Book 2:
Unseen Feet

ISBN 978-1-62010-328-9

3
Sophie Campbell
WET MOON
FURTHER REALMS OF FRIGHT

Wet Moon, Book 3:
Further Realms of Fright

ISBN 978-1-62010-329-6

WET MOON
4
DROWNED IN EVIL
Sophie Campbell

Wet Moon, Book 4:
Drowned in Evil

ISBN 978-1-62010-330-2

5
WET MOON
WHERE ALL STARS FAIL TO BURN
Sophie Campbell

Wet Moon Book 5:
Where All Stars
Fail to Burn

ISBN 978-1-62010-331-9

6
Sophie Campbell
WET MOON
YESTERDAY'S GONE

Wet Moon Book 6:
Yesterday's Gone

ISBN 978-1-62010-332-6

ONI PRESS
www.onipress.com

For more information on these and other fine Oni Press comic books and graphic novels, visit www.onipress.com. To find a comic specialty store in your area, call 1-888-COMICBOOK or visit www.comicshop.us.